THEORY-DRIVEN
EVALUATIONS

To Peter H. Rossi,
mentor and friend

THEORY-DRIVEN EVALUATIONS

HUEY-TSYH CHEN

SAGE Publications
International Educational and Professional Publisher
Newbury Park   London   New Delhi

For information address:

 SAGE Publications, Inc.
2455 Teller Road
Newbury Park, California 91320
E-mail: order@sagepub.com

SAGE Publications Ltd.
6 Bonhill Street
London EC2A 4PU
United Kingdom

SAGE Publications India Pvt. Ltd.
M-32 Market
Greater Kailash I
New Delhi 110 048 India

Printed in the United States of America

Library of Congress Cataloging-in-Publication Data

Chen, Huey-Tsyh.
  Theory-driven evaluations / Huey-Tsyh Chen.
    p.   cm.
  Includes bibliographical references.
  ISBN 0-8039-3532-3 (cl.)—ISBN 0-8039-5899-4 (pbk.)
  1. Evaluation research (Social action programs)   I. Title.
H62.C365   1990
001.4—dc20   89-24252
                                                                        CIP

97 98 99 00 01 10 9 8 7 6 5 4

Contents

Foreword

The expansion of liberal social programs and of related evaluations of social programs both abruptly came to a halt in 1980 after two decades of expansion. Some social programs were cut back drastically or inflation was allowed to undermine their value: The construction of additional public housing came to a halt; AFDC expenditures were cut back by the simple expedient of not correcting payment schedules to keep pace with inflation; evaluation research funded or required by federal agencies was cut back or kept level. Not all agencies were equally affected: The evaluation activities of the Department of Education declined drastically, but those of the Department of Labor were not as severely affected.

However, it did not take long before the regime discovered that it is necessary to have valid information about the state of society and the effectiveness of programs. The consequence has been an increasing reliance on evaluation and other social science research approaches to policy and program issues. Today, evaluation research is alive and flourishing, constituting the most exciting career a young social scientist may embark upon.

The abrupt decline in policy uses of social research in the early 1980s meant that evaluators both suffered and gained in the 1980s. On the down side, the cutback in evaluation activities has meant that some had to find other employment. Many of the evaluation research specialists, especially in the large research firms, found other employment: Many returned to academia. Some of the major evaluation research firms had to search for programs other than social to evaluate. Some large research firms that had diversified into evaluation in the 1970s

7

(e.g., the Mitre Corporation or the System Development Corporation) because the field was expanding at the time lost interest in evaluation. Another negative impact was a decline in interest in evaluation and other applied social research activities among graduate students in the social sciences and in the professional schools: After all, why get trained in a field in which job prospects were diminishing?

But there were positive results from the slowdown. The field was given a half decade's respite from the necessity to meet the demands for research and for training for research. This release from the need to meet current demand meant that evaluators could turn more of their energies to the task of consolidating and integrating what was learned in the 1960s and 1970s. Huey-tsyh Chen's book is surely part of that reaction: In an earlier period, he would have been too busy conducting evaluations to devote the time necessary to expand our formal understanding.

One of the most disappointing outcomes of the lessons of the 1960s and 1970s was to learn how difficult it is to design and carry through programs that effectively address major social problems. Indeed, a good case can be made for the proposition that the expected value of the outcome of an impact assessment is zero or close to it. The examination of evaluation theory and practice is heavily influenced by this finding.

Why is it that programs appear to fail? One attempt to answer this question looks at what might be at fault in evaluation methodology. The reasoning goes, "Programs to which a great deal of time, effort, and devotion have been given must do something positive. If we can't find it, then we are not looking for it properly." A second line of endeavor has been directed at a related question: "How is it that we have learned so little from all of the evaluations?" This line of effort has moved in the direction of maximizing the information about potentially fruitful interventions to be gained from evaluations.

Huey-tsyh Chen's approach to conceptualizing evaluation arises directly out of the attempt to answer these two questions. On one hand, Chen severely criticizes what he believes to have been the predominant approach to evaluation of the 1960s and 1970s, the black box impact assessment, which was often insensitive to the hopes and aspirations invested in the program by its typically diverse set of stakeholders. All too often, such assessments addressed issues that were not all of the goals imputed by program stakeholders. On the other hand, Chen criticizes the black box assessments on the grounds that they did not yield enough information useful for designing programs that work. Black box assessments mainly provided information on whether or not a program succeeded or failed to achieve a statistically significant impact. Why the program succeeded or (more often) failed was not (and could not) be addressed in such evaluations.

Evaluation theorists and practitioners will find much that is familiar in Chen's framework. The utility of this book lies primarily in its bringing together within a unified scheme the concerns of program operators, decision makers, stakeholders, and social scientists. And, even more important, following its prescriptions has great promise of providing information that can move our society appreciably closer to addressing its major social woes.

In my view, the most important message of Chen's book is that evaluation research is not a matter of technical methodological expertise. To be sure, the complete evaluator comes with a high level of technical expertise: She or he must know statistics, data collection strategies, measurement issues, and the like. But an evaluator would also be incomplete without substantive knowledge. If you know very little about labor markets, it is not likely you can design a reasonably fruitful evaluation of programs addressed to labor market issues. The importance of substantive knowledge is framed by Chen as the need for theory in the design and analysis of evaluation research. I would be more sympathetic to Chen's use of "theory" if that term did not carry with it such a load of unwanted meanings. For example, in sociology, "theory" is often equated with the abstract essays written by sociologists who are long dead. In other fields, theory is equated with sets of integrated mathematical statements concerning highly abstract properties. What is needed, in contrast, is general knowledge concerning our society. One cannot evaluate the impact of changes in our health care system on the level of health in our society without being thoroughly familiar with how health services are being delivered, how they are paid for, the competencies available in our medical knowledge, and so on. In my view, such knowledge is not theory. I also understand that what Chen means by "theory" is close to my description of what I mean by substantive knowledge. So, this disagreement is mainly over terminology rather than substance.

A second important feature of Chen's framework is its ability to incorporate both the normative and the causative into the same scheme. It is extremely important to identify those aspects of evaluation in which values are most directly engaged, if only to prevent evaluators from becoming modern-day, would-be "philosopher kings" unthinkingly imposing values, believing the process to be mainly technical in character.

If there is any gap in Chen's scheme, it is that there does not seem to be any place in it for the kind of descriptive research that often goes by the name of "needs assessment." Of course, there is no reason why his scheme should cover everything that anyone has ever called evaluation. In addition, there are good reasons for believing that "needs assessment" research belongs properly to the stage prior to the design of programs.

I believe that Chen's contribution will do much to focus the attention of evaluation practitioners and theorists on the critical developmental problems of our field. He has done us all a great service in his labors. His book appears at a critical juncture in the life course of applied social research: There can be no doubt that applied work has a strong future. This book provides some of that future strength.

—Peter H. Rossi

Preface

Major evaluation perspectives, which tend to be method oriented, have made important contributions to the development of program evaluation. However, the expanding field of program evaluation has outgrown its beginnings and there is a growing awareness of the necessity of developing a broader and more comprehensive conceptual framework for guiding evaluation practice. However, continued expansion of the scope of evaluation is difficult to achieve without dealing with issues of program theory. Currently, the notion of program theory is emerging as one of the major themes in the literature, but to date there has not been a book that provides a full-length treatment of this topic.

This book introduces a new, comprehensive framework for program evaluation that is designed to expand the scope and usefulness of this field. This framework has been designated the "theory-driven" perspective. This book is organized into five parts. Part I reviews the nature and problems of method-oriented evaluations and discusses the current movement toward theory-driven evaluations. Part II provides an infrastructure for the theory-driven perspective. Issues such as the nature and definition of program theory, the typology of theory-driven evaluations, the relationships between values and theory construction approaches, and general principles and guildelines for applying theory-driven evaluations are intensively discussed.

The actual illustrations of utilizing various types of theory-driven evaluations are the foci of Parts III, IV, and V. Part III discusses normative evaluations, which aim at providing information for improving program structure such as treatment, implementation environment, and outcomes.

Part IV discusses causative evaluations, which assess causal relationships among treatment, implementation environment, and outcomes. Parts III and IV discuss the basic evaluation types. Part V discusses some composite types, which systematically integrate two or more basic types. Part VI provides a summary and a forward look at the discipline. The research examples used in the discussions draw upon various areas, such as education, welfare, health, criminal justice, job training, family, communication, and so on, to attract a wider audience.

The presentation of this new perspective directly addresses the needs and concerns in both the professional and the applied areas of program evaluation. Professionals will find this book useful in stimulating and clarifying their own ideas and research interests. Evaluation practitioners in applied settings will find systematic strategies and guidelines that can enhance the quality and utility of their work. These strategies are illustrated by concrete examples from a variety of evaluation studies in different fields to better demonstrate their application.

For program planners and decision makers, this book will prove particularly useful in conceiving, constructing, and implementing a wide range of programs. Also, it should help them to clarify their expectations and needs and effectively communicate these to program evaluators. In addition, this book can also be used as a text for graduate and advanced undergraduate courses related to program evaluation.

This book has taken a much longer time to finish than was originally anticipated. It also took a zigzag path to completion. Initially, and that was a long, long time ago, the book was planned to be an edited collection of articles that would reflect the views and ideas behind theory-driven evaluations. However, after the articles had been collected, and when I began to write the introductory section of the book, the more I wrote the more I became convinced that, at the current stage, what was more urgently needed was a book that systematically introduced the theory-driven perspective. What began as a side issue in my work developed into a major preoccupation for the past several years. It certainly is a wonderful feeling to see the manuscript completed and published.

Pete Rossi has been the source of inspiration and moral support for the completion of this book. A long association with Pete as his former student and coauthor has proven to be an invaluable influence on my intellectual growth. I also am indebted deeply to Dave Cordray, Len Bickman, and Mark Lipsey for their many insightful comments on an earlier draft of the manuscript. Their comments have been very useful in revising it. However, I am totally responsible for any errors and controversial arguments in the book.

Special thanks are given to my colleague and friend, T. Neal Garland. Through his criticisms and suggestions on each chapter, the book at least appears to be more sophisticated and defensible than before. I also am grateful to my research assistants over the years—David Allen, Martin Kretzmann, Jim Quane, and Michelle Marks—for their help in gathering some of the material and critiquing sections of the manuscript. The manuscript has been revised numerous times. Beverly Riggin, the departmental secretary, has patiently typed most of the revisions of the manuscript. Irene Fort has also helped in typing the final version of the manuscript. They surely are as happy as I am to see the book finished. I am also grateful to the strong support from the Department of Sociology of the University of Akron on this project. Finally, my wife, mother, daughter, and son have provided me with the encouragement and joys that have been essential for the completion of this book.

—Huey-tsyh Chen

PART I

Introduction

Part I provides an overview of the traditional neglect of program theory and the popularity of method-oriented evaluations. The limitations and problems associated with method-oriented evaluations are identified. Furthermore, the current movement toward theory-driven evaluations and reasons for such a movement are discussed.

1. Method and Theory in Program Evaluation: A Question of Balance

THEORY IN PROGRAM EVALUATION: A NEGLECTED ISSUE

Theory is a frame of reference that helps humans to understand their world and to function in it. Theory is crucial in research (e.g., Rudner, 1966). Theory provides not only guidelines for analyzing a phenomenon but also a scheme for understanding the significance of research findings. Traditionally, however, theory has been neglected in the discipline of program evaluation. Until very recently, evaluation literature has rarely been concerned with the importance of theory in evaluating a program or with how to incorporate theory into evaluation processes. Influential evaluation books such as Guttentag and Struening's (1975) *Handbook of Evaluation Research* and Reicken and Boruch's (1974) *Social Experimentation* hardly focused upon or discussed the concepts and implications of theory. The *Evaluation Thesaurus* (Scriven, 1981) and the section on "Evaluation of Programs" in *Encyclopedia of Educational Research* (Talmage, 1982) have gathered the concepts and terminology commonly used in program evaluation, yet theory or related concepts are not included in these collections.

Furthermore, Lipsey et al. (1985) intensively reviewed a sample of 175 evaluation studies from a variety of journals. They found that most of those studies failed to integrate a prior theory into evaluations in terms of formulating program elements, rationale, and causal linkages. Lipsey et al. (1985) also noted that this lack of theory development appeared to be widespread throughout the evaluation community regardless of the authors' academic affiliations or program areas. The insensitivity to theoretical questions and issues and the prevalence of input/output types of evaluation has led Wortman (1983, p. 224) to comment that "program evaluation is a multi-disciplinary and (unfortunately) a largely atheoretical activity."

Chen and Rossi (1983) argue that, at the extreme, an atheoretical approach to evaluation is characterized by adherence to a step-by-step cookbook method of doing evaluations. Program evaluation in this situation can become a set of predetermined research steps that are uniformly and mechanically applied to various programs without concern for the theoretical implications of program content, setting, participants, implementing organizations, and so on.

The atheoretical view tends to result in a simple input/output or black box type of evaluation (Lipsey, 1987; Bickman, 1987b; Chen and Rossi, 1983). This type of evaluation is characterized by a primary focus on the overall relationship between the inputs and outputs of a program without concern for the transformation processes in the middle. Such simple input/output or black box evaluations may provide a gross assessment of whether or not a program works but fail to identify the underlying causal mechanisms that generate the treatment effects, thus failing to pinpoint the deficiencies of the program for future program improvement or development. A black box evaluation is usually not sensitive to the political and organizational contexts of input and output, and it neglects issues such as the relationship between the delivered treatment and the planned treatment, between official goals and operative goals, or between intended and unintended effects.

Whatever the results, the simple input/output or black box type of evaluation often will generate conclusions that are less than satisfactory. On one hand, an unqualified claim of program success that is based upon a black box evaluation may be difficult for policymakers or practitioners to apply. To use a medical example, if a black box evaluation shows a new drug to be capable of curing a disease without providing information on the underlying mechanisms of that cure, physicians will have difficulty in prescribing the new drug because the conditions under which the drug will work and the likelihood of negative side effects will not be known.

On the other hand, a claim of program failure based upon a black box evaluation may be even more misleading. Does failure imply that the theory on which the program is based is incorrect? Or is the failure due to a problem with implementation? Or is the strength of treatment too low? Or is the measurement of the treatment effect not sensitive enough? And so on. The finding of program failure in black box evaluations is vague and ambiguous. At most, little information is provided to assist in improving the program. At times, true program effects may be concealed by a gross estimation of the treatment effect in the black box evaluation, as demonstrated in the TARP Experiment (Rossi, Berk, and Lenihan, 1980) described later in this book.

Mitroff and Bonoma (1978) also argue for the importance of specifying prior theoretical assumptions in program evaluation in order to meet policy needs. They object to the belief held by some proponents of the experimental paradigm that overcoming methodological difficulties alone can make the data collected in an evaluation valid and scientifically precise without consideration of why the data were collected. They argue that "validity cannot be even approached until one learns to question his or her assumptions as closely as he or she questions the rigor with which data was [sic] generated" (1978, p. 256). Because scientific data can only be unearthed with the prior assumption of theory, Mitroff and Bonoma believe that evaluation requires a level of openness and flexibility in methodology that allows for inquiry into the background assumptions of the program and the data collection process.

Similarly, Wholey (1979, 1987) insisted that a program is not ready to be evaluated unless the theoretical basis of the program has been developed and carried out. An evaluation, according to Wholey (1979, 1987), is less likely to be useful under the conditions of unclear program objectives, lack of testable assumptions linking program components, and lack of sufficient resources and implementation efforts.

HISTORICAL DEVELOPMENTS AND THE NEGLECT OF THEORY IN EVALUATION

An intriguing question to raise is this: Why has program evaluation developed as an atheoretical activity? Taking the viewpoint of the philosophy of science (Kuhn, 1970), Shadish and Reichardt (1987a) argue that action and practice tend to precede theory development in any discipline. Program evaluation also falls within this trend. However, there are other interwoven reasons related to the historical conceptualization and focus of program evaluation that have particularly oriented program evaluation toward an atheoretical stance.

In the very early efforts to build program evaluation as a discipline, scientific research methods were greatly emphasized in many pioneer works in their attempts to define and conceptualize program evaluation. Perhaps this helped to promote evaluation as a new science that was clearly distinct from mere casual or arbitrary judgments in assessing program worthiness. For example, Suchman (1967, p. 7) viewed evaluation as "the utilization of scientific research methods and techniques for the purpose of an evaluation." Similarly, Scriven (1967, p. 40-41) defined evaluation as "a methodological activity which combines performance data with a goal scale." To underline the scientific status of this new discipline, the application of the scientific method has been emphasized. This emphasis is characteristic of what has been given the traditional and common label of the discipline of "evaluation research" (e.g., Weiss, 1972; Caro, 1977; Guttentag and Struening, 1975). Yet with such a great emphasis on research methods in conceptualizing and defining program evaluation, the implications of program theory tended to be ignored.

The focus on methodological issues has been further reinforced by the fact that, in spite of their many important contributions, the major evaluation perspectives have mainly been method oriented. For proponents of the experimental paradigm (e.g., see Campbell and Stanley, 1963; Reicken and Boruch, 1974; Cook and Campbell, 1979), an evaluation is best carried out by exactly following the classic randomized experimental design. In the classic experimental design, the treatment is manipulated in a controlled setting where subjects are randomly assigned to the experimental and control groups, variables are objectively measured, and experimental results are precisely analyzed with rigorous statistical methods. The merits of other designs or methods, such as quasi-experiments or preexperimental designs, are sometimes judged by the degree to which they approximate the experimental design.

In contrast, advocates of naturalistic approaches propose that qualitative or ethnographic methods serve best in doing an evaluation. According to Lincoln and Guba (1985), Guba and Lincoln (1981), and Patton (1980), evaluations are best carried out with minimum constraints on the antecedent conditions (independent variables) and the outputs of a research inquiry. They propose that qualitative or ethnographic investigations are superior to the more structured approaches usually involved in quantitative studies because the research format of naturalistic inquiry can be relatively free or fluid.

In the naturalistic approach, sensitive observers record behavior in "natural settings," and researchers analyze the resulting protocols with due regard for the humanity of the subjects and the desires of program operators, administrators, and other stakeholders. The full complexity of human behavior is thus given due attention, free of the constraints imposed by the research designs of the positivistic approaches.

Although the major concern in Cronbach's approach (Cronbach et al., 1980; Cronbach, 1982) is to incorporate program evaluation into the context of political and organizational processes to facilitate pluralistic decision making, his approach is closely related to qualitative methods. Cronbach maintains that flexible, qualitative methods are useful both in achieving the generalizability of evaluation results and in serving to enlighten program stakeholders.

Economists have developed sophisticated modeling processes in their evaluations of large-scale economics-related programs (e.g., Ferber and Hirsch, 1982; Hausman and Wise, 1985), but the major contribution of economists to the mainstream of program evaluation has been their introduction of econometric methods. The methodology of evaluation has been expanded considerably by the economists' demonstration that econometric methods are useful in dealing with nonexperimental data (e.g., Heckman, et al., 1987; Barnow et al., 1980) and by their intensive debates on the relative merits of econometric versus experimental methods.[1]

These major evaluation perspectives have made many important contributions to the development of program evaluation. However, in relying so heavily upon research methods as cornerstones of their approaches, they have also contributed to the traditional emphasis upon methodological and research issues to the neglect of program theory in doing evaluations.

The popularity of method-oriented evaluations has been further strengthened by the long and intensive debates between qualitative and quantitative camps about which research method is most suitable for evaluations (e.g., see Cook and Reichardt, 1979; Lincoln and Guba, 1985). On one hand, advocates of the experimental paradigm (e.g., Cook and Campbell, 1979) insist that rigorous methods such as randomized experiments—or at least strong quasi-experiments—should be used to assess program effectiveness. They believe that the use of preexperimental designs or qualitative methods tends to provide misleading information that confuses the decision-making process. Economists agree with the basic tenet of the experimental paradigm that internal validity is crucial in an evaluation, yet they disagree among themselves as to whether econometric methods are as effective as experimental methods in ensuring an unbiased estimate of treatment effect.

On the other hand, naturalists such as Lincoln and Guba (1985) and Patton (1980) argue that the rigidity of rigorous methods tends to alienate evaluators from stakeholders (those persons most directly affected by evaluation results) and prevents evaluators from understanding the stakeholders' perspectives and concerns and/or program operation processes. Similarly, Cronbach (1982) argues that the use of rigorous methods not only makes an evaluation rigid and narrow in scope but also exhausts scarce resources in dealing with trivial issues. Cronbach and many naturalists believe that flexible qualitative methods, rather than quantitative methods, best serve the needs of an evaluation. Guba and Lincoln (1981) and Lincoln and Guba (1985) even predict that in the future the naturalistic paradigm will gradually replace the experimental paradigm in program evaluation.

This conflict between the experimental and qualitative camps was dramatized in the debate between Robert F. Boruch and Milbrey W. McLaughlin (Davis, 1982). The controversy was concerned with the recommendation to Congress and the Department of Education that the federal government should mandate the use of experimental methods whenever appropriate. The debate was held at the 1981 annual meeting of the Evaluation Network and the Evaluation Research Society in Austin, Texas (Davis, 1982).

In the debate, Boruch (Davis, 1982, p. 12) argued that "if one wants statistically unbiased estimates of effects, then well designed field tests are warranted." He advocated that, if the experimental methods he recommended were implemented at federal or state levels, the quality of evidence of an evaluation would improve. This would eliminate the experience of many programs where real experiments had to be conducted after poor quasi-experiments or preexperimental research designs failed to evaluate the program appropriately.

However, McLaughlin (Davis, 1982, p. 14) argued just the opposite. She pointed out that the rigidity of experimental methods tends to lead an evaluator to "ask the wrong questions, use the wrong measures, and fails to provide information that validly informs policy and practice." Problems such as rigidity, high cost, and poor fit to the local program operations and program changes can make the use of experimental methods a waste of time and money in evaluation efforts.

The intensive conflicts and debates on research methods have generated information that is interesting and insightful for methodological development. However, this discussion may also create the impression that many or most problems in evaluation result mainly from methodological shortcomings and that the refinement of research methods alone will lead to the solution of many difficulties and problems in program evaluation.

FOCI AND PROBLEMS OF
METHOD-ORIENTED EVALUATIONS

Approaching an evaluation from the viewpoint of a research tradition provides the advocates with a shared view of the aims of program evaluation as well as a set of established techniques and procedures to carry it out. The use of a particular method allows the advocates of that perspective to intensively explore and deal with the particular evaluation issues with which they are primarily concerned. For example, the emphasis upon experimental designs and the development of various quasi-experimental designs not only has enhanced our understanding of issues relating to internal validity but has also helped prevent unsound and careless work in evaluation (e.g., Campbell and Stanley, 1963; Cook and Campbell, 1979). Campbell and his associates' checklist of threats to validity demystifies the sources of bias in applying a particular design in an evaluation and indicates the potential impact of these biases on the assessment of treatment effects.

Similarly, naturalistic approaches based upon qualitative methodology have helped us to explore and develop techniques to better understand multiple stakeholders'—especially program managers' and administrators'—needs and concerns. The use of qualitative methods provides evaluators with rich, firsthand information on questions such as how a program is implemented, what the patterns of interaction between stakeholders are, the kind of day-to-day problems that are confronted by program staff, and so on. This type of inquiry allows naturalists to work closely with stakeholders and to provide the timely information they need.

However, the overemphasis of both experimental and naturalistic perspectives on methodological issues also tends to narrow their focus.

These perspectives each tend to focus upon the area of program evaluation that corresponds to the strength of their methods. Other areas of program evaluation usually receive little attention and are sometimes argued to be less important. For example, the experimental paradigm (Campbell and Stanley, 1963; Cook and Campbell, 1979) deals mainly with issues relating only to internal validity, while other evaluation issues are given less priority by this perspective. Naturalistic approaches (e.g., Guba and Lincoln, 1981) mainly emphasize issues related to process evaluation, while the issues of outcome evaluation are not regarded from this perspective as very useful for stakeholders. Cronbach's (1982) approach places higher priority on achieving external validity, and issues of internal validity are regarded by him as trivial.

Currently, however, there is a growing consensus among evaluators that an evaluation must deal with multiple values and issues (e.g., Cook and Shadish, 1986). Adherence to a particular method prevents evaluators from developing strategies for dealing with more than a narrow range of issues. As a consequence, the traditional perspectives tend to be limited in scope and encounter difficulties in evaluation situations that require dealing with multiple issues.

Another problem of the individual method-oriented perspectives is that they are difficult to connect and seldom communicate with each other. It is well documented in research methods texts that each research method has its own strengths and weaknesses (e.g., see Babbie, 1986). Because this is the case, it is easy for an advocate of one particular research tradition to highlight only its strengths and attack other research traditions on their weaknesses. Accordingly, arguments for the replacement of one research method by another tend to generate only continuing debates, to further polarize proponents' positions, and to confuse the audience. An overly rigid adherence to any particular research method results in heightened differences that fuel continuing difficulties in communication.

The excessive advocacy of any one method might result in the exaggeration of that method's strengths and blindness to its weaknesses. For example, naturalists such as Parlett and Hamilton (1978) and Guba and Lincoln (1981) totally reject any merits of experimental or quasi-experimental methods. In the end, a "competition of research methods" may evolve that will hinder the development of a more comprehensive conceptual framework within which it would be possible for all research methods to make even greater contributions.

In spite of such debates, most evaluation studies still follow the framework provided by the experimental paradigm (Lipsey et al., 1985). As is reported from time to time, however, applications of the experimental paradigm in program evaluation are not always satisfactory. Among these complaints, Weiss and Rein (1969) report that using an experimental design to evaluate a broadly aimed and highly fluid program may lead to misleading and artificial results. Guttentag (1973) illustrates many difficulties involved in implementing experimental designs in the field, and Deutscher (1977) indicates that the inflexible structure of experimental methods can interfere with the detection of real program effects. Cronbach (1982) argues that evaluations that follow the experimental paradigm tend to focus on trivial issues that are not very useful for policy decisions. Evaluation studies following experimental designs have been found to have difficulties in maintaining the integrity of the design and have deficiencies in various methodological issues such as treatment integrity, statistical power, and the like (Lipsey et al., 1985).

Furthermore, the major purpose for doing evaluation is to provide timely and relevant feedback information for policy making. However, utilization studies indicate that many evaluation results are not used by decision makers (e.g., Weiss, 1977). Program stakeholders frequently report that evaluation studies fail to provide them with relevant and useful information (Chelimsky, 1977).

It might be thought that the naturalistic approaches are the perfect answer to this problem and that naturalistic evaluations would be popular. Judging from the evaluations reported in the major evaluation journals, however, and despite the optimism expressed by Lincoln and Guba (1985), the application of naturalistic approaches in program evaluations has been relatively limited in comparison with the experimental paradigm (Lipsey et al., 1985).

Part of the problem may be that the naturalistic approaches have not yet clearly demonstrated an ability to generate valid and generalizable information (Chen, 1988). Sadler (1981) points out that an evaluator's personal observations and intuitive analyses can result in biases in the naturalistic evaluation. Furthermore, Williams (1986b) points out that the application of naturalistic inquiries in the field may make it necessary to compromise evaluation standards and criteria. For example, naturalistic evaluators may insist on using an unstructured and inductive format in conducting an evaluation, while stakeholders want to know from the beginning of the evaluation what is going to be done, how, and by whom.

' With the growing awareness of the problems and difficulties associated with the traditional perspectives, there has been a concurrent interest in taking a more pragmatic view of research methods. Unlike hard-line naturalists such as Lincoln and Guba (1985), some naturalistic evaluators such as Williams (1986a) and Smith (1986) do not zealously reject quantitative methods; neither do they predict and advocate a new research era dominated by naturalistic approaches. They are willing to admit that both qualitative and quantitative methods have their strengths and weaknesses. As Williams (1986a, p. 85) suggests: "No single inquiry method will suffice for all evaluation needs."

Williams (1986a) does not believe that the naturalistic approach should be used blindly on every occasion. He suggests that naturalistic approaches may be most suitable under the following conditions: where the issues of the evaluation cannot be clearly defined before the evaluation begins, when a large group of stakeholders' informational needs and values must be dealt with, when the evaluation audience requires information about program processes, and so on.

Smith (1986) advocates the use of a combination of both qualitative and quantitative methods when the situation allows it. Smith admits that combining the qualitative and quantitative approaches can be expensive and requires not only the combination of many skills but also the accommodation of divergent viewpoints within the evaluation team. Nonetheless, she argues that the benefits outweigh the costs. Smith lists four circumstances under which a combined approach might prove most fruitful: when a complete description of the evaluation is necessary, when circumstances indicate that the results of a qualitative study can be generalized, when a combination of methods might enhance validity, and when qualitative feedback might be effective in influencing stakeholders' opinions. Smith (1986) believes the use of multiple methods can combine the best of the qualitative and quantitative worlds in one evaluation.

The idea of using multiple methods to overcome the shortcomings of any single research method is also shared by some evaluators from the quantitative camp (e.g., see Mark and Shotland, 1987). However, despite the potential advantages, the advocacy of multiple methods also presents some shortcomings of its own.

Reichardt and Cook (1979) point out factors that may prevent the use of multiple methods, such as the greater time and costs involved, lack of training programs for combined methodologies, and the persisting rivalry between research traditions. Furthermore, Shotland and Mark (1987) point out that evaluation results generated by the use of multiple methods may be difficult to interpret because different methods may address different questions, may generate conflicting results, and could also suffer the same inadequacies.

Furthermore, the simple advocacy of multiple methods alone is not adequate for providing guidance in actual practice because qualitative and quantitative methods each have their own unique assumptions, logic, and research procedures. There are no self-evident logical connections between these opposing methods. This is perhaps the reason why the advocates of one method-oriented perspective tend to debate instead of work with the proponents of other method-oriented perspectives (e.g., see Cook and Campbell, 1979; Guba and Lincoln, 1981). In fact, any suggestion that the assumptions, logic, and research procedures of a specific method be modified tends to threaten the existence and functioning of that method-oriented perspective. Without efforts toward conceptual integration, the advocacy of multiple methods may simply be expedient and similar to advocating a shotgun marriage.

Because each method, or even multiple methods, involves its own strengths and weaknesses, there realistically is no one best method for evaluation that can universally apply to every evaluation situation. Which method or methods should be used in an evaluation may be contingent upon external factors such as evaluation purposes, the maturity of the program, the availability of time and resources, stakeholders' and evaluators' values, and the political and organizational environments of a program. For example, where a program is still in the development stage, the issue of program effectiveness is too early to be judged and the randomized experiment may not be very useful for providing information for program improvement. Similarly, qualitative methods may not be useful when a program involves a large number of stakeholder groups and each has differing values and views on the program's purposes. For program management purposes, decision makers want to specify a set of goal dimensions of the program that clearly represent these stakeholders' views and values. Under this condition, quantitative methods may be more useful than qualitative methods in uncovering the underlying goal dimensions among a large number of stakeholders.

If the appropriateness of a research method or methods for any given evaluation can only be judged within a specific context, then without linking the evaluation process to the context, further efforts to advance research methods alone may not appreciably expand the focus and scope of program evaluation. The refinement of research methods is helpful, but what is most needed in the future for advancing program evaluation may be conceptual and theoretical efforts to systematically integrate these contextual factors and research methods. This is where incorporating program theory into evaluation processes becomes crucial. Program theory can provide guidelines for identifying which issues are most important in an evaluation, determining what method or methods are most relevant to address these issues, and suggesting how to apply the best method or methods for dealing with these issues. These kinds of concerns will be the fundamental force behind the new movement toward theory-driven evaluations.

THE MOVEMENT TOWARD
THEORY-DRIVEN EVALUATIONS

Currently, there is a new movement to shift program evaluation from method-oriented evaluations to theory-oriented evaluations. Lipsey (1987) argues that the traditional method-oriented or black box type of evaluation underrepresents the complexities of the treatment circumstances. He argues that, in reality, the treatment can deviate greatly from a simple dichotomously coded group membership, that exogenous variables can accompany or interact with the treatment, and that a broader range of outputs can be produced. Lipsey (1987) urges the development of a theoretical framework that will differentiate more richly the details of causal processes that can serve as a basis for planning and organizing evaluation activities.

Similarly, Trochim (1986b) has also criticized the mechanical application of randomized experiments and quasi-experiments as the primary means of assessing program effectiveness. Trochim (1986b, p. 3) argues that "this *ceteris paribus* mentality is inherently atheoretical and noncontextual. It assumes that the same mechanism works in basically the same way whether we apply it in mental health or criminal justice, income maintenance or education." Trochim believes that the causal mechanisms of a program should be examined within the framework of the program's theory.

Cordray (1986) argues that the traditional input-output assessment leads an evaluator to provide an improverished version of causal inference. Instead, he proposes that evaluation should broaden the evidential basis by actively considering plausible rival explanations, by examining implementation procedures, and by investigating mediating and contextual factors.

Chen and Rossi (1987) argue that method-driven evaluations tend to maximize one type of validity at the expense of others. To avoid this problem, Chen and Rossi (1987) point out the importance of program theory in simultaneously dealing with various types of validity.

The growing emphasis on the importance of program theory is also evidenced in some recent publications, such as the 1986 volume (edited by Cordray and Lipsey) and the 1987 volume (edited by Shadish and Reichardt) of *Evaluation Studies Review Annual* in which program theory is one of the major themes. Furthermore, a volume devoted to program theory in *New Directions for Program Evaluation* has been edited by Bickman (1987a). In this volume, Bickman (1987b) provides a list of benefits that can result from an articulation of program theory and its integration with program evaluation. Among other advantages, specifying the underlying theory of a program within the evaluation allows that theory to be tested in a way that reveals whether program failure results from implementation failure or theory failure. This will also help to clarify whether a program is being implemented under conditions in which it is appropriate. Program theory clarifies the connections between a program's operations and its effects, and thus helps the evaluator to find either positive or negative effects that otherwise might not be anticipated. It also can be used to specify intermediate effects of a program that might become evident and measurable before final outcomes can be manifested, which can provide opportunities for early program assessment in time for corrective action by program implementors. Finally, developing a program theory may be the best method of informing and educating stakeholders so that they can understand the limits of the program.

Given these positive functions, Bickman (1987b) is surprised that program theory has generally been slighted in the evaluation literature until recently and, in practice, has been largely ignored. In their chapters in the same volume, Conrad and Miller (1987), McClintock (1987), Scheirer (1987), Wholey (1987), and Shadish (1987) also share with Bickman (1987b) a desire to illustrate how incorporating program theory into an evaluation can enhance a program evaluator's sensitivity to planning, goal clarification, implementation, stakeholders' needs, and social change theories in general.

In addition, the current developments in this area are discussed in a special 1989 issue of *Evaluation and Program Planning* featuring the theory-driven approach. In this special issue, Chen and Rossi (forthcoming) point out issues relevant to formulating and using theory-driven evaluations. Finney and Moos (forthcoming), Scott and Sechrest (forthcoming), and Palumbo and Oliver (forthcoming) discuss the implications of program theory in treatment processes and implementation. Costner (forthcoming), Patton (forthcoming), Lipsey and Pollard (forthcoming), Trochim (forthcoming), Shapiro (forthcoming), and Chen (forthcoming) provide alternative views and strategies for formulating program theory. Cordray (forthcoming) and Bickman (forthcoming) discuss potential problems in theory-driven evaluations and possible strategies to deal with them.

This new movement toward theory-driven evaluations is not meant to detract from the significant contribution of research methods; as in many disciplines, research methods are useful tools for obtaining empirical knowledge and verifying hypotheses. However, as will become clear in later chapters of this book, this new movement argues strongly that it is not appropriate to perceive program evaluation mainly as an array of methods and data collection techniques. As a discipline, program evaluation must emphasize and develop its own unique, systematic, and theoretically based body of knowledge. Instead of being treated as ends in themselves, methods should be considered to be the means for facilitating the development of knowledge. As Bickman (1987c, p. 1) argues, "Evaluation is often referred to as a practical science, but both as a practice and as a science it requires theory."

The movement toward theory-driven evaluations is related to several important past developments in program evaluation. First of all, as discussed in the previous sections, this new trend may result from the growing recognition that concentration on methods alone may not be sufficient either to solve the current problems and difficulties in evaluations or to further advance the field of program evaluation in the future (e.g., Lipsey, 1987; Bickman, 1987b).

The intensive debates and conflicts between qualitative and quantitative camps have indicated that there is no shortage of methods in program evaluation. In fact, there is an abundance of advanced and sophisticated qualitative and quantitative methods available (e.g., see Cook and Campbell, 1979; Guba and Lincoln, 1981). At this stage of evaluation development, the problems and discontent currently raging may result not so much from a lack of research methods as from a lack of comprehensive conceptual frameworks or theories to link or integrate evaluation activities.

The need for focusing on program theory for the future advancement of program evaluation has been illustrated in the current development of the postexperimental perspective (Cook, 1985). Due to dissatisfaction with the limitations and problems of the experimental paradigm, some of its original advocates are attempting to expand and transform their traditional framework into a more general and comprehensive perspective that, hopefully, can better adapt to the political aspects of program evaluation.

This postexperimental perspective of "critical multiplism" has been developed in the last few years by Cook and his associates (e.g., see Cook, 1985; Shadish, Cook, and Houts, 1986). Generally speaking, critical multiplism asserts that evaluators should plan to use multiple methodologies, investigate multiple issues, and consider the views of multiple stakeholders. Cook (1985) believes that critical multiplism has distinct advantages over the traditional experimental paradigm. He claims that this perspective reduces the possibility of misinterpretation, provides more comprehensive information for policy processes, and makes an evaluation more rational and conscious of its values.

In its early stages of development, however, critical multiplism raises a major difficulty that cannot be resolved methodologically. An evaluation is carried out within the constraints of available resources and obviously cannot pursue all of the multiple options that might possibly be studied. Choices and trade-offs among these options are necessary and inevitable. These trade-offs, as noted by Shadish and Cook (1986), require guiding principles or theories rather than methodologies. Critical multiplism has yet to develop these. Shadish et al. (1986) note that the development of theories or guiding principles is the most urgent challenge that the advocates of critical multiplism currently face.

While methodological advancements will continue in program evaluation, we seem to have reached a stage where theoretical rather than methodological efforts are most needed. Perhaps an emphasis on a balance between methods and theory in program evaluation can help evaluators in examining the basic assumptions and dilemmas of an evaluation, in facilitating the development of strategies to deal with trade-offs, and in encouraging expansion of the scope of program evaluation.

This new trend may also result from the wisdom and experience accumulated in the past few decades and from the realization that the conceptualization and assumptions made about social intervention or planned changes may be too simplistic. The earlier works by theorists

such as Campbell (1969) and Scriven (1967) promoted the view that
the main purpose of an evaluation is to assess the overall effectiveness
of a program. Based on this information on program effectiveness,
decision makers then decide whether the program should continue or
be canceled.

However, it has been found that social interventions usually do not
work so predictably and that problems are not so straightforward.
Planned changes are usually implemented in an incremental fashion
(Lindblom and Cohen, 1979). Decision makers are mainly risk-avoiders
who prefer to alleviate present problems rather than initiate precipitate
changes. Because evaluation results are seldom applied to a go/no-go
decision situation (Cronbach, 1982), the information provided from the
traditional outcome evaluation tends not to be useful in decision-making
processes.

Frustrated with the low utilization of evaluation results, Weiss (1972)
has urged expansion of the scope of evaluation to include theoretical
issues. Weiss noted that simple input/output evaluations provide no
information on how and why a program worked or did not work and
cannot identify which elements of the program "amalgam" are the
essential ingredients for successful implementation. Weiss (1972) suggested
that the utilization of evaluation results would be greatly enhanced if
three basic elements were included: an analysis of the theoretical premises
of the program; specification of the program process or linkages between
inputs and program outcomes; and an analysis of the components of
the program—which ones are the most effective—and possible alternative approaches that could enhance program effectiveness.

Another reason for this new movement may relate to the recognition
of the need to understand how the treatment is implemented. The early
conceptualization of program evaluation was heavily influenced by the
laboratory experimental tradition in agricultural and other physical
science research (e.g., Fisher, 1935). In these areas, because researchers
often have full control of subjects and research conditions, the
experimental treatment can usually be precisely manipulated. For
example, in an agricultural assessment of the effect of a new fertilizer,
the new fertilizer can be precisely distributed to plants in treatment
areas, but not to those in control areas, by following the original plan.

However, a large body of implementation studies in intervention
programs provide highly convincing evidence that program implementation is extremely complicated and difficult within the human service
areas (e.g., see Williams and Elmore, 1976). For example, it has been

found that participating organizations may be receiving funds without committing themselves to implementing the program (e.g., McLaughlin, 1975). Even if it is implemented, the treatment may not be exactly the same as originally planned (e.g., Dobson and Cook, 1980). Furthermore, community political processes can easily hinder or deter the implementation of a program (e.g., Pressman and Wildavsky, 1973). Cooperative interorganizational relationships may be necessary for program implementation, but they may be so complicated that a program can hardly move ahead (Derthick, 1972). Also, with the discretion they have, implementors tend to proceed with a program according to their views and interests, and these are not necessarily consistent with the intentions of decision makers or program designers (Lipsky, 1980).

The difficulties and complications involved in implementation provide a serious challenge for evaluators to develop their own strategies and conceptual frameworks with which to deal with these problems, and they clearly cannot simply borrow from the traditions of physical science. Critics such as Sechrest and Redner (1979) and Leithwood and Montgomery (1980) have made a strong argument that evaluators should pay attention to implemented treatment rather than simply to planned treatment. A few studies that have examined this issue have revealed that the implemented treatment was not exactly identical with the planned treatment, regardless of the rigorousness of the designs used (e.g., Dobson and Cook, 1980). The traditional assumption is that, if the treatment is properly planned, then a coherent and proper implementation will follow. This assumption may have to change.

The revelation of the extent of the difficulties and complications present in implementation studies indicates that program stakeholders require considerable help from evaluators in order to improve program implementation. Argyris (1980) argues that the applicability of social research will be enhanced by understanding the ecological context within which the social action occurs. It is important for developing a new theoretical framework to integrate program implementation into the overall evaluation activity. Under this broad conceptual framework, evaluators not only can track the implementation and report on its progress, but they can also work jointly with program stakeholders to improve the program implementation in the course of their evaluation activities.

The need for an expansion of the conceptual framework from method-oriented to theory-oriented may also result from evaluators recognizing the importance of examining their evaluation activities from a broader perspective (e.g., Chen and Rossi, 1980; Mitroff and Bonoma, 1978). The emergence of program evaluation as a discipline relates to the general trend of growing rationalization and accountability in modern society. However, Weber (1947) cautioned that it is important to see the distinction between two types of rationality: formal rationality and value or substantive rationality. Formal rationality concerns efficiency in attaining specific short-term goals, while value rationality refers to the substantive purposes and long-term ends of individuals and groups. Because formal rationality is impersonal and bureaucratic, Weber saw an element of irrationality connected with it. Where formal rationality leads to the narrow specification and segmentation of social activities, overall purposes and goals are lost sight of and the attainment of narrow, short-term goals often results in unforeseen and unintended consequences.

Weber's argument is relevant to the conceptualization of program evaluation. When it is conceptualized narrowly as simply the measurement of goal attainment, as is common within the experimental paradigm, the emphasis is mainly on formal rationality. In such a case, evaluators are concerned only with the efficiency of the treatment in attaining given goals. The question of whether or not the goals are appropriate for the effectiveness of the program, or whether these rational goals and procedures could lead to unintended consequences, might not be considered. Evaluators may sometimes be serving only bureaucratic interests and neglect the broader implications of the program for human needs and purposes from the perspective of other stakeholders. To avoid such problems, a new conceptual framework for evaluation should be concerned with value rationality and should provide more insights into the real purposes of a program and its implications for wider social interests.

Generally speaking, the current developments of program evaluation clearly indicate a need for a theoretical perspective that not only is comprehensive enough to be sensitive to important evaluation issues in areas such as program implementation, underlying causal mechanisms, treatment designs, and program outcomes but also is sophisticated enough to provide guidance in dealing with multiple or even conflicting options. These concerns provide a basis for the development of a conceptual framework for the theory-driven perspective, which is the main focus of the next three chapters.

Before discussing the theory-driven perspective, however, it is important to point out that this emphasis on theory in an evaluation does not represent a rejection of using appropriate research methods.

As will be made clear in the later chapters of this book, a theory-driven evaluation requires the use of appropriate methods for data collection and empirical verification. The theory-driven perspective developed in this book disagrees with the current major evaluation perspectives in regard to their focus and conceptualization of evaluation, but recognizes their important contributions for devising various useful techniques and tools for conducting evaluations. The theory-driven perspective may be viewed as an expansion of previous contributions to program evaluation made by the traditional perspectives. This expansion can provide an agenda for the systematic integration of theory and methods.

NOTE

1. Their disagreements are highlighted in two journals that have recently devoted special issues to reviewing the use of state-of-the-art econometric methods for estimating treatment effects: *Evaluation Review* (1987, Volume 2, Number 4) and *Journal of Human Resources* (1987, Volume 21, Number 6).

PART II

The Theory-Driven Perspective

Part II of this book attempts to introduce the rationale, logic, and strategies of the theory-driven perspective. Three chapters are included in this part. Chapter 2 outlines the nature of program theory. Six basic domains in program theory are identified: treatment, outcome, implementation environment, impact, intervening mechanism, and generalization. On the basis of these six domains, three general categories of theory-driven evaluations are identified: normative, causative, and mixed. Furthermore, different kinds of theory-driven evaluations associated with these three categories are also discussed.

Chapter 3 focuses on the construction of program theory. This chapter starts by pointing out how theory construction is a value-laden activity. Four basic values in program evaluation are identified: responsiveness, objectivity, trustworthiness, and generalization. Depending on which value or values are used, three theory construction approaches are illustrated in detail: stakeholder, social science, and integrative. Strategies and implications of these theory construction approaches to the formulation of theory-driven evaluations are examined in detail.

Chapter 4 discusses issues in applying theory-driven evaluations. The role of the theory-driven evaluator and how it differs from the traditional evaluator's role are illustrated. Principles and guidelines are developed for facilitating the application of theory-driven evaluations.

Based on discussions in Chapters 2, 3, and 4, the definition of program evaluation as the concept is used in this book includes the systematic collection of empirical evidence for the purposes of:

(1) assessing the congruency between normative and actual program structures (including the structures of program treatment, implementation environment, and/or outcome); and

(2) verifying the program's impact, its underlying causal mechanisms, or the degree of its generalizability.

Both of these aspects, taken together, form the concept of program evaluation. The purposes of program evaluation are to refine or develop program structure and operations, to understand or strengthen program effectiveness and utility, and, therefore, to facilitate policy decision making regarding the program.

2. The Theory-Driven Perspective: The New Alternative

Based upon the current efforts toward developing theory-driven or theory-oriented evaluations discussed in Chapter 1, a comprehensive theory-driven perspective will be formulated in this book to facilitate the future development and utility of theory-driven evaluations. This chapter will examine issues concerning the nature of program theory and will outline a typology of theory-driven evaluations. Issues related to values, strategies, and guidelines for integrating program theory into evaluation processes will be discussed in Chapters 3 and 4. More detailed discussions of constructing various types of theory-driven evaluations will be the focus of the remaining chapters of this book.

THE NATURE OF PROGRAM THEORY

A social or intervention program is the purposive and organized effort to intervene in an ongoing social process for the purpose of solving a problem or providing a service. The questions of how to structure the organized efforts appropriately and why the organized efforts lead to the desired outcomes imply that the program operates under some theory. Although this theory is frequently implicit or unsystematic, it provides general guidance for the formation of the program and explains how the program is supposed to work. Because one of the central arguments in the theory-driven perspective is that program theory has to be integrated into evaluation processes, it is important to examine the nature of program theory.

In this book, "theory" is generally defined as a set of interrelated assumptions, principles, and/or propositions to explain or guide social actions. This definition is broader than the conventional definition of scientific theory.

For many social scientists, the term "theory" is usually defined as a set of interrelated propositions with the purposes of explaining and predicting a phenomenon (e.g., Kerlinger, 1986). However, this kind of definition is relevant primarily to one type of theory called "descriptive theory" (e.g., Lave and March, 1975). The purpose of a descriptive theory is to describe and explain a phenomenon. This kind of theory is rooted in the logical positivism advocated by philosophers of science such as Hemple (1965), Popper (1968), and Nagel (1979). Descriptive theory concerns what *is* and has no implication as to what people *ought* to do. This kind of theory is popular among the social sciences.

The type of theory that is evaluative in form is called "prescriptive theory." Prescriptive theory prescribes what *ought* to be done or how to do something better. An example of prescriptive theory is the rational decision model, which tells people how to make choices in order to maximize their expected utilities (Lave and March, 1975). Prescriptive theory prescribes how people *should* behave in ideal circumstances. It involves value judgments.

Current definitions of program theory have emphasized the nature of descriptive theory. The process of describing or explaining facts and relationships is highlighted. For example, Bickman (1987b, p. 5) defines program theory as "the construction of a plausible and sensible model of how a program is supposed to work." Lipsey (1987, p. 7) defines program theory as "a set of propositions regarding what goes on in the black box during the transformation of input into output; that is, how, via treatment inputs, a bad situation is transformed into a better one." Similarly, Wholey (1987, p. 78) views the purpose of program theory as being to identify "program resources, program activities, and intended program outcomes, and specifies a chain of causal assumptions linking program resources, activities, intermediate outcomes, and ultimate goals."

However, in addition to having the nature of a descriptive theory, program theory also has the nature of prescriptive theory. In program theory, the selection of criteria for judging program performance clearly involves value judgments. Issues such as how to design the treatment or how to implement the treatment also involve value judgments. Prescriptive theory in program theory includes the following characteristics: action orientation, concern with treatment design and implementation, and range or options in choosing outcome criteria. These prescriptive characteristics of program theory are discussed below.

Action Orientation

Program theory contains specific strategies for achieving a goal or solving a social problem. It implies that something ought to be done in order to improve the current situation. This characteristic of action orientation is very different from many descriptive social science theories.

An example will help to illustrate this point. In explaining the phenomenon of family violence, Goode's (1971) resource theory identifies a husband's lack of resources (e.g., income, prestige, knowledge) as the cause of the problem of family violence. Goode argues that the fewer the other resources a husband can command, the more likely he is to resort to violence in order to maintain superiority over other family members, such as the wife, who is traditionally assigned to an inferior role. By identifying the lack of resources as the cause, Goode's theory provides rich theoretical implications for explaining the problem of family violence. However, Goode's theory, at least in this form, is not a program theory because the theory does not prescribe purposive or deliberate actions for intervention. On the other hand, a theory that proposes remedies such as stress reduction and avoidance techniques as a means of exiting from escalating interactions qualifies as a program theory, regardless of whether the theory is sophisticated or not. The theory may be quite simplistic in assuming that a husband's lack of skills in handling stress leads to abuse of his wife, but the theory is action oriented and has specified what action strategies could be used to alleviate the problem.

Conceptualization of Treatment Format and Implementation Strategy

Because program theory is action oriented, how such actions are organized becomes an integral part of the concern of program theory. The action part of program theory usually involves issues such as how the treatment is constructed and implemented. A treatment can be designed in different formats in terms of components and strength. Program designers and decision makers usually make assumptions about the appropriate form of the treatment in designing a program. Program theory is concerned with how the treatment should be constructed for the purpose of intervention. Similarly, a given treatment can be implemented in terms of the types of implementors, modes of delivery, and so on. The implicit assumptions made by program designers about how the treatment should be implemented comprise one of the major focuses of program theory. Whether a program has an impact or not may depend on whether these prescriptive assumptions are correct. It is part of the task of program theory to make the assumptions in treatment design and implementation processes explicit in order to investigate and to feed back the information for decision-making purposes.

Range of Options in Choosing Outcome Criteria

Different stakeholders have different interests and values regarding a program. Depending on their frames of reference, they may have different preferences and concerns regarding what outcome criteria should be investigated. The outcome criteria finally selected in an evaluation are only a limited set of a large pool of potential outcomes that might be affected by the program. Which outcome criteria are chosen in an evaluation will influence evaluation results, creating problems. For example, the program administrators may prefer to choose the criteria related to the maintenance function of an evaluation, while funding agencies may be more interested in criteria related to output performance. A program that is judged highly according to a maintenance goal may not necessarily be judged highly according to output goals, and vice versa. Due to resource constraints, it is impossible for an evaluation to investigate all potential outcome criteria. The selection of outcome criteria to be used in an evaluation is a value-laden decision and also reflects the prescriptive aspect of program theory.

A combination of these three value-oriented characteristics of program theory with the causal aspect of program theory emphasized in the existing definitions described in the beginning of this chapter indicate that program theory has the nature not only of a descriptive theory but also of a prescriptive theory. This dual nature makes program theory a kind of theory that has long been advocated by John Dewey (1929, 1933). Dewey was against social scientists' mimicking natural scientists, who separated science and engineering. He argued that such separation of "science" from "practical application" when applied to social phenomena usually prevents social scientists from generating fundamental knowledge that could help to solve social problems. Dewey believes that social sciences and social practices should be integrated. His works imply an advocacy of the kind of theory that has scientific merits and that has the potential to be used in improving society.

CONCEPTUALIZATION OF PROGRAM THEORY

The discussion of the nature of program theory clearly indicates that program theory has both descriptive and prescriptive or scientific and practical concerns. To reflect these concerns, "program theory" is defined in this book as *a specification of what must be done to achieve the desired goals, what other important impacts may also be anticipated, and how these goals and impacts would be generated.* This definition implies that program theory consists of two parts. The first deals with what the structure of a program *should* be, including such things as treatments, outcomes, and implementation processes that are related to the values of the program; this part is related to prescriptive theory. The second part deals with what *are* the underlying causal mechanisms that link the relationships among program treatments, implementation processes, and outcomes; this part relates to descriptive theory.

For convenience, in this book the part of program theory related to prescriptive theory is called "normative theory," and the part of program theory related to descriptive theory is called "causative theory." Normative theory and causative theory are two subtheories within program theory. Normative theory provides guidance on what goals or outcomes should be pursued or examined, and how the treatment should be designed and implemented. Causative theory specifies how the program works by identifying the conditions under which certain processes will arise and what their likely consequences will be.

Normative theory can come from unexamined premises, assumptions, customary procedures, and/or prior knowledge and theory. It is usually taken for granted by program designers or other stakeholders and thus is not explicitly or systematically stated or examined. However, normative theory provides the rationale and justification for the program structure and activities. Normative theory guides program planning, formulation, and implementation.

Conversely, a causative theory usually is empirically based. It represents the empirical knowledge about the causal relationship between the treatment and the outcome. A causative theory specifies the underlying causal mechanisms that link, mediate, or condition the causal relationship between the treatment variable(s) and outcome variable(s) in a program. More specifically, causative theory covers issues such as the following: What kinds of relationships exist between the treatment and outcomes? What kinds of intervening factors could be mediating the effect of the treatment on the outcome variables? Under what kinds of contextual conditions will the causal relationship be facilitated or inhibited?

Evaluation of each of these theories serves important functions for program evaluation. An evaluation of normative theory is highly relevant to the program designers', managers', and administrators' daily activities and concerns. The specification and evaluation of the normative theory allow these program people to better understand the conceptualization and assumptions of the program and help them to identify the crucial issues in the program's design and implementation processes. As a consequence, by dealing with day-to-day program operation problems the evaluator can be responsive to program people's needs and can greatly enhance the utilization of evaluation results.

Furthermore, stakeholders need timely information in order to act and to make effective policy decisions. The evaluation of normative theory, as will be explained later, requires only that the consistency between the theoretical program structure and the implemented program structure be assessed. This can be carried out even in the very early stages of the program. The evaluation of normative theory can provide timely information to help stakeholders diagnose implementation problems and take action to deal with these problems by strengthening the program structure and/or implementation processes.

When the treatment of a program is constructed and implemented appropriately, the credibility of the program is enhanced. However, this does not imply that the program is also effective. In other words, although it is highly important to provide timely information for improving program activities, the evaluation of normative theory alone is insufficient to understand whether the program achieves its designated goals or to know the unintended consequences of the program. To understand program effectiveness, causative theory becomes important.

An evaluation of causative theory provides information both on the impacts generated by the program and on *how* the impacts were generated. Judging the quality of a social or intervention program is very different from judging the quality of goods such as automobiles and washing machines. The worthiness of an automobile may be judged in terms of the intrinsic merits of the final product, such as engine power, style, and interior design. The worthiness of a program, however, is difficult to judge without having information on the contextual and/ or intervening factors that help to make that program a success or a failure.

For example, an educational program might be demonstrated to substantially improve the academic performance of students. However, this information alone is not sufficient to judge the effectiveness of the program. The program could be sharply criticized if the students' performance is achieved through questionable means. If, for example, program implementors enhance the effectiveness of the program by applying techniques such as verbal threats or physical confinement for recalcitrant students, or simply throw the bad students out of the program, the value of that program is highly questionable. Causative theory is useful in providing information on these sorts of contextual and intervening factors.

The specification of a causative theory in an evaluation is especially useful for future program improvement. As discussed in the previous chapter, the traditional black box evaluation provides information simply on the failure or success of a program; if a program fails, this type of evaluation cannot give information about what went wrong, nor can it identify the weaknesses in the program. Black box evaluation provides program staff with little information they can use to improve the program. In contrast, as will be shown later, when the causative theory is mapped out in detail, the evaluation can pinpoint the weaknesses of the causal mechanism underlying the program, identify the contextual and intervening factors that hinder or facilitate program processes and outcomes, and suggest possible strategies for dealing with these programs.

DOMAINS AND DOMAIN THEORIES

The conceptualization of program theory discussed in the previous two sections implies that program theory contains several basic organized patterns called domains. Each domain has its own domain theory. As will be discussed later, each domain theory alone, or combined with other domain theories, provides important guidance for conducting various types of evaluation. These basic domains and their pertinent domain theories will be discussed in this section. A typology of theory-driven evaluations, based upon these domains and domain theories, will be developed in the next section.

Major Domains in Program Theory

There are six major domains in program theory. Three of them are pertinent to normative theory: treatment, implementation environment, and outcome. Three other major domains derive from causative theory: impact, intervening mechanism, and generalization. The importance of these six major domains in program evaluation is illustrated below.

Treatment Domain

The treatment is the basic, essential element that produces the intended changes within a social program. However, it is important to design the treatment within a structure that will allow for a systematic evaluation of treatment processes and outcomes. Furthermore, the delivery of treatment in many social programs is a complicated and difficult process. The treatment that was planned is not necessarily the treatment that is actually implemented. Strategies for examining the treatment that is actually implemented, as opposed to the intended or planned treatment, must be developed. This domain deals with issues such as the conceptualization and design of program treatments.

For example, in the Performance Contracting Experiment (Gramlich and Koshel, 1975), the treatment domain would specify how to conceptualize and design the treatment. The following questions would be relevant here: What is the nature of the treatment? Should the treatment consist of innovative instructional materials, teaching machines, the special payment system to the private firms (paid in proportion to the learning gains of students), and so on? How should these elements be organized? How should one measure the treatment?

Implementation Environment Domain

Program treatment can be implemented in different ways. How the program is implemented may affect program processes and consequences. The implementation environment domain attempts to understand within what environment the treatment is implemented. This domain is concerned with issues such as these: Is the treatment reaching the target group? Do the implementors possess the required qualities? Are the modes of delivery and organizational coordination appropriate? And so on. Information on the implementation environment is useful for improving the implementation processes and facilitating the interpretation of evaluation results.

For example, the implementation environment domain in the Performance Contracting Experiment would concern what kind of environment the treatment should operate in. More specifically, what kind of classroom atmosphere is desirable? Casual or formal? What kind of teaching staff is required? Licensed teachers, paraprofessionals, or teaching aides? What kind of curriculum schedule should be maintained? What kind of relationship should exist between program teaching staff and regular schoolteachers? And so on.

Outcome Domain

A program is created for the purpose of providing services or solving problems. These purposes are formally called goals or intended outcomes. Because goals or intended outcomes are what the program strives to achieve, they are crucial to stakeholders for two reasons. First, goals are usually used by stakeholders to guide their activities and to determine resource allocation. Second, goals are frequently used as criteria to assess the effectiveness of the program.

However, in addition to goals or intended outcomes, a program is also very likely to generate unintended outcomes that are ignored or are not foreseen by stakeholders. Traditional goal-attainment types of evaluation usually do not cover issues of unintended outcomes. However, when important unintended outcomes are neglected, the evaluation of program impacts may be too narrow or even misleading.

The outcome domain concerns issues of both intended and unintended outcomes. For example, the intended outcomes in the Performance Contracting Experiment were the increases of students' competence in mathematics and reading scores. The unintended outcomes might be the students' absenteeism or objections from regular teachers.

Impact Domain

The impact domain concerns assessing the impact of the treatment on the outcome. Efforts spent lead stakeholders such as decision makers to want to know whether the treatment is effective or in what direction the program is actually moving. The effectiveness of a program is difficult to know unless the relationship between the treatment and the outcome is well understood. This domain concerns issues related to providing a strong causal inference in the impact assessment. For example, the impact domain in the Performance Contracting Experiment concerns whether the treatment has an impact on the outcome variables such as mathematics score, reading score, or absenteeism. The impact domain has been the major focus in traditional evaluation and will continue to be one of the important evaluation domains in the future.

Intervening Mechanism Domain

This domain investigates the causal processes that link the implemented treatment to outcomes—that is, the processes by which the treatment produces or fails to produce the desired outcome. Program treatment usually affects program outcomes through some intervening process. An investigation of intervening mechanisms will provide information about why a program works or does not work and will help to diagnose the strengths and/or weaknesses of a program so that possible improvements can be made.

For example, one of the intervening mechanisms in the Performance Contracting Experiment may be the students' motivation for learning. The treatment in the experiment may be expected first to change students' motivation, which, in turn, may affect their mathematics and reading scores.

Generalization Domain

Sometimes decision makers and/or other key stakeholders have a clear idea about how evaluation results will be used in the future in a particular population, setting, or organization. In this case, it is important for evaluators to be aware of this expectation and plan the evaluation to provide information on how the evaluation results may be generalized from the current research system to the future target system. For example, the generalization domain in the Performance Contracting Experiment concerns issues such as whether the evaluation results can be generalized to other school districts or to other firms implementing a similar program. Even if a target situation is not specified, it is important for the evaluator to indicate to what type of situation the results can be generalized.

The relationships among these domains are illustrated in Figure 2.1. Figure 2.1 indicates the two systems involved in an evaluation: the research system and the generalizing system. The research system is the system in which an evaluation takes place. The generalizing system is the system to which evaluation results will be generalized and within which they will be used in the future.[1] Within the research system, the treatment domain on the left side of the diagram deals with the nature of the treatment. The outcome domain on the right concerns which outcome variables should be examined.

In the research system, the impact domain deals with assessing the relationship between the treatment domain and the outcome domain. The intervening mechanism domain concerns the intervening processes that link the treatment domain and the outcome domain. The implementation environment domain indicates how the program is implemented. Furthermore, causal relationships between the treatment and the outcomes or the intervening mechanism are conditioned by the contextual factors represented by the implementation environment. Following conventional usage, the arrows from the implementation environment indicate these conditioning influences (see Heise, 1975). For example, the success of a job training program may be contingent upon whether the job skills provided by the program meet the demands of the local market. The domain of the implementation environment is also directed toward this type of issue.

The generalization domain, at the bottom of Figure 2.1, addresses the issue of whether the processes and outcomes generated in the research system, on the left of the diagram, can be generalized or applied to the generalizing system, on the right hand of the diagram. Because the generalizing system usually has a different implementation environment, the evaluation findings in the research system may not be automatically generalizable to the generalizing system. Special effort must be taken to build into the evaluation features that enhance generalizability. In short, the generalization domain deals with the issue of how to enhance generalizability.

Domain Theories

The theory-driven perspective argues that six domain theories are required to evaluate these six domains.

The following three domain theories are part of the general normative theory:

(1) *Treatment theory* specifies what the nature of the program treatment should be.

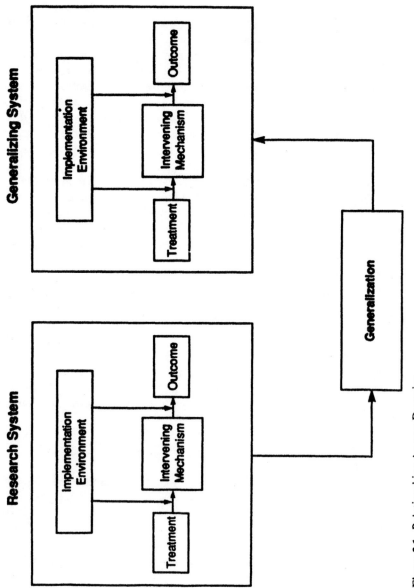

Figure 2.1. Relationships Among Domains

(2) *Implementation environment theory* specifies the nature of the contextual environment within which the program should be implemented.

(3) *Outcome theory* specifies what the nature of the program outcomes should be.

The following three domain theories are related to the general causative theory:

(4) *Impact theory* specifies the causal effect between the treatment and the outcome.

(5) *Intervening mechanism theory* specifies how the underlying intervening processes operate.

(6) *Generalization theory* specifies the generalizability of evaluation results to the topics or circumstances of interest to stakeholders.

A systematic combination of all six domain theories constitutes a superordinate theory of the program. It is desirable for evaluating the subordinate theory of a program, but this does not imply that these six domain theories have to be evaluated simultaneously in every evaluation. Due to time and resource constraints, an evaluation may often require that only one or a few of the domain theories be evaluated in accordance with the specific concerns of stakeholders. For example, stakeholders may mainly be concerned with the following issues in the normative domain theories: the appropriateness of the delivered treatment in terms of intensity and amount; whether or not certain features of the implementation environment, such as mode of delivery, hinder the treatment delivery processes; and the true nature of the goals the program is actually pursuing.

When the program is mature and routinized, program effectiveness or generalizability becomes a salient issue. An evaluator may be asked to evaluate one or more of the causative domain theories such as impact, intervening mechanism, and generalization. Generally speaking, it requires more time and effort to evaluate causative domain theories than normative domain theories.

Furthermore, the normative domain theories and causative domain theories are not disconnected from each other. In fact, the information found in evaluating normative domain theories, such as that on treatment, implementation environment, and outcome, provides the knowledge of contextual and intervening factors needed to explain or interpret the empirical findings in the causative domains of impact, intervening mechanism, and generalization. For example, information on the nature of the treatment, implementation processes, and outcomes can help explain why the treatment does or does not have the intended impact. This provides insights into the intervening processes that suggest how they operate and to what extent they may produce similar results in different programs or contexts.

On the other hand, the evaluation findings from the causative domains can eventually provide information on the performance of the normative domains and can indicate how to improve these domains, such as how to redesign the treatment structure, what implementation factors must be considered in the future, and what outcomes should be given more attention in the future.

TYPOLOGY OF THEORY-DRIVEN EVALUATIONS

These six domain theories (treatment, implementation environment, outcome, impact, intervening mechanism, and generalization) allow us to systematically derive two general categories of theory-driven evaluations: basic and composite. Basic types are derived directly from each type of domain theory. Composite types are constructed from combinations of these basic types, which produce various new types of evaluations.

Basic Types

Based upon the six domain theories, the following six basic types of evaluations can be derived. The relationships between theories and these six basic types are illustrated in Figure 2.2. Because each basic type will be discussed in detail in later chapters of the book, this section is intended to provide only a brief overview.

Normative Treatment Evaluation

This type of evaluation focuses on identifying the normative structure of the treatment, examining the actual treatment delivered in the field, and assessing the congruency between the normative and implemented treatment. For example, by working with program designers and other

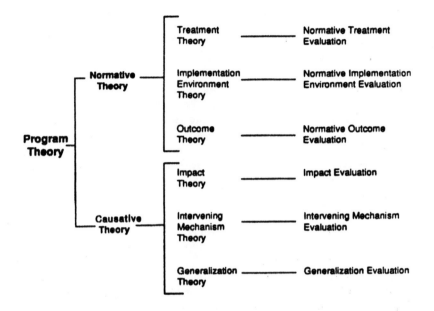

Figure 2.2. Relationships Between Theories and Basic Evaluation Types

stakeholders, Brekke (1987) has specified the normative theory of treatment in a community support program for the chronically mentally ill. Empirical data on program operation were then collected to assess the congruency between theoretical and implemented treatment. Brekke (1987) has demonstrated the usefulness of this type of evaluation for program managers and administrators in improving program operations.

Normative Implementation Environment Evaluation

This type of evaluation focuses on identifying the normative implementation environment, examining the actual implementation environment in the field, and assessing the congruency between the theoretical implementation environment and the actual implementation environment. For example, the normative implementation environment of a drug treatment program for youngsters may specify that therapeutic sessions for drug-addicted youngsters should not be carried out in an environment that emphasizes coercion or physical punishments. After the normative implementation environment is specified, then empirical data are gathered to assess its congruency with the actual implementation environment.

Normative Outcome Evaluation

Normative outcome evaluation involves systematically identifying or clarifying a set of program goals or outcomes for facilitating the processes of program planning and management. Normative outcome evaluation is especially useful when multiple stakeholders are unclear concerning what specific goals they are pursuing or have conflicting goals that are difficult to reconcile. The multiattribute utility analyses proposed by Edwards et al. (1975) serve as one example of a normative outcome evaluation that generated a set of goals that were acceptable to multiple constituents.

Impact Evaluation

The purpose of this type of evaluation is to assess the impact of the treatment on the outcomes. This type of evaluation is different from the traditional summative evaluation in two aspects: First, the impact evaluation emphasizes the generation of a broad evidence base in evaluating program impacts. To achieve this, evaluators are required to actively and creatively use stategies and designs, especially those that are theory guided, to strengthen evidence for causal inferences. Strategies such as patched-up designs (Cordray, 1986) and pattern matching (Trochim, forthcoming) are good examples. Second, the impact evaluation emphasizes the need to be sensitive to important intended and unintended outcomes. This requires clarifying stakeholders' policy-relevant goals and proposing outcomes that are theoretically plausible for investigation (Chen and Rossi, 1980). Either of these two aspects may serve as the basis for an impact evaluation.

Intervening Mechanism Evaluation

This type of evaluation attempts to expand the scope of the evaluation by incorporating intervening processes. The intervening mechanism evaluation provides information on causal processes between the treatment and the outcome. For example, in evaluating a juvenile delinquency program, Chandler (1973) demonstrates that the treatment variable (role taking) affects the outcome variable (delinquent behavior) through the intervening variable of social egocentrism. Furthermore, the causal process identified through the intervening mechanism evaluation not only provides information that is important in terms of better understanding the potential of a program but also provides a diagnosis of the potential problems that can be used for future program improvement.

Generalization Evaluation

This type of evaluation attempts to integrate the issues of generalization into evaluation processes. This type of evaluation looks beyond the specific results of an implemented program in a future-oriented view of how to enhance the generalizability of the evaluation results to other situations that may be of interest to the stakeholders. Because the ultimate purpose of doing evaluation is application, generalization evaluation addresses important issues in program evaluation. Chen and Rossi (1987) argue that, in designing a generalization evaluation, the evaluator should consider issues such as the structure and operating procedures of the future organization that will implement the program, potential contingencies that could affect the operations of the treatment, and possible shifts and changes in the implementation environment.

Composite Types

Different combinations of the above basic types can produce a large number of composite types of theory-driven evaluations. For example, one type of normative evaluation can be connected with other normative evaluations. Or, one type of causative evaluation can be integrated with other causative or normative evaluations. It is beyond the scope of this book to discuss all the possible composite types of theory-driven evaluations. Instead, two composite types of theory-driven evaluations that might be more related to current concerns and developments than others will be discussed in detail in later chapters of this book. These two composite types are briefly discussed below.

Normative Treatment-Impact Evaluation

This composite type is constructed from the combination of a normative treatment evaluation with an impact evaluation. One of the functions of this type of evaluation is to pinpoint crucial components in the treatment that affect the outcomes. As an example, a program often contains a number of components, and stakeholders may want to know which components contribute more to program effectiveness. A normative treatment-impact evaluation attempts to systematically elaborate these treatment components in the impact evaluation to provide information on the relative effectiveness of each component.

Normative Implementation Environment-Impact Evaluation

This composite type is constructed from the integration of an implementation environment evaluation with an impact evaluation. One of the reasons for program failure is slippage between planning and implementation. The incorporation of implementation environment evaluation into an impact evaluation can provide useful contextual information for improving the effectiveness of a program. For example, a factor in the implementation environment (perhaps capital investments in traditional techniques) may have resulted in the failure of an agricultural extension program to persuade farmers to adopt an innovative technique. An impact evaluation that only indicated program failure may not be as useful to decision makers in improving the program in comparison with a normative implementation environment-impact evaluation that identifies the exact factor of the implementation environment that caused the failure or success of the program.

Because program theory must be incorporated into evaluation processes regardless of which type of theory-driven evaluation is used, it is important to understand the various approaches to theory construction and to have a set of guidelines and principles to direct the construction of program theory. The next two chapters attempt to discuss these issues. The application of basic types and composite types of theory-driven evaluations will be discussed in detail following Chapter 5.

NOTE

1. The concepts of research and generalizing systems will be illustrated in detail in Chapter II.

3. Constructing Program Theory: Values, Approaches, and Strategies

PROGRAM THEORY AND VALUES

The most essential task when applying theory-driven evaluations—regardless of which type, or types, is adopted—is the construction of program theory. However, the construction of program theory is a value-laden activity. "Values" are defined in this book as ideas or meanings of what ought to be. They are attributed to or shared by a group or community. Values are involved in the construction of program theory in a number of ways. Values can affect what goals or outcomes should be used to judge the worth of a program, what causal processes should be investigated, and how to conceptualize and measure the variables concerned. Depending upon the values that underlie the program, different program theories will be generated. Even when evaluating the same program, theory constructed from the stakeholders' values may be quite different from theory constructed from the evaluators' professional values and expertise.

For example, in evaluating the impact of an office automation program in an organization, an evaluator can formulate a program theory by taking the managers' values. The theory may suggest that the automation system will facilitate communication and coordination between units, hence it will enhance productivity. Alternatively, based upon his or her own values, knowledge, or experience, an evaluator may construct an alternative program theory for the same office automation program.

This theory may specify that office automation will provide managers with a powerful means of surveillance for controlling workers' activities, such as their pace and speed. Hence, it could create dissatisfaction among the workers.

Because the construction of program theory is value laden, it is legitimate to raise concerns such as these: Should an evaluator only accept stakeholders' values when formulating program theory, irrespective of his or her own values? Or should evaluators mainly follow their professional values in formulating program theory? Or should both stakeholders' theory and evaluators' theory be incorporated in the same evaluation?

These vital questions are difficult to address without knowing what the basic values are in program evaluation. To facilitate the understanding of strategies for formulating program theory, the next section will provide an intensive discussion of basic values in program evaluation as well as problems in achieving these values.

EVALUATION OF EVALUATION:
BASIC VALUES OF PROGRAM EVALUATION

One of the major tasks of an evaluation is to judge the merits of a program. However, prior to an evaluation, there is a fundamental question to ask: How can we know if a program evaluation will be useful or of high quality? Obviously, a set of values for judging evaluations is needed. These values are defined here as the fundamental ideas of a useful and estimable evaluation. These values are important for both knowing the appropriateness of an evaluation and providing general guidance on what is expected of the evaluation at hand.

What are the fundamental values by which we can judge whether or not a given evaluation is useful and of high quality? Unfortunately, this is a very difficult question—but a question we must answer. Different theorists disagree profoundly on what the fundamental values are and on how to classify them. The traditional classification of values in quantitative research has been the distinction between internal and external validity proposed by Campbell and Stanley (1963). According to Campbell and Stanley (1963, p. 5), internal validity is concerned with the question: "Did the experimental treatment make a difference in this specific experimental instance?" External validity, on the other hand, asks: "To what populations, settings, treatment variables, and measurement variables can this effect be generalized?" This classification has been revised by Cook and Campbell (1979). One important feature in their revision is the subdivision of the values of internal and external validity into two additional subcategories: statistical conclusion validity and construct validity. The former refers to the appropriateness of drawing conclusions from the statistical evidence in research; the latter refers to making generalizations about higher-order constructs from research operations.

In spite of the popularity of these classifications, there have been strong disagreements regarding the priority of these values. Campbell and Stanley (1963) and Cook and Campbell (1979) argue forcefully that the prime priority in evaluation should be internal validity. They view internal validity as the sine qua non of research. In order for any research finding to have external validity, it first must have internal validity, with all sources of spuriousness carefully eliminated so that there is a true result that can be generalized. Similar arguments are also made by Cook and Campbell (1979).

On the contrary, critics such as Cronbach (Cronbach, 1982; Cronbach et al., 1980) strongly argue that external validity, rather than internal validity, is the more important value in evaluation. Because a profitable evaluation is one that can draw stakeholders' attention to relevant facts and maximally influence their decisions, Cronbach argues that it is essential for evaluators to design evaluations that allow them to extrapolate information from domains such as population, treatment, measurement, and setting.

Another issue, in addition to the disagreement over priority, is that the classifications provided by Campbell and his associates do not cover other important values. One of these values is responsiveness. Stake (1975) and Guba and Lincoln (1981) point out that, because evaluation has specific stakeholders to serve, an evaluation should respond to the needs and views of these stakeholders and should highlight the different views and needs held by different stakeholder groups. Other frequently mentioned values, such as objectivity (Scriven, 1971), justice (House, 1976), and relevance, timeliness, and broadness in scope (e.g., Rossi and Freeman, 1985; Posavac and Carey, 1989; Cronbach et al., 1980), are also left out of the traditional classification.

Lincoln and Guba (1985) have developed a classification of values that mainly pertains to qualitative research. These authors argue that the trustworthiness of qualitative research is based upon criteria such as true value, applicability, consistency, and neutrality. Each of these values is parallel to the following comparable values in quantitative research: internal validity, external validity, reliability, and objectivity. These two sets of values are more different in terms of how they can be achieved (quantitatively or qualitatively) than in terms of their meanings.

More recently, Lincoln and Guba (1986) have argued that authenticity should also be an important concern in qualitative research, but they concede that their concept of authenticity has not been fully developed yet. Authenticity may cover criteria such as fairness, conscientiousness, enrichment (ontological authentication), appreciating other stakeholders' views and needs (educative authentication), stimulating actions (catalytic authentication), and generating desirable change (tactical authenticity). In general, authenticity (Lincoln and Guba, 1986) appears to be an elaboration of the value of responsiveness (Guba and Lincoln, 1981; Stake, 1975).

All of these elaborations and variations in values and value classifications may be useful for helping their advocates to illustrate their viewpoints. However, for the purpose of a general discussion of the relationship between values and other evaluation issues, a parsimonious scheme of values is needed. The parsimony may be achieved through combining two or more related values to form a more general value. For example, the values of relevance and timeliness can be incorporated into the general value of responsiveness. Another example is, for convenience, that the value of internal validity can include issues of both internal and statistical conclusion validity, as has been implied in Campbell and Stanley's classification. Furthermore, if the focus of a discussion is on the meanings of values themselves rather than on what methods are used to implement these values, then there is no need to have two labels for the same value—one for quantitative research and another for qualitative research.

Based upon these strategies, a scheme of fundamental values for program evaluation is developed in the following pages. This scheme deals with the following values: responsiveness, objectivity, trustworthiness, and generalizability. There is no claim that this scheme exhausts all the values in program evaluation. However, as will soon be shown, this scheme includes those values of most concern to many evaluators. There is also no claim that this is the most parsimonious classification. Alternative classifications can always be constructed. However, as will be demonstrated later, this scheme serves particularly well for the purpose of discussing the relationship between values and program theory. The meanings and implications of this value scheme are discussed below.

Responsiveness

Cronbach et al. (1980) point out that the traditional concept of evaluation focuses on the interests of just one stakeholder group, such as decision makers. However, because decision making in democratic societies is characterized by pluralism, the evaluation that lets one single group set the question for its attention tends not to be useful (Cronbach, 1982). A great majority of evaluators (e.g., Stake, 1975; Patton, 1980; Guba and Lincoln, 1981; Cronbach et al., 1980) accept that evaluation results should be relevant and useful to the needs and concerns of not only decision makers but also other stakeholders such as program managers, program staffs, and clients. This value is called responsiveness.

Evaluations are rarely, if ever, done out of purely academic curiosity; they are done to provide useful information for program stakeholders in order to improve program operations and ultimately to improve society. From the stakeholders' perspective, it is desirable that the evaluator understand their viewpoints, beliefs, and interests, so that the evaluator may provide the information the stakeholders want. From the evaluator's perspective, it is both personally and professionally satisfying to do a good evaluation that results in action and change.

A number of evaluation utilization studies have pointed out factors that are related to responsiveness. One is timeliness, that is, making sure that the stakeholders get the information while there is still time to use it. Davis and Salasin (1975) claim that lack of timeliness is frequently cited as a major reason for nonuse of evaluation reports. Another factor related to nonuse is relevance. Anderson (1975) indicates that program staff frequently do not view evaluation results as being relevant to their decision-making processes. Another factor in responsiveness is broadness, that is, taking in the whole range of program consequences. Mushkin (1973) argues that a useful evaluation must be broad and flexible enough to include all of the intended and unintended consequences of the program.

Given that an evaluation is constrained by time and resources, it is impossible for an evaluator to satisfy all the interests raised by every group or coalition (Raizen and Rossi, 1981). An important issue is to which groups' interests should the evaluator pay more attention. There has been strong disagreement among evaluators on this issue. Wholey (1979, 1987) assigns a high priority to federal and state decision makers and managers. Stake (1986, 1978) prefers to give priority to local implementors and other related interest groups. For the sake of justice, House (1976, 1980) insists that the evaluators should advance the interests of the least privileged groups. Taking the view of pluralism in decision-making processes, Cronbach (1982) and Lincoln and Guba (1986) favor an evenness idea, which takes interests among primary stakeholder groups equally.

The evenness approach is perhaps more attractive than other approaches. An evaluation needs strong support from powerful groups in order to be funded or carried out. It is usually not feasible for an evaluator to ignore powerful interests in doing an evaluation. The evenness approach argues for taking the powerful groups' interests seriously. In addition, the evenness approach enhances justice in the sense that it attempts to raise disadvantaged groups' interests to a level similar to others. Because the evaluator is only one of the constituents in policy processes, there is no guarantee that the final priority assignment will exactly follow the evenness idea. However, evaluators should have the responsibility at least to bring the powerful groups' attention to the problem of neglect of disadvantaged groups' interests and to negotiate for a fair consideration.

Objectivity

The meaning of objectivity can be better understood through the following contrast made by Scriven (1971, pp. 95-96): "'Subjective' means unreliable, biased or probably biased, a matter of opinion, and 'objective' means reliable, factual, confirmable or confirmed, and so forth." Furthermore, objectivity is attained through intersubjective agreement (Scriven, 1971) rather than through requiring evaluators to purge all their values. Based upon Scriven's work, "objectivity" in this book refers to the expectation that evaluators' personal preferences or loyalties do not contaminate evaluation results and that results yielded by certain research techniques or procedures are replicable by others by using the same techniques and procedures.[1] A number of authors have commented on the importance of objectivity in program evaluation. Reicken and Boruch (1974) argue that evaluations must be objective in order to ensure that the results are valid and reliable. Caplan (1977) points out that decision makers are more likely to use evaluation studies that are objective. Drawing from their experience, Braskamp et al. (1987) point out that clients frequently hire external evaluators to guarantee objectivity in the evaluation process. Even internal evaluators are told by policymakers that they need to be perceived as objective and, therefore, they need to keep some distance from administrators.

Cronbach's (1982) concept of reproducibility is also related to objectivity. His approach asks whether another evaluator using the same procedure would get the same results, which would indicate that the original evaluation was carried out objectively. In addition, it asks whether an evaluator faced with the same situation would design a similar evaluation, which would indicate that the evaluation was designed objectively.

Scriven (1967, 1971, 1972, 1983) has made important contributions in advancing the understanding of the relationship between objectivity and evaluation. Scriven points out that the very credibility of an evaluation depends upon its objectivity. Because an evaluator who stands to gain or lose by the results of an evaluation cannot carry out a study without bias, Scriven argues that ideally an evaluator should not have a personal stake in the success or failure of the program. Furthermore, Scriven (1972) takes the concept of objectivity further to argue that even evaluators' merely knowing stakeholders' designated goals can create a problem in objectivity. The awareness of program goals may make evaluators develop tunnel vision, thus decreasing opportunities to detect the real impacts and, therefore, producing biased results.[2]

Trustworthiness

"Trustworthiness" is defined in this book as an assurance that an evaluation will provide convincing evidence that can be trusted by stakeholders or others in their utilization of evaluation results.[3] This value is related to the concept of "internal validity" in the experimental paradigm and to the concept of "nonspuriousness" in econometrics. In all three cases, the main concern is with the elimination of confounding factors in the research. Lately, even naturalists such as Lincoln and Guba (1985, 1986) have also come to believe that this criterion, under the name "true value," is essential to naturalistic evaluations. In spite of criticisms from other perspectives (e.g., Cronbach, 1982; Lincoln and Guba, 1985), the experimental paradigm, so far, has made the most important contribution to dealing with the issues of trustworthiness. Campbell and his associates' (e.g., Campbell and Stanley, 1963; Cook and Campbell, 1979) identification of a checklist of threats to validity demystifies the sources of biases in a study. Their checklist not only indicates the possible effects the threats may have on the research but also provides the evaluator with a basis for planning to deal with them. Furthermore, Campbell and his associates also provide various experimental and quasi-experimental designs for ensuring trustworthiness in evaluation.

Although the experimental paradigm will continue to play an important role in dealing with trustworthiness in the future, some of the experimental paradigms' conceptualizations and applications are in need of change or further development. Cordray (1986) and Trochim (1986b) have criticized the traditional application of the design taxonomy provided by the experimental paradigm as being too passive and rigid. Similarly, Chen (1988) points out that the randomized experiment is a powerful design, but some strong statements, such as that the randomized experiment is the best method to ensure internal validity in all situations, might be overstated. In practice, problems such as difficulty in maintaining design integrity and participants' reactivity in the field can quickly diminish the power of randomized experiments.

This book uses the concept of trustworthiness to emphasize that there are a number of ways to skin a cat. Under different conditions, trustworthiness can be achieved by a variety of methods and strategies. According to this view, unlike that of the experimental paradigm, we can recognize the merits of the experimental methods without the necessity of rejecting the merits of other strategies and methods for achieving the same ends. Perhaps the less we insist that there is only one best method in all situations (either quantitative or qualitative), the more we will develop new strategies and methods for achieving trustworthiness. Currently, there are efforts under way to expand the traditional view of how to achieve trustworthiness. Some of the original supporters of the experimental paradigm (e.g., Cook, 1985; Shotland and Mark, 1987) assert that each method has its own strengths and weaknesses and thus trustworthiness can be better achieved by applying multiple methods. Alternatively, Cordray (1986), Chen and Rossi (1987), and Trochim (1985, forthcoming) argue in favor of systematically elaborating the theoretical patterns underlying a program in order to broaden the evidence base as a general strategy for enhancing trustworthiness.[4]

Generalizability

"Generalizability" refers to the extent to which evaluation results can be applied to future pertinent circumstances or problems in which stakeholders are interested. Generalizability implies that evaluation results gathered from past program activities will be used by stakeholders for decision making in the future. This future-oriented aspect of program evaluation has been well illustrated by Cronbach (1982). Cronbach pointed out that there is always a time gap between the sample domains (which he labels "utos") in an evaluation and the future domain (which he terms "*UTOS") to which results will be applied. Unless evaluators provide information about the past history of a program so that decision makers can extrapolate evaluation results to future domains (*UTOS), the evaluation will have little value.

Generalizability can also mean that evaluation results can be used outside of the boundary of a specific program. Mushkin (1973) argues that decision makers almost always want to be able to apply the results of an evaluation beyond its specific purpose. He points out that decision makers tend to be more interested in broad issues than in the specific and narrow results provided by most evaluations. They tend to look at the program in a broad sense and hope that what they learn can be applied even beyond the limits of the program being evaluated. For example, a school lunch program may be evaluated in terms of its success in improving children's nutrition, but decision makers may also regard it as a farm income program, an education program, or an income redistribution program and wish to gauge its effectiveness in these areas. Such information is useful to decision makers who are considering expanding or modifying their program.

STAKEHOLDER VERSUS SOCIAL SCIENCE APPROACH IN FORMULATING PROGRAM THEORY

Because the construction of program theory is value laden, a focus on different values will generate different theory construction approaches, which, in turn, will produce different program theories. Based upon different values, two approaches to formulating program theory have been proposed: stakeholder and social science approaches.

Stakeholder Approach

This approach strongly emphasizes the value of responsiveness in constructing program theory. The stakeholder approach refers to the construction of program theory in a way that is highly responsive to key stakeholders' perspectives, views, ideas, and/or expectations. The rationale underlying this approach is that, because it is usually the stakeholder who sponsors the evaluation and utilizes the evaluation results, program theory has to reflect the key stakeholders' values in order to be useful. The stakeholder approach has been systematically developed and applied by Wholey and his associates (e.g., Wholey, 1979, 1987; Rutman, 1980) although Patton (1980, forthcoming) and Trochim (1985, forthcoming) have also made contributions in this area.

The construction of program theory is one of the crucial elements in Wholey and his associates' work (e.g., Wholey, 1979) on evaluability assessment, that is, an assessment of the feasibility of evaluating a program for the purpose of improving program performance. According to Wholey and his associates, in constructing program theory, the stakeholder approach requires evaluators to obtain clues or hints from both relevant documents and interviews with multiple stakeholders. Relevant documentation includes the program's legislative history, regulations and guidelines, budget justification, monitoring reports, and reports of program accomplishments. Key policymakers, managers, and interest groups would be questioned regarding their assumptions and expectations about the relationships among program resources, program activities, and expected outcomes. These interviews and site visits reveal program priorities, expected program accomplishments, relationships between objectives, the resources needed to accomplish the objectives, problems and difficulties facing the program, and information needs.

Based upon the documentation review and interviews, evaluators can construct a tentative model and discuss the model with key stakeholders, highlighting the differences in expectations discussed above. This process should facilitate agreements on the intended program theory in terms of program resources, activities, intended outcomes, important side effects, and assumed causal links among resources, activities, and outcomes. After the differences are resolved, a formal program theory can be completed.

Program theory as constructed by Wholey and his associates can be present in a PERT chart, which links resource inputs through a chain of events to final objectives. The program theory usually outlines a chain of administrative events demonstrating how one administrative step (e.g., allocation of resources) leads to another step (e.g., training of staff) and so on. Wholey (1987) stresses that the purpose of the construction of program theory is mainly to clarify and develop the key stakeholders' theory underlying the program. Evaluators should not rely on their own knowledge or expertise to construct program theory. Wholey (1987) insists that theory should be emergent from the data rather than imposed by a prior structure or hypothesis.

Social Science Approach

Alternatively, a social science approach that emphasizes the value of objectivity in constructing program theory has been proposed by Chen and Rossi (1980, 1983). The social science approach argues that program theory should be derived from information on both how the program is actually operated and existing social science theory and knowledge.

Chen and Rossi (1980, 1983) are concerned that evaluators' uncritical acceptance of key stakeholders' values may not reflect the reality of the program. Because of vested interests, key stakeholders' perspectives and views may overly emphasize the desirability rather than the plausibility of the program. A desirable version of theory, in spite of its intuitive appeal to stakeholders in the short run, may not necessarily be the best for providing enlightening information on the program.

Furthermore, because key stakeholders' understanding of both social problems and the theory of a program are usually based upon common sense or hunch, the construction of program theory based exclusively on the stakeholders' perspective may not be sufficiently sensitive to capture the complicated causal processes underlying the program. Evaluators who formulate program theory based upon uncritical acceptance of stakeholders' values and viewpoints may be off the mark. For example, it is well known that official goals often are not operative goals (Perrow, 1961). An evaluator who relies mainly on the stakeholders' views in specifying outcomes may focus too much attention on official goals that are not seriously pursued by the staff. On the other hand, those areas most likely to be affected by operative goals may not be included in the evaluation.

Unlike Wholey (1987), Chen and Rossi (1980, 1983) insist that evaluators should utilize their own expertise and knowledge in constructing program theory. Program theory based upon knowledge of both how the program is operated and social science theory may provide a better opportunity to understand program structure, processes, and consequences. Chen and Rossi (1980, 1983) do not object to the inclusion of the key stakeholders' views in formulating program theory. In fact, they suggest that theories constructed from both perspectives should be included in the evaluation. However, Chen and Rossi (1980, 1983) do not provide detailed procedures or guidance for integrating the perspectives.

STRENGTHS AND LIMITATIONS OF
STAKEHOLDER AND SOCIAL SCIENCE APPROACHES

Both stakeholder and social science approaches are useful when the evaluation requires maximization of either the responsiveness or the objectivity of the evaluation. For example, if the evaluation situation only requires managerial consulting to provide immediate information useful in clarifying the stakeholders' program theory, the application of the stakeholder approach may be sufficient. Similarly, if the evaluation situation requires an impartial and systematic investigation of how causal mechanisms underlying the program operate, the use of the social science approach may be appropriate.

However, when an evaluation situation requires dealing with more than one basic value, the use of either the stakeholder or the social science approach is not sufficient. The need to develop a theory construction approach that can deal with multiple values has been supported by knowledge utilization literature (e.g., Weiss, 1977). This literature clearly indicates that decision makers frequently assess the usefulness of an evaluation by considering its implications for multiple values rather than for one single value. Holzner and Fisher (1979) argue that the frames of reference used by stakeholders in social reform when appraising knowledge claims involve two central components: truth tests and relevance tests. They (1979, pp. 232-33) define "truth tests" as "decision points concerning evidence; the grounds for accepting or rejecting truth claims include the obvious empirical as well as formal rational tests." On the other hand, "relevance tests" are defined as "decision situations in which the potential significance of an item or line of inquiry is assessed with regard to the inquirer's cognitive interests." Truth tests emphasize scientific values while relevance tests emphasize political values. Holzner and Fisher's argument suggests that stakeholders in social reform tend to utilize knowledge that has both scientific and political merits. Decision makers' frames of reference for knowledge utilization have been empirically examined by Weiss and Bucuvalas (1980b). They interviewed 155 upper-level officials in federal, state, and local agencies in the fields of mental health, alcoholism, and drug abuse regarding how they evaluated the usefulness of actual research reports. Decision makers were asked to rate reports in terms of 29 criteria, such as technical quality, objectivity, applicability, congruence with potential users' ideas and values, and the political acceptability of the findings.

Factor analysis showed that three basic frames of reference were associated with the chance of a research study being used: *relevance* (How closely and clearly did the content of the study relate to the administrator's area of responsibility?); the *trust test* (Do the results match up with previous experience, knowledge, and values?); and the *utility test* (Does the research show how to make plausible changes in things that can plausibly be changed? Does the research challenge any current philosophy, program, or practice? Does it offer new perspectives or does it support the status quo?). Weiss and Bucuvalas's study empirically demonstrates that decision makers use multiple scientific and political criteria rather than any single criterion in judging the usefulness of a research project. The truth test is oriented more toward scientific values such as objectivity and trustworthiness, while relevance and the utility test are oriented more toward the political values such as responsiveness and generalizability. If decision makers' and other key stakeholders' frames of reference are likely to consider multiple values, as indicated in the utilization studies, this requires the construction of a program theory that takes multiple values into consideration. A theory construction approach that is more comprehensive than either the stakeholder approach or the social science approach is needed.

INTEGRATIVE APPROACHES

Integrative approaches attempt to build two or more values into the theory construction process of an evaluation. Chen and Rossi (1987) and Costner (forthcoming) have expanded the social science approach to deal with two other basic values: trustworthiness and generalizability. The trustworthiness of an evaluation can be enhanced through the incorporation of program theory. For example, if a substance-abuse treatment program is evaluated as successful overall, the evidence of a positive treatment effect can be strengthened when the theoretical patterns of the treatment also support the claim of success. The theory may suggest that those who attended most of the treatment sessions will do much better than those who attended only a few sessions. If this theoretical pattern is actually found, the claim of the treatment effect is enhanced. If, however, program participants improve regardless of how many sessions were attended, the treatment effect is questionable. Issues on program theory and trustworthiness will be discussed in more detail in Chapter 8.

Furthermore, Chen and Rossi (1987) argue that program theory can be formulated in a way that incorporates issues of generalizability. If generalizability is a concern, it is important to have a program theory that foresees the expected circumstances under which the evaluation results will be utilized and that incorporates those expectations when designing the program. For example, if a service-oriented program will eventually be implemented by ordinary administrators rather than by a special group of enthusiastic and highly innovative professionals, the generalizability of the evaluation will be higher when the evaluated program is run by ordinary administrators, and the evalutor has built that expectation into the evaluation processes. Issues on generalizability and program theory will be further discussed in Chapter 11.

Chen and Rossi (1987, pp. 101-2) suggest the following guidelines in constructing a program theory that can deal with generalizability:

1. Specify the conditioning variables, interaction variables and intervening variables, which realize the causal relationship between the treatment variables and outcome variables both in the research system and in the prospective system in which the program will be installed.

2. Develop an understanding of the ways in which the program in question would operate, including the population elements to be served, the agencies to be given administering responsibilities, and the potential distribution of contingencies and interactions involved.

3. Develop a sampling strategy and an administrative apparatus for the evaluation which mimics as closely as possible the images of the future setting of the program developed under (2) above.

This discussion of integrative approaches would not be complete without providing efforts to integrate the social science and stakeholder approaches. It is highly desirable to expand Chen and Rossi's (1980, 1983, 1987) conceptual framework to cover the value of responsiveness. This book attempts to fill this gap.

Any integrative approach that incorporates the value of responsiveness needs dual theorizing processes to integrate the social science and stakeholder approaches. On one hand, the evaluator should use the stakeholder approach to clarify and refine the key stakeholders' theory through interviews and documentation review as described in the previous section. On the other hand, based upon the social science approach, the evaluators should apply their knowledge, expertise, and understanding of the program to construct an alternative program theory.

During these dual theorizing processes, alternative and often multiple program theories are likely to be generated. The evaluator and key stakeholders need to review and discuss the implications of these theories in terms of issues such as the following: What are the merits or limitations? What kinds of information will be provided by these theories? How will the information be relevant to policy decision-making processes? And so on. Because any evaluation is constrained by resources and time, it is very likely that not all of the theories generated by the integrative approach will be included in the evaluation. The evaluator has to negotiate with key stakeholders to determine a version of program theory that fits the concerns of both stakeholders and evaluators. Evaluation is carried out after a consensus on the program theory has been reached. Through these dual and collaborative theorizing processes, the integrative approach has a better chance than other approaches to meet the requirements of the four basic values.

The final version of the program theory produced by the integrative approach is very likely to be a synthetic form of theory that covers issues of concern to both stakeholders and evaluators. However, in some situations it is still possible that, during the discussion and negotiation processes, the key stakeholders and the evaluators may agree that the final version of theory should be the one produced by either the stakeholder or the social science approach. Even so, this does not reduce the merit of the integrative approach, because the decision to use either the stakeholder or the social science approach to construct program theory is made by mutual understanding and consensus between key stakeholders and the evaluators rather than by an arbitrary decision of one party. The mutual understanding and consensus may facilitate the utilization of evaluation results.

PROBLEMS IN THE INTEGRATIVE APPROACH AND STRATEGIES FOR DEALING WITH THEM

Like other theory construction approaches, the integrative approach also has its limitations. To facilitate appropriate use of this approach, this section attempts to discuss these problems and proposes some strategies for dealing with them.

Problems in Pursuing Multiple Values

In spite of its merits, the integrative approach is not without its problems. Obviously, the use of a integrative approach may require more resources and time. However, in addition to the resource and time constraints, there is a less obvious, but equally important, problem; the fundamental dilemma of pursuing four basic evaluation values simultaneously. There is a trade-off between responsiveness and objectivity. The value of objectivity requires evaluators to be impartial (Scriven, 1971). The credibility of an evaluation is damaged when the evaluators begin to take the stakeholders' side or let stakeholders influence the evaluation foci and procedures. However, the strategies necessary to pursue responsiveness almost inevitably run against objectivity. To be highly responsive, the issues that should be used to judge program efficiency or effectiveness, and the plan for carrying out the investigation, tend to be determined or influenced by stakeholders' needs and interests. For the purpose of generating timely and relevant information, flexible and fluid research methods are preferred over standardized and replicable methods in data collection and research procedures. Evaluation may be designed in a fashion that is tailored more to fit the political reality than to pursue scientific truth. The higher the responsiveness, the higher the possibility that the evaluator's role as an objective observer is undermined. The trade-off relationship between trustworthiness and generalizability has been well documented in the literature (e.g., Cook and Campbell, 1979; Cronbach et al., 1980).

According to the experimental paradigm, to achieve trustworthiness, an evaluation ideally must have well-controlled, easily manipulable research conditions. The sample must be homogeneous and not too large. Intrusions or disturbances must be eliminated. The subjects must be randomly assigned to different experimental conditions. The research procedures must be followed exactly as planned, with no change allowed.

The research focuses intensively on a very few precisely measured variables.

But all of these features, which are similar to those in a laboratory setting and are intended to deal with trustworthiness, seriously limit generalizability. The structural arrangement, established for specific purposes, makes it very difficult to study the program in different contexts for generalization purposes, such as with different settings, groups, time, and administrative procedures. Furthermore, it is well known that a tightly controlled experiment is most likely to generate problems of reactivity, which further limits the generalization of research results.

In addition, there is also a trade-off relationship between trustworthiness and responsiveness. To assure trustworthiness, the evaluation often needs a rigorous design, which usually requires a lengthy period of time to plan and implement in the field. It must focus upon a few highly specific and measurable issues, with a research procedure that is highly fixed and standardized. However, these requirements for trustworthiness may also reduce responsiveness, which requires factors such as timeliness, flexibility, and the addressing of broad and general issues.

Sequential and Balancing Strategies for
Dealing with Conflicting Values

These fundamental dilemmas in pursuing multiple values imply that it is impossible for the integrative approach to maximize all four basic values (responsiveness, objectivity, trustworthiness, and generalizability) at the same time in an evaluation without problems in resource and time constraints. Chen (1989) indicates three strategies for dealing with multiple and conflicting values: maximizing, sequencing, and balancing.

Among them, the maximizing strategy urges stakeholders and evaluators to agree upon one of the basic values as of prime importance and to maximize that particular value. This strategy may provide a justification for using less comprehensive approaches such as the social science approach or the stakeholder approach, but it is not a satisfactory solution for dealing with multiple values. The other two strategies (sequential and balancing) discussed by Chen (1989) provide a better solution for the integrative approach in dealing with value dilemmas and are, therefore, discussed in greater detail below.

The Sequential Strategy

When the different values assessed by the integrative approach produce multiple theories and each is considered to be important, the sequential strategy suggests evaluating different theories in a time sequence. Depending on which theory is evaluated first, there are various ways to utilize the sequential strategy. For example, an evaluation can be carried out initially by evaluating the theory formulated by the stakeholder approach in order to maximize the value of responsiveness. After the program has been fine-tuned, the social science approach can be applied in subsequent evaluations to formulate a theory that attempts to deal with other values such as trustworthiness, objectivity, and/or generalizability. Similarly, another version of the application of the sequential strategy is to apply the social science approach for constructing program theory, which can maximize values of objectivity and trustworthiness, and then replicate the evaluation under different pertinent conditions to determine the generalizability or responsiveness of the results. This application of the sequential strategy may be favored by those advocates from the experimental paradigm tradition.

By dealing with different values at different times, a sequential strategy can effectively deal with multiple values. However, to replicate an evaluation two or more times can often substantially increase the cost and length of time involved. Unless there is strong support from the key stakeholders, it is not likely that this strategy will be considered feasible.

Balancing Strategy

The alternative balancing strategy, which is closely tied to the development of the theory-driven perspective (Chen and Rossi, 1987), can be used to deal with multiple and conflicting values. The balancing strategy assumes that, if an evaluation must deal with multiple values instead of constructing a program theory to maximizes one basic value at the expense of others, it may be better to allocate resources and energy to construct a theory that balances these four values. This balancing strategy will not result in the achievement of maximizing one value. But because it deals with multiple values simultaneously, the balancing strategy may be more likely to produce information that at least meets the minimum standards of both scientific and political requirements in program evaluation and that, therefore, is more useful for pluralistic decision-making purposes.

The advantage of using a balancing strategy is that it prevents evaluators from having tunnel vision and ignoring crucial issues in constructing program theory. The benefits obtained from investing resources and efforts in constructing a theory that fully achieves one of the basic values will follow the principle of diminishing returns. For example, five hours spent interviewing a stakeholder certainly means a greater understanding of that particular stakeholder's view of the program than would be the case with no interview at all. However, fifty additional hours spent interviewing the same person may not result in a significantly increased understanding. Given the resource constraint, the most important difference between five hours and fifty hours of interviews is that doing only the five-hour interview produces a good basic knowledge of the stakeholder's view but saves many resources that can be used to deal with other value dimensions. While the fifty hours may provide more refined and detailed knowledge of the same stakeholder, it is much more than sufficient for the evaluators' purposes and may greatly reduce the time and effort available for other important areas. Instead of putting forth resources to gain a trivial increment for either scientific or political values, the theory-driven perspective argues that the remaining resources should be allocated to other values, where larger gains may result.

The balancing strategy is compatible with those social science theories that also deal with conflicting values. For example, system theorists argue that a system has multiple and conflicting functions (e.g., maintenance and adaptation), and that the health or survival of a system depends on a balanced distribution of resources among those functions (e.g., Etzioni, 1960; Yuchtman and Seashore, 1967). Excess allocation of resources to a single function is dysfunctional. System theorists would argue that, if a program evaluation has multiple and conflicting value dimensions, the appropriate way to carry it out is to work for balance among these value dimensions rather than to maximize one of them.

More specifically, the balancing strategy is related to Herbert Simon's model (1955, 1956) for human decision making. Simon argues that, because of the limited human cognitive capacity for processing information and the uncertainty of future events, individuals and organizations are unable to order all the possibilities in a single utility scale and maximize the intended utility. Accordingly, Simon believes that actual decision making is likely to be done by finding a "satisficing" or "good enough" choice rather than by finding a maximizing choice.

Simon's argument has important implications for the balancing strategy. The discussion, above, of the basic values indicated that decision makers and other stakeholders hold multiple values rather than a single value in their frames of reference. Moreover, like most people, they have difficulty ordering their preferences on a utility scale. If Simon is correct, they prefer to have a satisfactory choice as a compromise among the different basic values. In this sense, the balancing strategy will come closer than other strategies to meeting the needs of decision makers.

If the situation requires an evaluation to deal with multiple values, the balancing strategy may be more preferable than other strategies for constructing program theory. Gosset (who used the pen name "Student" in all his writings), an eminent statistician and the inventor of the t-test, held a balancing view very similar to that of the theory-driven perspective. Gosset (e.g., "Student," 1936a, 1936b) disagreed strongly with Fisher's (1935) position that one should maximize trustworthiness at the expense of generalizability. Gosset forcefully argued that applied research should have implications for generalizability. He believed that both trustworthiness and generalizability should be dealt with in a research study, even though this might entail a sacrifice of some rigor or precision.[5]

Based upon these theory construction approaches and strategies for dealing with multiple values, some general principles and guidelines for conducting theory-driven evaluations will be developed in the next chapter.

NOTES

1. The value of objectivity contradicts the value of responsiveness. This issue will be explored in a later section of this chapter.

2. Scriven's goal-free evaluation will be discussed in Chapter 9 of this book.

3. The reason for using the term "trustworthiness" in this book rather than the more popular term "internal validity" is partly because of Campbell's (1986) own dissatisfaction with the internal validity label. An even more important reason is that the term "internal validity" implies that an evaluation is invalid if it does not meet each of the validity criteria specified by Campbell and Stanley (1963) and Cook and Campbell (1979). Or it may even imply that the experimental method is the best method to achieve internal validity in all situations. The use of the term "trustworthiness" is an attempt to avoid this connection. Furthermore, the definition of trustworthiness used in this book is somewhat different from Lincoln and Guba's (1985) usage.

4. This issue will be discussed in detail in Chapter 8.

5. The debate between Gosset and Fisher and its implications will be discussed in detail in Chapter 11.

4. Applications of Theory-Driven Evaluations

The conceptual framework of the theory-driven perspective outlined in the previous two chapters is very different from traditional evaluation perspectives. Accordingly, the role of the theory-driven evaluator and the principles for applying theory-driven evaluations are also different from the traditional ones. This chapter attempts to outline the theory-driven evaluator's role and to provide guidance and suggest principles to be followed in constructing and conducting theory-driven evaluations.

THE THEORY-DRIVEN EVALUATOR'S ROLE

The role of the theory-driven evaluator is much more broad and encompassing than that of merely providing information requested by decision makers or program staff. Instead, she or he should be a source of important and unanticipated information concerning a variety of policy issues relevant to a program, such as program planning, implementation, evaluation, and utilization of evaluation results. The evaluator is in a position to provide information that key stakeholders might otherwise ignore or misconstrue.

Evaluators should use their expertise, knowledge, and experience to provide an appropriate agenda for investigation and communicate their views to key stakeholders to promote the formulation of acceptable evaluation strategies. Accordingly, it may be useful for theory-driven evaluators to regard themselves as one of the stakeholders and to be concerned with doing a useful, high-quality evaluation. The evaluator and other key stakeholders can negotiate with each other to produce an evaluation design that will generate useful information and contribute to a pluralistic policy-making process. In doing so, a theory-driven evaluator may be required to take on the role of constituent and consensus generator.

As the evaluator is typically the only one among the stakeholders who possesses the expertise and familiarity with the scientific viewpoint that enables him or her to recognize the issues and problems most relevant to the evaluation, it is the evaluator's responsibiity to see that these issues are discussed and incorporated into the overall evaluation. In other words, as one of the constituents, evaluators should present their own professional ideas and views about which theoretical issues must be addressed, explain to the other stakeholders why they are important, and show how they can best be investigated. Evaluators cannot passively accept the values and views of the other stakeholders; as evaluation experts, they should present their professional views having in mind the planning of a useful evaluation.

The role of constituent does not imply that the theory-driven evaluator attempts to substitute his or her values and views for those of the other stakeholders. Rather, this role requires evaluators to express their professional opinions on what issues should be addressed and what financial and administrative supports will be required to achieve these purposes. As one of the constituents, evaluators should rely on their training, experience, and knowledge of the program to inform or bring to the stakeholders' attention important issues in the evaluation that might otherwise receive less attention or emphasis. After all, evaluators are paid to produce a good evaluation.

Furthermore, because evaluations are often carried out with limited resources and under rigid time constraints, the stakeholders' multiple and conflicting values and needs may create conflict and disagreements in establishing priorities and in creating agendas for the evaluations. Some consensus has to be reached among stakeholders before an evaluation can begin. In order to achieve some agreement upon which domains or issues the evaluation will focus and what theories will be formulated to accomplish these aims, the evaluator may also have to play the role of consensus generator. Evaluators must solicit consensus among stakeholders. After the stakeholders' views on evaluation domains and different types of theory-driven evaluation have been well communicated and understood, the evaluators should bring multiple stake-holders into an open discussion or even create a formal forum for reaching a consensus.

Open discussion may enable the multiple stakeholders to mutually comprehend each others' perspectives on evaluation domains and theories in a more purposive way than was previously the case. Increased understanding among stakeholders of the plural perspectives that constitute an organization might not only decrease perceived antagonism among stakeholders but might also increase the cohesiveness of that organization as a functioning unit. Here the evaluator acts as a mediator searching for consensus among stakeholders. If a compromise is not possible at the level of an open discussion, the evaluator intervenes more directly and actively utilizes his or her understanding of the organization's potential to reach a compromise position among the divergent stakeholders' perspectives.

If the number of stakeholders is small or if disagreements among them are not great, open discussion will usually enable them to effectively reach agreement and allow the evaluators to create a workable design for conducting the evaluation. However, when the number of stakeholders is large and there are divergent interests, evaluators may have to use the special consensus-promoting methods discussed in Chapter 5 to achieve agreement.

APPLYING THEORY-DRIVEN EVALUATIONS

Based upon the conceptual framework of the theory-driven perspective outlined in Chapters 2 and 3, the section below attempts to summarize some general guidelines and principles to be considered when designing and executing a theory-driven evaluation. The specific strategies and techniques for carrying out various types of theory-driven evaluations will be discussed in detail in the rest of this book.

Planning Stage

In the planning stage of the theory-driven evaluation, in-depth communication and negotiation between evaluators and key stakeholders are required to identify concerns such as these: What issues related to which domain or domains are the main concern in the evaluation? What type or types of theory-driven evaluation are relevant for addressing the issues? What theory construction approach will be most appropriate to use?

Furthermore, resource and time constraints and trade-offs among different values or issues are common in an evaluation (Cordray, forthcoming). To be comprehensive, these trade-offs and constraints need to be understood by both the evaluator and the key stakeholders before they decide which strategy will be used. During these discussions, it is the evaluator's duty to explain the issues related to theory-driven evaluation and theory construction and how they are relevant to a particular program or key stakeholder.

Some of the more important areas the evaluator should address are these: What procedures will be required in using any particular type of evaluation? What potential kinds of information can be expected from these evaluations? What kinds of resources and time frames are required in alternative types of evaluations? How will the evaluation results be utilized in decision-making processes? A systematic review and discussion of the strengths and limitations of alternative evaluations can facilitate negotiation between the evaluator and stakeholders in their efforts to reach agreement regarding the most appropriate types of theory-driven evaluation and the theory construction approach that can be used within the resource and time limitations of a particular program.

During these theorizing processes, alternative and often multiple evaluation strategies are likely to be generated. The evaluator has to inform stakeholders of the approximate cost and time frame necessary to carry out each of these evaluation strategies. The evaluator has to discuss and negotiate with stakeholders in order to determine the optimal theory-driven type and approach suitable, given the resource and time constraints. These planning processes will enhance the likelihood of designing a theory-driven evaluation that ensures an evaluator will pay attention to the crucial issues and may increase the stakeholders' utilization of evaluation results. The following is a set of principles that may provide useful guidance in planning a theory-driven evaluation.

(1) *The dual concern principle.* This principle states that the theory-driven evaluation should balance the dual concerns of the stakeholders' needs and the evaluators' professional judgment and standards. For the evaluation to be responsive, the stakeholders should have input into choosing the type of theory-driven evaluation to be used and helping to create theories that specify the evaluation processes. To be credible and generalizable, however, the design of an evaluation should not be subordinated to or overwhelmingly dominated by the stakeholders' wishes or views.

A program evaluation that is designed solely around the stakeholders' own perceived needs is often problematic. Stakeholders may fail to raise or foresee important issues because of their training, ideology, immediate concerns, or overinvolvement with the program. If the evaluator follows only the stakeholders' views in determining which evaluation domains to focus upon or which type of theory-driven evaluation to implement, important issues will often be neglected and only limited information will be provided by the evaluation. The evaluator's professional concern can be used to prevent this by prompting the evaluator to point out the important theoretical issues that need to be recognized by the stakeholders.

For example, the decision makers may originally propose an outcome evaluation that emphasizes the impact domain. The evaluator, however, might recognize that the intervening mechanism or generalization domain is crucial to that particular evaluation. The evaluators must bring these concerns to the attention of the decision makers and explain why these domains must also be examined.

Based upon his or her understanding of the program's operation, professional training, and existing theory and knowledge relevant to the program, the evaluator can propose studying the domains and domain theories that will be most useful for policy considerations. It is the professional concern of the evaluator that must compensate for the stakeholders' lack of knowledge or biased priorities.

(2) *The program deficiency principle.* This principle suggests that the particular type of theory-driven evaluation selected should be the one that can deal with the domains in which program problems are most evident. Depending on the nature of the program being evaluated, evaluations will find fewer problems in some domains than others. For example, in some programs, treatment implementation is straightforward and simple, such as mailing out welfare checks every month. Similarly, in some health programs, goals are specific and clear and represent a strong consensus among the stakeholders. In an antismoking program, there is probably little disagreement that the goal of the program is to help people quit smoking. When these domains do not present problems, evaluation resources can be shifted to other evaluation domains.

In some cases, the program deficiency principle can serve evaluators as a guide for setting a sequential strategy regarding which domains to focus upon first. For example, in the study by Kress et al. (1981), the most serious problem in the program was the outcome domain. Decision makers and program staff had lost sight of what their goals were. They needed help in clarifying these goals before pursuing other evaluation activities. In this case, the evaluator begins with a normative evaluation focusing on the issues in the outcome domain. Later on, when decision makers and program staff are ready for a more comprehensive evaluation, the evaluators can concentrate on other types of evaluations.

(3) *The formative and summative principle.* The third principle is called the formative and summative principle. This principle is applicable to composite types of evaluations such as the normative impact evaluation. As indicated in Chapter 2, in a composite type of evaluation, the information on the normative aspect is much more accessible in the early stages of evaluation activities, and useful evaluation information can be derived quickly. At the beginning of the normative part of an evaluation, the evaluator can formatively feed this information back to decision makers and other stakeholders to facilitate program improvement. If a program has problems, the earlier they are identified and corrected, the more money and resources will be saved. Of course, changes in the program will mean that more time must be allowed for stabilization before the evaluation can continue, and the changes may also require the evaluator to reexamine the design and then execute the causative part of the evaluation.

(4) *The method contingency principle.* Traditionally, as discussed in Chapter 1, many efforts have been expended in developing and arguing for one best method for doing evaluations in all situations. The method contingency principle argues that there may be no single best method or design that universally applies to every evaluation situation. In spite of its intrinsic merits, the usefulness of a research method or design in an evaluation may often depend upon the evaluation purposes, the maturity of the program, the possibility of participants' reactivity, and the capability of maintaining the integrity of the research. The method contingency principle urges evaluators to seek or even develop methods that better fit the evaluation context. The contingency principle has the potential to diminish antagonism among advocates of the quantitative, qualitative, and mixed methodologies. According to this principle, the quality of an evaluation is high as long as the issues of a particular theory-driven evaluation have been adequately addressed— regardless of the research method(s) used.

The four principles discussed here are useful in helping to select appropriate type(s) of theory-driven evaluation(s). Use of these principles will ensure that the resources available are distributed such that the crucial issues in a program will be adequately covered in the evaluation without neglecting either the expectations of the stakeholders or the professional concerns of the evaluators.

The Execution Stage

After the particular type of the theory-driven evaluation has been chosen and the theory pertinent to that particular evaluation has been constructed, empirical data are needed to verify the theory. The empirical verification of program theory in the theory-driven evaluation generally involves two kinds of procedures. Which procedure is used will depend upon whether the evaluation tests the causative theory or the normative theory underlying the program.

In terms of logic, evaluation of normative and causative theories requires specifying the theory first; that is, what the theoretical structure of the program should be according to the normative theory or what the theoretical relationships among variables are according to the causative theory. In terms of testing procedures, tests of a causative theory in domains such as impact or intervening mechanism are highly similar to the hypothesis testing usually carried out in social science research. For example, after causative theories have been formulated, sophisticated statistical methods such as structural equation models are frequently used to determine whether the causative theory is empirically supported.

However, although it shares the same logic, the test of normative theory in domains such as treatment and implementation is usually not as complicated as the statistical procedures used in testing causative theory. The normative theory specifies what the program structure should be, and the evaluator monitors or observes whether the expected program structure is actually utilized in the implementation processes (see Brekke, 1987; Rossi and Freeman, 1985).

For example, if the stakeholders adhere to a normative theory of treatment for an educational program indicating that disadvantaged students must receive two one-hour tutoring sessions every day to improve their achievement scores, then the evaluation process is to observe whether the disadvantaged students actually attend the classes, if the teacher teaches the class adequately, and so on. If there is consistency between the theoretical expectation and the empirical data, the normative theory is verified. Otherwise, it is rejected.

The information obtained from an assessment of normative theory can be immediately fed back to stakeholders for helping program planning and operations. Except for being more specific, the test of a normative theory and the utilization of its results are parallel to evaluability assessment as proposed by Wholey and his associates (e.g., Wholey, 1979; Rutman, 1980), which examines whether the program is evaluable or whether it is possible to develop an evaluable program.

Both the theory-driven and method-driven types of evaluation use research methods to do evaluation, but in different ways. A method-driven evaluation may tailor an evaluation to meet the requirements of a particular method. A theory-driven evaluation, however, constructs an evaluation based upon theory first, and then a particular method is selected because it is useful for verifying the theory. The role of the method selected is to test the theory rather than to supersede the theory. Because the theory-driven perspective is not method bound, the theory-driven evaluation can take advantage of using various qualitative or quantitative methods as long as the method is appropriate to serve the theoretical purposes.

DEALING WITH POLITICAL AND
SCIENTIFIC REQUIREMENTS

Generally speaking, the logic underlying the application of theory-driven evaluation resembles that of an organization, in that they both have to contend with forces from both open and closed systems in order to function properly. An open system perspective emphasizes the fact that a system has to interact with its environment in order to survive, while the closed system perspective treats a system as self-contained and insulated from environmental interaction. Both perspectives are useful in studying organizations. On one hand, an organization is affected by environmental forces such as governmental laws and legislation, economic conditions, resources, and competitors. To survive, the organization has to interact with its environment (an open system view). The organization has to respond to environmental turbulence and uncertainty. On the other hand, the organization has to produce services or products, and the production process requires stability and freedom from interruption (a closed system view). The organization has to strive for integration of these two concerns in order to perform effectively.

In order to deal with this dilemma, Thompson (1967) argues that organizations operate in both open system and closed system modes. On one hand, an organization must act like an open system, intensively monitoring the uncertain environment and developing strategies to deal with the uncertainty. After the production process has been determined, however, the organization must also operate like a closed system and seal off its technical core from environmental intrusion in order to operate efficiently.

The dilemma of environmental uncertainty and the need for internal stability faced by organizations is similar to the dilemma of scientific and political requirements in program evaluation. The political environment is turbulent, rough, and unstable, while the scientific evaluation operation must be operated in a controlled, predetermined way (Weiss, 1975). Accordingly, to solve the dilemma, the evaluator must also act in both open and closed system modes when doing theory-driven evaluations.

The open and closed system strategy suggests that, in the early stage of designing the evaluation model, an evaluator must lean more toward an open system mode, monitoring and learning about the political environment in order to cope with uncertainty. In this planning stage, when the open system mode is being used, the evaluator may have to play an active role in interacting with stakeholders in order to understand their needs, concerns, and theories regarding the program. Many times, stakeholders such as decision makers, program managers, program administrators, and clients have difficulty in clearly conceptualizing their problems and needs, and the evaluators have to help them diagnose problems and make explicit their own theories and concerns. Furthermore, to ensure that important program structures, processes, and concerns are not ignored, the evaluator should also use his or her expertise and knowledge to construct alternative theories.

Through these learning and searching processes, the evaluator identifies what the stakeholders' theory is, how the stakeholders will use the information in the future, what the crucial issues in the evaluation domains are, what type(s) of theory-driven evaluation is most appropriate, what previous studies, theory, and knowledge are relevant to this particular program, and so on. Based upon this information, the evaluator then negotiates with key stakeholders to reach a workable evaluation theory. In doing so, a theory-driven evaluation may be designed in a way that enhances the probability that it will be responsive to stakeholders' needs and sensitive to political processes.

After crucial issues have been identified, the particular evaluator moves into a closed system mode. At this point, the evaluator has to buffer environmental intrusions that may disrupt the evaluation operation and prevent it from generating valid and reliable information.

Although the closed system mode dominates at this stage, it does not mean that the open system mode is totally eliminated. Learning and monitoring must continue, given that the research setting is far from being a laboratory and the evaluator cannot totally seal off enviromental intrusions. The evaluator must still monitor the political environment and deal with it to protect the technical core of evaluation. For example, if new demands on the evaluation are raised by decision makers, the evaluator has to assess whether the operating evaluation process can be expanded to meet them. If it cannot, the evaluator may have to reject the new demand or propose an additional evaluation to protect the integrity of evaluation activities. Through the use of the open and closed system principle, an evaluation can better meet both its scientific and its political requirements.

Based upon the infrastructure of the theory-driven perspective elaborated thus far, the rest of the book attempts to systematically discuss a number of important types of theory-driven evaluations and illustrate in detail how to apply these evaluations.

PART III

Normative Evaluations: Basic Types

Part III focuses on a detailed discussion of normative evaluations. This category of evaluations attempts to provide information that helps to focus on clarifying and identifying the structure of a program both in theory and in actual implementation. Three basic types of normative evaluations are discussed in this part.

Normative outcome evaluation, as discussed in Chapter 5, attempts to provide stakeholders with timely information with which to clarify issues related to program goals or to improve the linkages between goals and program activity. Normative treatment evaluation, examined in Chapter 6, focuses on issues of program treatment and discusses strategies and methods to assess the consistency between normative treatment and implemented treatment. Chapter 7 discusses the normative implementation environment evaluation. This type of evaluation attempts to assess the consistency between the normative implementation environment and the actual environment under which the program is implemented.

5. Normative Outcome Evaluation

A program does not stay static. Program goals can evolve or change from time to time due to changes in political or organizational climate, policies, program staff, program structure, clients, and so on. As a consequence, decision makers and/or program managers may need help in understanding the outcome domain of the program for facilitating decision-making processes. Normative outcome evaluation attempts to help stakeholders to identify or clarify the nature of program outcomes, especially goals, for the purposes of program planning and management.

As indicated in Chapter 2, the outcome domain consists of both intended outcomes (goals) and unintended outcomes. In a broad form, the normative outcome evaluation should deal with both issues. In doing so, normative outcome evaluation attempts to help stakeholders clarify or identify which goals the program is pursuing, or should pursue, and what possible unintended outcomes might be generated by the program. However, in actual applications, normative outcome evaluation tends to focus mainly on goals. This focus partly results from the fact that unintended outcomes take a lot of time and effort to identify or understand. On the other hand, goals are the reasons for creating the program. Goals not only are already understood by stakeholders but also are considered by them as highly important for the program. Goals are a natural area of focus in the outcome domain, especially in the early stages of the program. Unintended outcomes are not usually considered by stakeholders as an important issue until stakeholders feel that it is necessary to have a comprehensive understanding of program impacts.

An even more important reason for stakeholders to focus on goals in the outcome domain is that goals are closely related to program planning and management processes. Program goals serve many important functions for decision makers', managers', and administrators' day-to-day activities. More specifically, these functions are as follows:

(1) Legitimating the existence of the program. Program goals provide an important source of legitimacy for a program by exemplifying the values that justify its existence. Goals present the program with a highly positive and acceptable image, which is necessary in order to gain support from the public or from related organizations.

(2) Binding political coalitions. Establishing a program or a policy requires support from various coalitions or interest groups. Goals or normative outcomes serve as an important motivation for uniting various coalitions to work for the existence or survival of a program.

(3) Resource acquisition. Program goals serve as a means for a program to acquire needed financial and human resources from the external environment. With highly appealing goals, stakeholders can solicit pertinent agencies, institutions, and the public for resources to operate the program.

(4) Budget allocation. By describing the desired aims and missions to be pursued, goals serve as general guidelines for decision makers to determine the budget for an area. Based upon goals, ideally, the higher relevancy or contribution of a unit or department to program goals, the more resources should be allocated to that unit or department.

(5) Criteria of performance and effectiveness. Because goals represent the rationale for the existence of a program, they serve as logical criteria for evaluating administrators' performance or the effectiveness of the program.

(6) Bases for designing the program. Goals provide general bases for designing treatment and for organizing program activities. For example, designing the structure and operation of a prison system that emphasizes a custodial goal is very different from designing the structure and operation of a prison system that emphasizes a rehabilitative goal.

Functions 1, 2, and 3 can be regarded as political functions, while Functions 4, 5, and 6 can be regarded as operative functions. The problem is that, in the same program, the statements of goals that are needed to serve political functions can be very different from the statements of goals needed to serve operative functions.

To serve the political functions well, it is ideal to state the goals in the most desirable and vague terms possible both to avoid conflict of interests and to get support for the program. However, to serve the operative functions well, the goals ideally should be stated in as specific, clear, and measurable terms as possible in order to avoid confusion and conflict in operating the program.

The political functions of the goals are emphasized in the start-up stage when coalition building is necessary, and goals in this stage usually are stated in vague and idealistic terms to attract political support (Weiss, 1975). Due to their familiarity with the political arena, decision makers, program designers, and other key stakeholders are experienced and skillful at constructing these kinds of goals. However, after a program has succeeded in the political arena and resources have been funded for operating the program, the operative function of programs becomes more important. Unfortunately, the transition from vague and idealistic goals to a set of specific and measurable goals that can be agreed upon by key stakeholders and that can be used to mobilize their resources and efforts can be very difficult for stakeholders to manage. It is often in the implementation stage that stakeholders begin to recognize problems in their program goals. Stakeholders are likely to pose the following questions: How are program goals to be adequately translated into specific goals for action purposes? Do program activities truly reflect the intentions of the original program? Is there a consensus among stakeholders on a set of specific goals for operation? How is it possible to measure or monitor the specific goals for program planning and management purposes? It is here that evaluators can provide assistance. Identification of normative goals may prove most helpful. Normative outcome evaluation serves the purpose of helping stakeholders to examine program operation.

"Normative outcome evaluation" is defined as *an attempt to assist stakeholders in identifying, clarifying, or developing the goals or outcomes of a program for program improvement.* However, because goals play such an important role for program planning and management purposes, this chapter intends to cover three types of normative outcome evaluation that associate closely with program goals. These evaluations serve the purposes of helping stakeholders to uncover the goals underlying a program, to develop a consensus on a set of goals for operation, or to clarify and develop a theory that links goals and related program activities. These three types of normative outcome evaluations are goal revelation, goal consensus, and goal realizability evaluation. Because the purpose of these three types of normative outcome evaluation largely involves specifying stakeholders' normative theory of program goals, methods that can facilitate in uncovering, clarifying, or developing stakeholders' views and concerns are particularly useful for these evaluations.

GOAL REVELATION EVALUATION

In many decentralized programs, diversified activities and functions are in operation. After a while, decision makers or program managers may lose sight of what goals the program is actually pursuing. Decision makers may lose sight of the direction of the program. Decision makers may want to understand the underlying structure of these diversified activities and functions in order to facilitate program planning or management. They may need to have a set of fundamental goals that adequately represent stakeholders' views and beliefs. Goal revelation evaluation is useful in these situations. More specifically, goal revelation evaluation refers to examining and uncovering the major goal dimensions underlying stakeholders' beliefs and views.

Because goal revelation evaluation attempts to uncover the underlying structure of goals from the stakeholders' views and beliefs, the stakeholder approach is particularly useful in constructing a stakeholders' normative theory of goals. However, when there are many diverse groups, with many different viewpoints on a program, their ideas of program goals may appear to be highly divergent, muddy, and difficult to understand. In order to better construct the stakeholders' normative theory of goals, statistical tools may be needed to extract underlying fundamental goal dimensions of stakeholders' views and beliefs for policy utilization. Data reduction techniques such as multidimensional scaling, factor analysis, cluster analysis, small area analysis, and so on (e.g., Tatsuoka, 1988) are especially useful in uncovering stakeholders' underlying goal dimensions.

More specifically, goal revelation evaluation involves two steps. The first step involves the stakeholders' identification of important program goals. The second step involves constructing important goal dimensions from these responses. The second step may require using a data reduction technique to facilitate uncovering the underlying goal dimensions.

Goal revelation evaluation is well illustrated by Trochim (1985) in studying the goals of a university health service. The research procedure required the staff of the service center to answer questions regarding their views of what the health service should be or should do. The data, then, were analyzed by multidimensional scaling analysis. Three goal dimensions were found: effective patient flow, improved system and data management, and staff morale. Trochim (1985) has shown that information on goal dimensions is useful in planning and evaluating programs.

Although the stakeholder approach is the most relevant in the goal revelation evaluation, the social science approach is also useful in sharpening the conceptualization of underlying goal dimensions. The benefits of using the integrative approach to constructing a theory of normative goals has been demonstrated by Litwin (1987). In his study of the goal dimensions of social programs for the elderly, Litwin (1987) found that two theories of social programs for elders are relevant. The first is the disengagement theory. This theory assumes that the later years of an elderly person's life are a period of decreasing social interaction and diminishing social responsibility. Accordingly, programming for senior centers should assume an increasingly compensatory role in providing services to meet needs and responsibilities over which the elderly have decreasing control. On the other hand, the action theory assumes that social activities provide the elderly with role support for reaffirming their self-concepts. Therefore, in planning a program for the elderly, program planners should emphasize training the elderly for new roles of social responsibility. The program should stress productivity and negate debility.

Litwin (1987) showed that these prior theories provide a useful conceptual framework for constructing items to measure stakeholders' views and for conceptualizing the goal dimensions. After applying a small area analysis of data, three goal dimensions were found: social and cultural programming, voluntary community action, and specialized services. The data indicate that the elderly community centers in this study viewed their function primarily from an action theory perspective.

GOAL PRIORITY CONSENSUS EVALUATION

In some situations, the stakeholders have clear ideas about which goals are to be pursued by a program, but they need to know the priority among these goals so that resources can be allocated more efficiently within the program. However, when multiple stakeholders are involved in a program, each of them may insist that their goals should be set at a higher priority than others. If the decision makers believe that a specification of the priority of goals is useful for policy purposes, then a consensus among multiple stakeholders on this priority is needed. This is the main task of goal priority consensus evaluation. Goal priority consensus evaluation is defined as efforts to generate consensus among stakeholders regarding the priority of program goals.

If there are only a few stakeholders involved, consensus on priority among goals may be achieved through open discussion. However, when the number becomes larger, it may become more difficult to reach consensus through open discussion. Sophisticated consensus generation methods may be required to achieve consensus. Three popular consensus generation methods are discussed below.

The Delphi Method

The Delphi method (e.g., Dalkey, 1969; Brown, 1968) searches for consensus through the staging of several consecutive questionnaires that are completed by key stakeholders. Each questionnaire comprises a series of problems, potential solutions, and strategic choices. The data gathered from these questionnaires are made available to stakeholders, and this forms the basis of the next questionnaire in the series. Consensus is a product of this process of elimination and refinement, and thus the final decision should be a negotiated settlement among the perspectives of the multiple stakeholders. Dalkey (1969) has identified three crucial requirements that must be met for this method to succeed:

(1) Stakeholders must have anonymity. Opinions are kept anonymous and stakeholders are kept apart until the process is complete. Thus opportunities for dominance in any one group are minimized from the inception of the process.

(2) The ability of the stakeholders to clarify and refine their decisions on the basis of new information is essential. The Delphi method requires the continuous commitment of stakeholders if it is to succeed. The dropout rate can be high.

(3) Statistical presentation of the data at each stage of the process enables the evaluator and the stakeholders to determine how close a consensus has been achieved and to make adjustments to their decisions so that political compromise can be made. These statistical data aid the evaluator in objectively presenting the information gathered.

Otherwise, data can be easily misrepresented or even subjected to political manipulation.

The Delphi method has a wide range of applications. Among others, it has been used by the National Institute on Drug Abuse in a nationwide evaluation of drug-abuse treatments in terms of their objectives and relative strengths (Jellson, 1975). Further, the comprehensiveness of this technique has been demonstrated by Keeney and Raiffa (1977) in their assessment of utility functions in educational budgeting, corporate planning, and even determining an airport location. An example of how to apply the Delphi method to clarify the relative importance of treatment outcomes of a mental health program has been illustrated by Clark and Friedman (1982). They utilized the Delphi method to clarify outcomes among a group of 23 administrators and clinicians. Through an interactive group discussion, voting on weights for outcomes, and feedback, the stakeholders finally reached a consensus on ranking nine outcomes in priority and assigning relative weights. It was found that the most important outcome was the improvement of client ability to be self-supporting, followed by the reduction of symptoms of mental problems. The least important was the outcome of involvement with friends and the outcome of alcohol or drug abuse.

The Nominal Group Process

The nominal group process, like the Delphi method, is a structured technique that attempts to obtain both objective and subjective information regarding an organization through a discussion among stakeholders (e.g., see Fink et al., 1984; Delbecq et al., 1975). It differs from the Delphi method in that it is a qualitative method (Van de Ven and Delbecq, 1972). The nominal group process moves through several successive stages, the first of which is to bring together all the stakeholders in a meeting. The evaluator then divides the stakeholders into smaller units, called nominal groups, consisting of no more than eight individuals who share some defining characteristic, such as being operational staff, clientele, or administrators. The evaluators provide an exploratory question that is used to elicit a response to a key area of evaluative inquiry from the stakeholders. For example, Van de Ven and Delbecq (1972, p. 339), in conducting research on comprehensive health planning (CHP), asked their nominal groups to "list the subjective and objective barriers you have experienced when trying to obtain health-care services in this community." This list is made on a strictly individual basis and prior to any discussion among stakeholders. The evaluators then ask each member of each nominal group to individually present the key idea from his or her list. The process is repeated until all the ideas have been presented to the nominal group. Each idea is charted on a group or composite list.

The next stage of the process is a highly structured discussion of these collected ideas. The stakeholders intensively review each idea by discussing it in detail. Following this discussion, each stakeholder privately ranks the ideas in terms of their potential utility. Their rankings are then discussed on a group basis and the stakeholders are again asked to privately rerank in the light of their discussions. These revised ballots are then collected and assigned numeric values between 0 and 100 that reflect the relative priority given to each idea. Finally, all the nominal groups are brought together for a discussion in which the findings of each nominal group are clearly outlined. The advantages of the nominal group method include a consensus-oriented development of evaluation hypotheses, relatively low cost, and high speed of implementation. Delbecq and Van de Ven (1971) provide a good illustration of the use of the nominal group to help the planning process of a community action agency. They organized meetings involving the following key stakeholder groups in the successive phases of program development: (1) clients and first-line staff, in program exploration; (2) external resource people and internal specialists, in knowledge exploration; (3) key administrators and resource controllers, in priority development and local adaptation; (4) organizational staff, in program proposal building; and (5) all constituencies, in final approval and evaluation designs.

Multiattribute Utility Method (MAUT)

MAUT is a technique used to identify and isolate the individual elements in the decision-making process. Edwards and Guttentag (1975), for example, list several dimensions that may contribute to the decision-making process in the provision of remedial educational. Educational utility can be measured in terms of cost-effectiveness, teaching talent, potential for student gain, provision of facilities and materials, location, and political and/or cultural determinants. MAUT is a method by which organizational options derived from the multiple perspectives of stakeholders are isolated and ranked through a process of discussion, negotiation, and consensus generation. Like the Delphi method and the nominal group process, MAUT is a highly structured process that begins with the identification of the entity to be evaluated and the specification of the issues of utility (desirability) that are the subject of evaluation. These preliminary stages are conducted in a way that gives stakeholders the opportunity to circulate their views. Each idea is given a numeric value, for example along a dimension from 1 to 10; these values are called "weights." Through further discussion, each of the ideas and its weight are assessed and evaluated in terms of its probability of adoption and then reranked according to this dimension. The benefits of this method are similar to those noted in the nominal group process. Ideas are refined through a process of discussion among stakeholders and disagreement is ideally limited to subjective estimations of the ideas' probability of organizational adoption. Thus the evaluation is focused on those areas where decisions must be made.

These methods of achieving a working consensus among multiple stakeholders and of enhancing their understandings of the entity to be evaluated are important issues for planning a theory-driven evaluation. Once a consensus has been reached, the misunderstandings between stakeholders and the evaluator can be minimized. Edwards et al. (1975) have applied MAUT to develop goals for the Office of Child Development (OCD). A group of key stakeholders was assembled to develop a list of goals for programs of benefit to children and their families. These goals were evaluated through a cyclical process of ranking, weighting, and discussing. Eventually an agreement was reached that the following five goals for programs were prioritized in order of importance above all others for OCD: is consistent with departmental policy, influences national child-care policy positively, consists of prototype/high-leverage activities, produces tangible short-term results, and makes public leadership more sensitive to children's needs.

GOAL REALIZABILITY EVALUATION

As discussed in the first section of this chapter, goals that serve good political functions may not necessarily serve good operative functions. While vague, abstract, and/or idealistic goals may provide important functions in attracting public support or in building coalitions, the vagueness, idealism, and/or abstractness of the goals will very likely create problems in implementation, such as poor coordination, resource wasting, or the pursuit of goals opposite to the program designers' or decision makers' intentions (e.g., see Derthick, 1972; Nakamura and Smallwood, 1980).

Hence, the degree to which program goals are appropriately structured can affect the results of a program. One of the important functions of the goal realizability evaluation is to help key stakeholders diagnose the problems in program goals or to develop a set of specific goals for guiding program operation.

However, a set of specific and measurable goals does not necessarily imply that program activities such as resource allocation and implementation efforts will be systematically organized to pursue these goals. If program activities are not organized or mobilized in such a way as to achieve these goals, one can hardly expect that the program will be effective. Another function of the goal realizability evaluation is to assess whether resources and activities are organized toward the specific goals.

"Goal realizability evaluation" is defined here as the effort to diagnose problems in program goals and activities or develop the appropriate structure of program goals and activities. More specifically, depending on the purposes, there are two kinds of goal realizability evaluation: diagnostic and developmental, which are elaborated in detail below.

Diagnostic Goal Realizability Evaluation

The purpose of diagnostic goal realizability evaluation is to diagnose problems in the structure of program goals and activities. The evaluator first applies the stakeholder approach to clarify the stakeholders' normative theory of goals. A set of program goals will be clarified through reviewing pertinent documents, interviewing key stakeholders, and/or carrying out field observations. Based upon these goals, the evaluators can examine the following two areas:

(1) Whether program goals are creating difficulties in operating the program. Stakeholders' program goals may be too vague, idealistic, or ambiguous. As a result, these program goals cannot provide consistent guidance for program staff to operate the program and may even confuse or mislead their operations. The evaluator can examine whether these goals lack specificity, consistency, and measurability and see if these problems have created confusion and difficulty in implementation. If program goals are indeed detrimental to the operation of the program, the evaluator can point out to key stakeholders the sources of the vagueness or ambiguity for future improvement of the goal structure.

This area of evaluation is illustrated by the evaluation of the Work Incentive Program (WIN) by Rodgers (1981). According to Rodgers

(1981), one of the problems in the WIN Program was the vagueness of the program goal. One of its main purposes was to move welfare recipients from welfare to employment. However, the program never clearly spelled out the exact meanings and criteria of the work requirements for those enrolled in the program, and the vagueness of goals created confusion for implementors in enforcing the work requirements. As a result, only a small fraction of WIN participants ever received job-related services.

(2) Examining the consistency between program goals and activities. In some situations, program activities may not be adequately pooled or structured together for achieving program goals. The evaluator can examine whether resource allocation and implementation efforts are incongruent with program goals. If they are incongruent, the evaluator can point out the dissociation between goals and activities to help stakeholders improve the linkage between them in the future.

This area of evaluation is also illustrated in the study of Rodgers (1981) on the WIN Program. In his examination, Rodgers (1981) points out that the program activities were organized in a way that provided little incentive for the staff members to enforce the work requirement. The assessment of staff performance and the allocation of funds to the program were largely determined by the number and quality of placements rather than by the enforcement of work requirements. This incentive structure encouraged staff to select only the best participants for job placement and to apply work requirements indiscreetly.

Developmental Goal Realizability Evaluation

Alternatively, the evaluator can use goal realization evaluation to work together with key stakeholders in joint efforts to develop an appropriate structure of program goals and activities. Because this type of evaluation goes further than just diagnosis of the problem, it is called "developmental goal realizability evaluation." In this type of evaluation, the evaluators help stakeholders to develop both a set of specific goals suitable for guiding program operations and a systematic arrangement of program activities that closely aim at achieving these goals.

The characteristics of developmental goal realizability evaluation are similar to those of evaluability assessment (e.g., Wholey, 1979). The only difference is that developmental goal realizability focuses more specifically on issues related to goals and activities, while evaluability assessment covers many broad issues related to formative evaluation

(Rutman, 1980). Nevertheless, the construction of the format of goal realizability greatly benefits from the work of evaluability assessment. More specifically, the developmental goal realizability evaluation involves the following steps:

(1) The evaluator applies the stakeholder approach to develop a stakeholders' theory of program goals through activities such as reviewing pertinent documents, interviewing key stakeholders, and/or conducting field observations.

(2) Where the goals identified at Step 1 tend to be vague, abstract, or inconsistent, the evaluator may need intensive discussion with key stakeholders to clarify and develop a set of specific, measurable, and consistent goals that are not only acceptable to key stakeholders but can serve as guidance for program operation.

(3) The evaluator also works with stakeholders to develop their theory of how program activities are supposed to achieve these goals. The administrative procedures, according to stakeholders, that are necessary to achieve these goals are systematically arranged in a flowchart or timetable that outlines a chain of events such as resource allocation, personnel hiring, equipment purchasing, implementing group or organization creation, effort coordination, and so on.

(4) The evaluator checks whether the stakeholders' theory on the linkage between program activities and specific goals is actually being pursued. If there is no discrepancy between the specific goals and program activities, the evaluator can reassure the stakeholders that the program is moving in the right direction. The evaluator contributes to making the stakeholders' theory on program structure of goals and activities explicit. This, in turn, may make program operation more consistent in the future. However, if a discrepancy is found, the evaluator can point out the sources and suggest strategies to reorganize program structure to better align specific goals and program activities.

The closest example of the developmental goal realizability evaluation is Wholey's (1987) discussions of the evaluations of Tennessee's Prenatal Program and the Aid Association for the Lutherans' Fraternal Benefit Program. In these two evaluations, Wholey (1987) demonstrates the procedures and usefulness of the evaluators who work with key stakeholders in clarifying and developing both a set of realistic and measurable goals and the theory that links program activities to these goals.

In spite of the attractiveness of goal realizability evaluation, for either diagnosis or development purposes, it is important to point out its strengths and limitations to assure its appropriate utilization. The diagnostic goal realizability evaluation can be regarded as an evaluation that attempts to assess the necessary conditions for program effectiveness. If the results of diagnostic evaluation indicate that a program does not meet the test of goal realizability evaluation, this can mean that the program is structured inappropriately in terms of program goals and activities; hence the program is not likely to be effective. The developmental goal realizability evaluation is useful to help stakeholders reorganize the structure of goals and activities to enhance the possibility of successful outcomes.

On the other hand, a program may have a sound structure of goals and activities, as indicated by the results of a diagnostic goal realizability evaluation or developmental goal realizability evaluation. This only means that the program is being conducted in a manner that is close to stakeholders' normative theory of program goals and activities. The sound structure of goals and activities does not imply that the program will be effective. Goal realizability evaluation should not be used as direct evidence of program effectiveness. The type of evaluation that addresses program effectiveness is causative evaluation, which will be discussed in Chapters 8, 10, and 11.

6. Normative Treatment Evaluation

CONCEPT AND ISSUES

Program activities such as fund-raising, personnel management, equipment purchasing, facility maintenance, and so on relate more to the existence of the program than to the production of intended changes. As an example, a program to increase awareness of cancer might focus more on raising money to pay the staff than on educating the public. In order to produce impacts, the treatment in a program has to be constructed and implemented to do so. When key stakeholders of a program seriously pursue its goals, issues regarding the nature of treatment and how the treatment is actually delivered become important.

"Treatment" is defined here as those organized services, materials, or activities that are directly delivered to the clients or subjects and are essential in order to generate the desired changes. For example, the treatment in the Housing Allowance Experiment was payments to participating households. The treatment in the Kansas City Prevention Patrol Experiment was the preventive patrol. In the above two experiments, the treatment mainly consisted of one component such as payment or the preventive patrol. However, it is more common for social or intervention programs to consist of multiple components. For example, the treatment in an abuser treatment program may consist of presentations on family violence programs, group therapy sessions, and teaching the abusers stress reduction and avoidance techniques.

The design of the treatment for a program is not a simple matter. There are multiple options in constructing the treatment format for almost any program. Program designers have to contemplate which formats may better suit the program. For example, in the Housing Allowance Experiment, program designers had to think through the issue of how to set the amount of the payment. Should the payments be set at the same fixed dollar amount for every participating household? If not, what criteria are relevant to determine the amount of payments for a household? Should factors such as household income, housing conditions, number of rooms, or number of children be considered? Similarly, in formulating the treatment in an abuser treatment program, designers may confront such problems as the following: What are the major themes and lengths of the presentations? What kind of group structure and processes will be emphasized? What stress reduction and avoidance techniques will be taught? Should the treatment include the spouses' involvement? And so on.

Because the format of treatment can be designed in many different ways, program designers usually use some sort of normative theory, sophisticated or not, to guide their choices in designing the treatment. The normative treatment theory can come from the program designers' wisdom, experience, or hunches, or it can come from existing social science theory and knowledge (Wang and Walberg, 1983; Lipsey, 1987). Regardless of the sources, the normative treatment theory provides a rationale for the treatment and specifies the appropriate format of the treatment. For example, the decision to use the treatment (supplementary income payments to poor families) in the New Jersey-Pennsylvania Income Maintenance Experiment reflected the program designers' normative theory that the new payment system would be more humane and administratively efficient than the traditional welfare payment system.

Accordingly, based upon program designers' and other key stakeholders' normative theory, the appropriate format of the treatment can be derived. The appropriate format of the treatment derived from a normative treatment theory is called the "normative treatment." Normative treatment can be regarded as the format of the treatment that designers and decision makers believe should be maintained during implementation to assure the program the best chance for success. The normative treatment of a program requires appropriate implementation in the field.

To further complicate issues, if stakeholders want to know the impact of the program in the future, then the treatment format has to be designed in a way such that systematic information can be gathered for assessing the impact. Frequently, this implies that some control or comparison groups that do not receive the same treatment also have to be built into the treatment format. Accordingly, the nontreatment condition in the control or comparison groups is also part of the normative treatment that needs to be maintained with integrity in the field.

As will be discussed in the next section, due to the complexity of the implementation process, normative treatment may not necessarily be the treatment that is actually delivered to the clients or subjects. The treatment actually implemented by the implementors is called the "implemented treatment." Evaluation literature has frequently indicated that a discrepancy between normative and implemented treatment is not uncommon in many programs (e.g., see Pressman and Wildavsky, 1973; Hall and Loucks, 1977). Furthermore, implemented treatments are usually found to be much less adequate than normative treatments, especially in decentralized programs. For example, according to program designers, the normative treatment of an educational program may require the use of innovative teaching materials and equipment and that classes be taught by specially trained teachers on every school day. The implemented treatment may use less innovative teaching materials and equipment and be taught by regular teachers. Because the discrepancy between normative and implemented treatment can directly affect the success opportunities of the program, information in this area is important for understanding program processes or program improvement. Normative treatment evaluation attempts to deal with issues in these areas.

"Normative treatment evaluation" refers to the assessment of the congruency between normative treatment and implemented treatment. It is particularly useful when the format of the treatment is complicated (e.g., has many components), when the delivery of treatment demands the implementors' intensive personal efforts (such as teaching or conducting therapy), or when the implementation of treatment requires much coordination within an organization or between organizations.

The following sections of this chapter first attempt to provide a political and organizational understanding of the discrepancy between normative and implemented treatment. After that, the strategies for carrying out normative treatment evaluation will be discussed.

The normative treatment evaluation serves the important purpose of assessing and improving treatment implementation processes. Normative treatment evaluation can immediately indicate whether the implemented treatment is appropriate in comparison with the normative treatment specified in the theory. The information is useful for stakeholders in judging whether the integrity of the treatment is problematic and whether actions should be taken to improve them. In this sense, the normative treatment evaluation can provide timely information for improving the program.

THE IMPORTANCE OF
NORMATIVE TREATMENT EVALUATION

Normative treatment evaluation may not be important in physical science research. Physical science research is usually carried out in laboratory settings, where treatment implementation in the research project is under the control of the researcher. He or she can manipulate the treatment precisely to ensure that research subjects, such as animals or plants, do or do not receive the exact quality or quantity of treatment throughout the experimental period. In other words, the normative treatment as planned is usually the exact implemented treatment received by the subjects in this type of research. There may be little need for concern about subjects who fail to receive the normative treatment as planned or about the possibility of contamination between the control group and the treatment group in laboratory settings.

However, the procedure of treatment delivery used in physical science research cannot be exactly copied when dealing with treatment implementation in the areas of social intervention. In social intervention, treatment implementation is a much more difficult and complicated process. As will be discussed in the next chapter, the implementation literature (e.g., see Derthick, 1972) has demonstrated that program staffs frequently experience problems in implementing intervention programs.

There are several important reasons why treatment implementation in social or intervention programs is much more complicated and difficult than in physical science research and why special strategies must be devised to deal with these problems. These reasons include the following:

(1) Program implementors often do not implement the treatment according to the original design. Program managers and implementors may deliver treatment to participants based upon their own interests, values, ideologies, preferences, abilities, training, and so on. Lipsky (1980) observed that "street-level bureaucrats" (the lower-level personnel who are in direct contact with the clients), with their power of discretion,

have tremendous impact on actually shaping the direction of programs. They may often deliver the treatment differently from the program designers' or evaluators' expectations.

In some extreme cases, program implementors may use resources intended for delivery of treatment for purposes not related to the original program intentions. An example of this problem was found in McLaughlin's 1975 study of the implementation of Title I of the Elementary and Secondary Education Act. In this program, McLaughlin found, that despite the billions of dollars of program money spent yearly, few identifiable treatment activities in the local schools could be directly associated with program treatments aimed at helping disadvantaged students.

More often, however, the treatment is delivered to the participants in a way that deviates from the requirements of an evaluation design. Posavac and Carey (1985) report this problem in an early evaluation of the effect of an information/counseling program for postcoronary inpatients. It was found that nurses had distributed part of the treatment (a program textbook) to those patients in the control group who demanded more information. The nurses, in opposition to the researchers' requirements, had different views on providing the treatment to the control group and, until the posttest part of the evaluation was carried out, the nurses acted accordingly. As a consequence, the structure of the treatment design was not appropriately maintained.

In a study of the adoption of educational programs in schools, Hall and Loucks (1977) found that implementation of educational innovations may not simply be an all-or-nothing phenomenon, as planned. In fact, the classroom teachers in both the experimental and the control groups adopted innovations at different levels.

(2) Delivered treatments may not be uniformly accepted by the participants. Treatment delivery in human services is subject to each participant's cooperation and acceptance. In laboratory research, the researchers can force the research subjects to absorb the treatment— for example, by injecting drugs into mice. In social interventions, however, the evaluators, or even program managers and implementors, do not have that kind of absolute control over participants. The major inducement for human participation in an evaluation or other research project is the benefit of receiving treatments, but this is not always sufficient. Participant attrition is a problem in many social programs and is a particularly serious problem among control group participants. In some situations, the program managers or administrators have

problems recruiting a sufficient number of people to attend the program (e.g., the Housing Allowance Experiments) or preventing them from dropping out (e.g., the Negative Income Tax Experiment). Experimental conditions easily deteriorate if the differential attrition rate between groups is not random (e.g., see Hausman and Wise, 1985; Ferber and Hirsch, 1982).

Even when the participants can be persuaded to remain in the program throughout the evaluation period, there are still no guarantees that the program treatment components will be uniformly accepted by the participants. They may or may not participate in all of the program activities. For example, some individuals may participate in all of the training sessions in a job program while others may attend only a few. In the same manner, recipients in the food stamp program can use food stamps for various items. Some use food stamps to improve the nutrition of family members; others sell the stamps in order to buy liquor, cigarettes, lottery tickets, and so on. Still other recipients exchange food stamps for luxury items. Thus participants in a program may not respond uniformly to the program treatment.

(3) Participants in the control group may be exposed to the treatment or to an equivalent alternative. Although treatments are withheld from the control (or comparison) group, the evaluators or program staff do not have much control over the members of the group. Participants in the control group are not static or inactive; they are free to engage in many activities that may alter the treatment design. They may have access to treatment or seek equivalent alternatives during the program period. As was shown by the first-year evaluation of *Sesame Street*, those in the control group were also viewers of the program (Ball and Bogatz, 1970). Because the program was widely broadcast, it was accessible to any family that owned a television set. As a consequence, the original experimental conditions of encouraged viewing versus nonencouraged viewing were not maintained. The problem was resolved by abandoning the experimental conditions as a treatment variable. Instead, the treatment variable was measured by the amount of time spent viewing the program.

The same difficulty occurred in a study of the effect of handgun-related crimes. Citizens or criminals living in a state with strict gun control laws are free to travel to other states with lenient gun control laws to obtain a gun. The strictness of gun control laws among states is not a valid reflection of handgun accessibility because of the free transportation of guns between states (Wright et al., 1981).

(4) Problems in creating and maintaining an effective implementation organization for treatment delivery and evaluation purposes. Sometimes, the program designers and implementors have difficulty in creating an effective organization that is capable of appropriately scheduling and maintaining delivery of treatment. For example, in the Performance Contracting Experiment (Gramlich and Koshel, 1975), implementation was much more difficult than the companies had anticipated. In spite of the fact that the program would be evaluated one year after delivery, many firms had difficulty supplying their own teaching materials, maintaining the teaching machines and other hardware, paying their teachers incentive payments, and so on, even after the programs were formally started. Similar findings occurred in a study of the effects on subsequent parole behavior and recidivism after the administration of group therapy sessions to adult male prisoners (Kassebaum et al., 1971). The program treatment, in this study, was a weekly session of group counseling. However, it was found that the quality of the counseling sessions was far from satisfactory. Problems of inadequate staff, low morale, absenteeism, and so on caused the sessions to deteriorate.

Sometimes the hierarchical delegation of authority, from top to bottom, may not be well communicated, received, understood, or carried out. The discrepancy between the treatment as it was planned in the policymakers' minds and treatment actually delivered by the implementors may be wide, especially when the decision makers and program implementors have different perspectives, interests, motivations, and preferences regarding the program (Bardach, 1977).

A good example illustrating this point is a well-known incident that took place during the Cuban missile crisis. In 1961, President John Kennedy ordered his secretary of state to remove U.S. missiles from Turkey because he thought the missiles might precipitate a war with Russia (Allison, 1971). However, the order was not implemented. The State Department officials in Turkey believed that this action would weaken our relationship with Turkey, an important member of NATO. The Turkish government also strongly opposed the action. The failure to remove the missiles from Turkey subsequently led to difficulties for the United States in dealing with Russia's placement of missiles in Cuba.

(5) Environmental influences. Significantly, unlike laboratory researchers, the evaluator and program stakeholders of human services programs have little control over changes in the external environment in the form of social, economic, and/or legislative intrusions that may upset the integrity of treatment structure.

The study of the effect of public housing on morbidity and mental health in Baltimore by Wilner et al. (1962) provides a good example of this. In this study, the treatment group—about 400 families—consisted of those originally living in a slum area but subsequently moved to a new public housing project. The control group consisted of a matched sample of those who were slated to remain in the slum area. The control group was found to be a problem. A substantial number of control families unexpectedly moved to better housing—both public and private—in the city. As a consequence, the planned variation in the experimental conditions was reduced. This unexpected development was a result of the general improvement of housing quality and availability in Baltimore during the research period. The general improvement of conditions and the sample attrition both upset the original experimental conditions.

Similarly, one of the reasons New Jersey was selected for the Negative Income Tax (NIT) experiment was that, at the time, New Jersey had no AFDC plan covering families with unemployed fathers (AFDC-UP) (Rossi and Lyall, 1976). It was hoped that the control groups would not be contaminated by any equivalent treatment alternative. However, soon after the program was started, an AFDC-UP plan was launched in New Jersey that covered intact households. The new welfare plan was generally comparable to the NIT program. For some families, the new welfare plan's payments were even more generous than NIT payments. The environmental change severely damaged the original treatment conditions, and there was a substantial amount of attrition from both experimental and control groups. As a consequence, Rossi and Lyall (1976) suggested that the findings of the NIT experiment could not be used for estimating the magnitude of treatment effect, but instead provided information on labor force response to NIT as a replacement for generous welfare plans.

Even if there is no environmental intrusion on treatment conditions, it is still possible that administrative necessities may contaminate them. As mentioned above, in the Kansas City Preventive Patrol experiment, three treatment conditions were designed: reactive, preventive, and controlled. However, it was found that the treatment conditions were not neatly maintained after the program was in operation. The reactive beats were supposed to be the ones with minimum police visibility. It was found in the field (Larson, 1975) that the number of patrol-initiated activities, instead of decreasing, increased from 5,948 to 6,057. This was attributed to such factors as police officers being dispatched across beat boundaries to provide services.

NORMATIVE TREATMENT EVALUATION FOR
ASSESSING THE INTEGRITY OF TREATMENT

When the stakeholders' evaluation need is mainly for understanding the consistency between the normative and the implemented treatment, the normative treatment evaluation can be designed to serve this purpose. In this evaluation, the evaluator has to work with stakeholders to explicitly specify a treatment format based upon the normative treatment theory and then evaluate it.

Specification of the Normative Treatment Format

The evaluator and stakeholders have to work together to specify theoretically what the appropriate treatment components and/or strengths in the normative structure should be, as discussed below.

Treatment Components

A social or intervention program usually contains more than one treatment component. For example, to name a few, the payment guarantee level and tax rates were identified as two critically important components in the Income Maintenance Experiments (Rossi and Lyall, 1976). Similarly, an innovative program for toilet training by Foxx and Azrin (1973) consisted of a package of treatment components including a distraction-free environment, manual guidance, and a variety of reinforcements for the young children. Similarly, a youth consultation service program for improving schoolwork studied by Borgatta and Jones (1965) contained treatment components such as therapy and caseworker's contact.

Treatment Strength

The treatment in an intervention program often varies in strength. If this is the case, it is important to clarify the treatment strength that is required according to the normative treatment theory, because an inadequate strength of treatment can result in the failure of a program. The importance of treatment strength in intervention programs has been highlighted by Scott and Sechrest (forthcoming). They argue that the finding of little or no effect in many programs may be because the treatment strength was so weak that it would have been unreasonable to expect any effect. Three dimensions of treatment strength are useful to the evaluator and stakeholders in making the normative treatment theory explicit: amount, frequency, and duration.

(1) Amount. Treatment "amount" refers to the amount of a treatment or treatment component the program participants receive. For example, a component such as counseling can be administered at different levels, such as one hour, two hours, or more. Evaluators and program stakeholders can work together to determine the appropriate treatment levels for evaluation.

(2) Frequency. "Frequency" refers to how often the treatment is administered to the participants. In an alcoholism treatment program, individual therapy can be held twice per day, once per day, one session every two days, once per week, and so on. It is possible that if the frequency of treatment strength is too low the treatment effect may not be sustained. However, if the frequency is too high, the participants may not be able to adequately absorb or deal with it or could even be upset by the treatment process. If the frequency of treatment is a concern, stakeholders and the evaluator can work together to determine the appropriate frequency of the treatment.

(3) Duration. "Duration" refers to the length of time the treatment processes are continued. The treatment process must continue during a certain period of time in order to have an effect. If the treatment duration is too short it may not work, while if it is too long resources could be wasted. Again, if duration is a treatment issue, then the appropriate treatment duration has to be specified by stakeholders and the evaluator.

In doing normative treatment evaluation, there needs to be a consensus between the evaluator and stakeholders regarding what the essential components and their strengths in the normative treatment should be. For example, in an alcoholism treatment program, the stakeholders and the evaluator may agree that the following treatment components are essential for the program: individual therapy, Alcoholics Anonymous meetings, group therapy, and exercise sessions. The agreement on a set of crucial treatment components and/or their strengths is important to start the normative evaluation. When agreement is difficult to reach or when there are a large number of major stakeholders involved, the consensus-promoting methods discussed in Chapter 5 can be used to resolve the disagreements.

Evaluation of the Normative Treatment Format

After the structure of the normative treatment has been specified, the evaluator can proceed to gather empirical data to evaluate whether the implemented treatment is consistent with the normative treatment. There are various quantitative and qualitative methods available for this evaluation, as discussed below.

(1) Interview or survey of the implementor. In this approach, the evaluator first identifies the crucial treatment component(s). Then various interview or survey techniques (e.g., face-to-face or telephone interviews, mailed questionnaires) can be used to question the program implementors regarding the level or magnitude of their implementation of the treatment component(s). For example, Hall and Loucks (1977) developed and applied a treatment implementation scale to measure the level of treatment components actually used in an education program. This scale contained seven levels, ranging from the level of no use, through the level of mechanical use, to the level of renewal. A face-to-face interview was carried out with teachers to determine the level of usage of the innovative program. It was found that teachers in the treatment group were not uniformly implementing the program treatment, but they varied from level to level in their adoption of the treatment. The same scale was also used to measure the teachers in the control group. It was discovered that a substantial number of them had also adopted program treatment at varying levels.

(2) Interview or survey of program participants. Evaluators can interview or survey the participants or their close associates or relatives in order to measure the extent to which program treatments were implemented. For example, in the evaluation of *Sesame Street* (Ball and Bogatz, 1970), parents were asked to record the amount of time their children spent viewing the program.

Similarly, in order to determine whether a given amount of aerobic dance has effectively reduced cholesterol levels, a researcher can survey program participants regarding the number of hours per week they actually do aerobic dance. To determine the effects of a weight loss program, the researcher could measure the implemented treatment by comparing the program participants in amount of high-fat foods consumed, the amount of exercise done, amount of nondiet drinks consumed, and so on.

(3) Field observation. Evaluators can also collect firsthand information themselves by observing and measuring the implemented treatment directly. This method is more easily and efficiently applied when the treatment is administered to a group of participants in a confined setting. This is, perhaps, why this approach has been increasingly popular in the study of educational programs (e.g., see Wang

and Walberg, 1983). For example, in examining the implemented treatment of the Delinquency Research and Development Project, which emphasized an innovative teaching method to improve delinquents' school performance and reduce their delinquency, Kerr et al. (1985) utilized field observation to measure the degree of implemented treatment. They first constructed scales (called Interactive Teaching Maps) that were relevant to the program treatment components in terms of the frequency and the fidelity with which teachers used various teaching techniques and that measured students' classroom behavior. Trained observers were sent to classrooms to observe classroom activities and code the behavior according to the scales. They found that program treatment was implemented differently by various teachers as well as across the program sites.

(4) Program records. The implementation organization may keep ongoing official records as to the level or magnitude of the treatment components delivered to program participants. These records can be useful in measuring the implemented program treatment. Though the implementing organization may not keep this kind of record, if evaluators plan the evaluation at an early stage of program implementation, they can negotiate with the program staff in order to gather this information.

In a study of a domestic abuse treatment program, Bersani et al. (1988) used program records to measure implemented treatment. The program participants were those men convicted of domestic violence for the first time. The actual sentence of those convicted was set aside until the offender had completed a court-sponsored treatment program. Program treatment contained a series of counseling sessions (usually eight sessions), and the implementing agency kept attendance records for each participant. It was found that the offenders attended the sessions differentially: About 37% of them missed more than two sessions; about 10% did not attend any sessions.

(5) Combination methods. An evaluator can measure the implemented treatment by combining two or more of the above data collection methods. Palumbo et al. (1984) developed a scale to measure the level of treatment implementation of the Oregon Community Correction Act. Palumbo et al. first identified a set of dimensions that they believed were important in treatment implementation. Then, various data were gathered to determine the level of treatment implementation in each dimension in different counties. These data were collected through telephone interviews of upper-level implementors, such as judges, county

commissioners, and so on; through mailed questionnaires sent to lower-level implementors, such as probation officers and service providers; and through examination of various official records and court documents. It was found that legislation had been implemented at different levels for different dimensions from county to county.

APPLICATIONS

The normative treatment evaluation provides stakeholders with information on whether the treatment is being implemented in a way that is congruent with the normative treatment specified by theory. This kind of evaluation can provide information on day-to-day program activities within a short time after the initial implementation of the treatment. Stakeholders, by judging the information provided by this kind of normative evaluation, not only can gain a good understanding of how the treatment is being implemented but can also take immediate action for improving the treatment implementation processes if necessary.

There are different ways to apply the normative treatment evaluation. The simplest form of application is tracking whether or not the normative treatment has been categorically implemented or received. For a simple example, the normative treatment of an adult literacy program may specify that an 80% attendance rate is crucial for the participant to adequately learn the materials. In the evaluation, stakeholders may judge that the normative treatment is quite successfully implemented if most of the students attend 90% of the classes. The stakeholders may regard the treatment implementation a total failure if the evaluation finds that only one-third of the students attend 80% or more of the classes. Similarly, a federal program may require all local agencies to develop a computer-based system for processing applications and other information. The normative treatment evaluation can be carried out to discover whether or not the local agencies actually have implemented the system.

In many situations, the implementation of treatment is not simply a yes or no question. The actual treatment tends to vary in different degrees from the normative treatment. Key stakeholders may be concerned with the exact degree of treatment implementation. Under this condition, the normative treatment evaluation needs to measure the degree to which the treatment has been implemented. Some programs require clients to attend multiple sessions, such as therapy or job training.

In this type of program, as discussed in the previous section, the attendance record can provide a measure of the degree of treatment implementation.

However, in many programs, the degree of treatment implementation cannot be measured simply by the frequency of attendance. A treatment implementation scale may need to be developed to measure the degree of treatment implementation. For example, as discussed in the previous section, Kerr et al. (1985) developed an implemented treatment scale for measuring classroom activities. Similarly, Hall and Loucks (1977) developed a treatment implementation scale to measure the adoption of educational innovation.

Furthermore, the treatment in a program may involve a complicated set of components rather than a single component. Under this condition, the application of the normative treatment evaluation requires the development of an intensive measurement system to reflect the normative treatment and to measure the implemented treatment.

This type of application is illustrated by Bickman's (1985) discussion of an evaluation of statewide services delivered to preschool children. In this evaluation, the stakeholder approach was utilized to specify a normative treatment structure. A set of essential program components and related activities were identified. For example, the family intervention component contained the following activities: family assessment, parent education, parent support, and so on. The appropriateness of each activity was measured by criteria such as degree of implementation, frequency, and duration of activity. A checklist of a combination of these measures was made to assess program components, and experts were invited to rate their relative importance. An aggregation of the experts' ratings of specific activities and overall components served as basis for the normative treatment.

Service providers were asked how the activities offered in their projects related to the questions in the checklist. Information on the implemented treatment was obtained from an aggregation of the answered checklists. The implemented treatment activities and components were then compared with the experts' ratings. The consistency between the normative and implemented treatments was used as a guide for judging the quality of the state's preschool programs.

Usually the results of the normative treatment evaluation can be utilized in the following ways. If the results of the normative treatment evaluation show that there is a congruency between the normative treatment and the actual treatment, this indicates that the implementation of the treatment is sound. The evaluators not only help key stakeholders to identify or clarify their normative treatment theory but also provide them with empirical evidence to confirm that the integrity of the treatment has been well maintained in the field. Then program managers and administrators are encouraged to proceed with their routine operations.

However, if the results of the normative treatment evaluation show that there is incongruency between the normative treatment and the actual treatment, this often indicates problems in the implementation of the treatment and suggests that program operations need modifications. Evaluators can help key stakeholders in developing strategies to cope with the problems.

In fact, the evaluator can contribute to this troubleshooting process even more if he or she can provide further information on the reasons for the incongruency, the prospective remedial actions, and the potential strategies available for improving implementation processes. These will be the major issues in the next chapter.

Furthermore, the function of normative treatment evaluation is not limited to assessing the integrity of the treatment. The normative treatment evaluation can also be designed in such a way that it can be later integrated with the impact evaluation for better understanding or improving program effectiveness. These strategies for integrating normative treatment evaluation into impact evaluation will be discussed in detail in Chapter 12.

7. Normative Implementation Environment Evaluation

Normative treatment evaluation can reveal whether or not there is a discrepancy between the normative treatment and the implemented treatment, but it often cannot exactly pinpoint the sources of the problems. For an understanding of where the implementation processes went wrong, a normative implementation environment evaluation is required. Before discussing the normative implementation environment, it is important to examine the concepts of implementation environment, normative implementation environment, and evaluation of the normative implementation environment.

A social or intervention program cannot automatically deliver itself, nor is it implemented within a vacuum. Social or intervention programs must be implemented by a program staff, within a setting, organized by an implementing organization within a community context. Consequently, the processes and outcomes of a program may be conditioned by environmental factors such as implementors, setting, implementing organizations, or community structures as well as by the factors more commonly considered in a program environment.

The "implementation environment" is defined here as the pertinent environmental factors under which the program is implemented that have the potential to condition the implementation processes and program consequences. For example, a halfway house operated in a friendly and supportive neighborhood may have different implementation qualities and program outcomes than an otherwise similar program operated in a hostile neighborhood. Consequently, the neighborhood is a factor in the implementation environment of the halfway house. Similarly, the implementation processes and program consequences may depend upon who implements the program. A program implemented by skillful and enthusiastic implementors may have results quite different from the same program implemented by unskilled or indifferent implementors. The implementors' characteristics, then, are also part of the implementation environment.

These efforts to bring the implementation environment into the scheme of program evaluation parallel many social science theories that are based on the belief that human behavior can be better understood by examining the relationships that exist between structural or ecological contexts and social factors (e.g., Durkheim, 1951; Hawley, 1950; Barker, 1968; Bronfenbrenner, 1977). These theories, which are found in many disciplines, have suggested that human behavior is shaped and constrained by external environmental factors such as social structure, culture, physical arrangements, and so forth.

The importance for an evaluation of examining the implementation environment has also been demonstrated by many implementation studies that indicate that program failures often result from implementation failures (e.g., see Sabatier and Mazmanian, 1982; Williams, 1980; Derthick, 1972; Pressman and Wildavsky, 1973). According to Williams (1975), program implementation is the Achilles' heel in human services management. He claims that the major difficulty faced by decision makers today is not so much in developing what appear on paper to be reasonable policies, but in converting these written policies into appropriate operations in the field. Program stakeholders obviously can benefit more from an evaluation if it can provide information for strengthening the implementation process.

In the effort to incorporate the implementation environment into an evaluation, it is first necessary to formulate a normative theory of the implementation environment of the program. This theory specifies the normative implementation environment under which the treatment can be appropriately implemented. For example, the normative implementation environment theory may specify that the treatment of a program must be implemented by a certain type of implementor, using a particular mode of delivery, and so on. As will be explained later, both the stakeholder approach and the social science approach can be used to formulate the normative theory of the implementation environment. An agreement between the evaluator and stakeholders on the normative implementation environment is necessary in order to carry out the normative implementation environment evaluation.

The purpose of a normative implementation environment evaluation is to assess the congruency between the normative implementation environment and the actual environment under which the program treatment is implemented. By indicating discrepancies between the normative and actual environments, this evaluation can provide timely feedback to stakeholders on the sources of problems within the implementation environment. Based upon this information, program managers and administrators can take immediate actions to improve the implementation process.

THE CONCEPTUAL FRAMEWORK OF THE IMPLEMENTATION ENVIRONMENT

However, in spite of its usefulness, application of the normative implementation environment evaluation is hindered by lack of a conceptual framework to guide the evaluator and stakeholders in specifying the relevant implementation environment. Unlike normative treatment evaluation, where the meaning of treatment is conceptually clear, in the normative implementation environment evaluation the implementation environment can mean anything external to the treatment. Without guidance from a conceptual framework, it is difficult for an evaluator to know the areas in the external environment appropriate for investigation. This section will focus on the development of a conceptual framework for the implementation environment.

Traditionally, the environment is generally classified into two categories: the micro environment (the environment created by the program) and the macro environment (the environment in which the program exists) (Conrad and Roberts-Gray, 1988). However, a more refined distinction is needed in order to better understand the nature of the implementation environment. Based upon the previous work of Chen and Rossi (1983), this section develops a refined distinction in which the implementation environment is conceptualized as containing seven related dimensions: participant, implementor, delivery mode, implementing organization, interorganizational relationship, micro context, and macro context. The first four dimensions can be regarded as the environment created by the program; the remaining three dimensions can be regarded as the external environment the program inhabits or with which it is connected. All of these may affect the success of implementation processes and condition the consequences of the program.

Participant Dimension

Every program, if it is implemented, involves people who receive or are exposed to the treatment. These people are participants in the program. For example, the participants in mental health programs are patients; in welfare programs, they are the welfare recipients; in neighborhood crime prevention programs, the residents; and so on. The participant dimension concerns the relationships between participants and a program. Issues such as the participants' characteristics, as well as their acceptance or reactivity to the program and the implementation processes, are important in this dimension.

A social or intervention program usually sets eligibility standards to distinguish which people should or should not receive the treatment. It is important for key stakeholders to address issues such as the following: What exactly are the eligibility rules to be applied? Who should be potential program participants? How are the participants admitted to the program? Are the participants consistent with the target groups as in the original plan? In fact, a program may be regarded as resource wasteful or a failure if the participants are not the target group.

Furthermore, the success of program implementation may, at least partially, depend on the participants' receptivity (e.g., level of compliance) and their attributes (e.g., education). If the participants refuse, resist, or do not cooperate with the treatment delivery, then clearly the program has serious implementation problems and can have no effect. Hence, program implementation and effectiveness are contingent on the participants' acceptance of the program treatment. For example, the success of any educational broadcasting program is first conditioned by the percentage of the potential audience listening. The overall success (although the effect is small) of *Sesame Street* is due to its success in attracting a large proportion of its intended audience of nursery-school- and school-aged children in poor families.

Furthermore, even when the participants accept the treatment, treatment effectiveness may still be conditioned by their experience, background, motivations, values, attitudes, social demographic characteristics, and so on. A treatment found to be effective for a certain group of participants may not be effective for others. A program treatment might be more suited to the highly motivated rather than the less motivated, to men rather than women, to blacks rather than whites, to highly educated rather than less educated, and so forth (e.g., see Rossi and Lyall, 1976; Somers and Stromsdorfer, 1972).

Generally speaking, the participants' receptivity and attributes may condition the implementation processes and outcomes of a program. Information provided by evaluators concerning the participant dimension can make it easier for users to understand program impacts, improve implementation strategies, and discover ways to tailor programs to meet the needs of different groups as well as to facilitate the future planning of similar programs.

Implementor Dimension

Program treatment is usually delivered to participants through implementors. How the implementors deliver the program makes a major difference in the success of the program implementation. Therefore, implementors are also one of the important dimensions of the implementation environment. The implementor dimension addresses the relationship between the implementor and the implementation processes. Issues such as the implementors' attributes as well as their relationships with the participants are important concerns in this dimension.

Implementors' attributes can directly affect the quality of implementation. Many treatment implementations, such as teaching, rehabilitating, consulting, and so on, require special training, education, and skill for appropriate treatment delivery. Qualified implementors are essential for the success of implementation. Furthermore, organizational theories (Maslow, 1943; Herzberg, 1966; Lawler, 1973) have consistently pointed to workers' motivation and commitment as essential to providing high-quality work.

Similarly, the relationship between the implementors and the participants may also determine the success of the implementation. Many studies in psychotherapy have showed that therapists who cannot develop good rapport with clients tend to produce low-quality treatment implementation (e.g., Garfield and Bergin, 1978).

The importance of the implementor in an evaluation usually depends on the level of interaction between the implementor and the participant in the delivery of treatment. Whenever a program requires high levels of interaction or contact, key stakeholders and the evaluators should seriously consider including the implementor dimension in the evaluation processes. Many labor-intensive social programs, especially those with an educational, therapeutic, or rehabilitative purpose, fall into this category. On the other hand, if the treatment delivery requires only the mailing of letters, such as with welfare checks, the implementor dimension may be less important.

Delivery Mode Dimension

The delivery of treatment requires both structural and administrative efforts for organizing and coordinating the operation procedures, facilities, implementors, and participants. How the arrangements are made can determine the quality of implementation. For example, problems such as conflicting treatment schedules or ill-prepared facilities obviously hinder the delivery of treatment. Furthermore, structural and administrative efforts usually create a kind of social climate or milieu that can influence the treatment implementation in characteristic, constant ways (Moos, 1974, 1988). Some social climates will be more supportive than others. Some social climates emphasize order and control, thus encouraging compliance or rebellion, depending on people's feelings about order and control. Delivery modes refer to both the structural and the administrative arrangements and/or social climates that convey the treatment to the participants.

According to this conceptualization, a program treatment, when it is delivered in the field, consists of not only the treatment but also the mode of delivery of the treatment. For example, an educational program consists not only of the treatment, such as teaching activities, but also of the delivery mode, which includes such aspects as classroom regulations, the time and place of meeting, the class size, use of teaching aids, and classroom climate. In a psychiatric hospital, treatment outcomes are conditioned by factors such as the staff-patient ratio, the interaction patterns between patients, the extensiveness and flexibility of the rules and regulations patients have to obey, the attitudes of the staff who enforce the rules, layout, the general level of social support, and whether or not the air-conditioning is operative. Because program treatment requires a mode of delivery, the delivery system may condition program processes and outcomes. Some modes of treatment delivery may enhance the treatment effect while others may hinder it. Including the mode of delivery as an additional factor within the evaluation provides information on program implementation that may clarify how best to specify an evaluation model or structure a social program for future application. This implies that evaluators who work with programs need to develop measurements and tests to evaluate these factors.

The study of the delivery mode dimension has been hindered by difficulty in measuring the concept. Lately, however, the development in this area is very encouraging. A number of useful instruments for measuring delivery mode have been constructed and have been demonstrated to be useful (see Conrad and Roberts-Gray, 1988). The most important contribution in this area appears to be Moos's work (e.g., see Moos, 1974, 1988; Finney and Moos, forthcoming). Moos has systematically developed a number of measurement instruments, such as the Community-Oriented Programs Environment Scale and the Ward Atmosphere Scale, for measuring the delivery mode or social environment of psychiatric wards, classrooms, correctional institutions, community-oriented programs, and so on. Moos's most comprehensive instrument is the Multiphasic Environmental Assessment Procedure (MEAP) containing measures of the following four aspects of the program delivery mode: physical and architectural features, organizational policies and services, suprapersonal factors, and social climates.

Implementing Organization Dimension

The implementing organization is responsible for socializing, training, coordinating, and supporting the individual program implementors as well as for structuring the delivery system. Sometimes the structure and process of an implementing organization may condition the results of implementations and outcomes. Many of its characteristics, such as its resources, its particular type of authority structure and personnel composition, its existing standard operating procedures, and the system of incentives employed to achieve coordination of activities among personnel and departments, may affect the amount and specific form of the treatment delivered.

Organizational theory should provide a general basis for developing knowledge in this area. Organizational theories imply that the fit between the nature of treatment and the nature of organizational structure are crucial in treatment implementation and organizational effectiveness. Organizational theories such as those of Perrow (1967), Thompson (1967), and Woodward (1965) argue that, generally speaking, organizational technology (or treatment implementation in the context of program evaluation) can be classified as routine (few exceptions and easy-to-analyze problems) and nonroutine (many exceptions and difficult-to-analyze problems). Examples of routine technology are automobile assembly lines or bank teller departments. Examples of nonroutine technology are the transformation processes in aerospace projects or filmmaking projects.

In order to be effective, routine technology should be implemented in a mechanistic structure characterized by high vertical differentiation (a large number of hierarchical levels), high formalization (use of rules and regulations to control members' behavior), and high centralization (decision making is concentrated at upper levels). However, nonroutine technology should operate under an organic structure characterized by flexible and adaptive structures with emphasis on lateral communication, loosely defined responsibilities, and nonauthority-based influence. These arguments imply that social or intervention programs that operate with routine technology, such as welfare programs, require mechanistic structures, while programs that operate with nonroutine technology, such as counseling and noncustodial psychiatric clinics, require organic structures.

Interorganizational Relationship Dimension

Implementing organizations function in constant relationship with other organizations. Some of these relationships are required by law, such as those between regulatory agencies and the organizations they regulate; some are formal and contractual, such as those between funding and implementing agencies; some are relatively informal, such as the system of referrals between primary care physicians and specialists. Some of these relationships may be amicable and cooperative, others may be adversarial, or competitive, or both. Through this network of relationships, implementing organizations acquire resources, gain legitimacy, and develop channels for seeking advance and assistance.

The nature of the interorganizational processes in which an implementing organization is involved may affect program implementation or outcome. Very often social service agencies are linked together weakly, with each agency giving high priority to its own goals and interests and low priority to those of other agencies. In such a system, if an agency begins a treatment whose success is dependent upon the cooperation of other agencies, the treatment outcome will be directly conditioned by the degree of cooperation the agency obtains.

Inappropriate interorganizational processes usually lead to a setback in program implementation, which often results in program failure—as many implementation studies have noted. For example, the New Towns-in-Town program (Derthick, 1972) and the Oakland manpower program (Pressman and Wildavsky, 1973) show how the jurisdictional and coordinative requirements of multiagency programs can create uncertainty, confusion, and delay and eventually undermine the entire enterprise.

Micro-Context Dimension

In many situations the program-treatment-related environment is not the only environment with which clients must interact. Clients also have to interact with other environments, which, though not directly related to the treatment, may constrain the outcome of the program. The term "micro context" refers to the immediate social units, such as family and peer groups, within which the clients live during or after the treatment. Some micro contexts may favor the implementation of a program and consequently strengthen its effects. For example, a drug-abuse treatment program may cure patients more easily if the clients' families show a large measure of support. Generally speaking, if the micro context provides substantial social support, is highly cohesive, and so on, a program treatment will be more easily applied and the results will be more successful. On the other hand, if the micro context is stressful, disruptive, and nonsupportive, the program treatment may be more difficult to apply and less effective.

Social science research on the relationships between social support and human health or well-being (e.g., see Cobb, 1976; Caplan, 1979; House, 1981) strengthens the argument that the micro context is one of the important dimensions in the implementation environment. Several studies on alcoholism treatment programs show that social support in the micro context is related to program processes, such as completion of the treatment. For example, Janzen (1977), Berenson (1976), and Cantanzaro et al. (1973) found that social support from family members increased the likelihood of an alcoholic's completion of the treatment program.

Macro-Context Dimension

The macro context is the broadest and most general level of the social, political, economic, and cultural structures within which a program takes place that affect its outcome. This includes such things as regional and national cultures, political movements, levels of economic activity, historical processes, and social changes. The macro context may condition program implementation, intervening processes, and/or program outcomes.

Organizational literature provides many insights into how the macro context can influence the operation of organizations (e.g., Lawrence and Lorsch, 1967). An organization has to cope appropriately with the uncertainty in the external environment in order to function well or even survive. In general, organizational theorists such as Burns and Stalker (1961) argue that organizational effectiveness depends to some extent on the fit between structure and environment. They argue that mechanistic structures may be more effective in a stable environment and organic structures may be more effective in an unstable environment.

Based upon the idea of the fit between the characteristics of the environment and the characteristics of the organization, the population ecology model (e.g., Aldrich, 1979) goes further to argue that the environment selects certain kinds of organizations to survive and others to perish. This perspective implies the importance of an organization finding a niche (a domain of unique environmental resources and needs) where the organization can produce the outputs desired by the environment.

The application of the conceptual framework in normative evaluation will be the topic of the rest of this chapter. However, in addition to normative evaluation, the conceptual framework of the implementation environment is also useful in causative evaluation. This application will be discussed in Chapters 11 and 13.

NORMATIVE IMPLEMENTATION ENVIRONMENT EVALUATION: STRATEGIES AND PROCEDURES

In general, normative implementation environment evaluation assesses the congruence between the normative and actual implementation environments. According to the conceptual framework discussed above, the normative implementation environment evaluation addresses issues such as these: Are the participants receiving treatment consistent with the target group specified in the normative implementation environment? Are the actual implementors of the treatment consistent with the normative implementors as planned? Is the setting or implementing organization under which the treatment is implemented consistent with the setting or implementing organization specified in the normative theory? More specifically, normative implementation environment evaluation involves two stages. The first stage is to specify the normative implementation environment. The second stage is to gather empirical data on the actual implementation environment for assessing the congruency between the actual and normative implementation environments.

Specifying the Normative Implementation Environment

The specification of the normative implementation environment requires a normative theory. Key stakeholders usually have an implicit theory about what the required normative implementation environment should be for the program treatment to generate the desired processes and outcomes. In the theorizing process, it is important for the evaluator to apply the stakeholder approach to render the stakeholders' own theory explicit.

In some cases, there are formal policies, regulations, or guidelines regarding treatment implementation, and these are also useful sources in the theorizing process. For example, a state agency may have formal regulations requiring local mental health agencies to maintain credentialed doctors and nurses, certain patient-staff ratios, health and safety requirements, and so on in order to have a license.

Furthermore, the evaluator can also apply the social science approach to derive some dimensions of the normative implementation environment that may otherwise be ignored by the stakeholders. Based upon the conceptual framework of the implementation environment, the evaluator and stakeholders can discuss the dimensions of the implementation environment that are crucial to implementing the treatment. After the relevant dimensions have been identified, the required elements of these dimensions must be specified explicitly. For example, the stakeholders and evaluators may theoretically specify that the implementor and mode of delivery dimensions in a therapy program for prisoners are the most crucial dimensions contributing to both desirable treatment process and outcomes. Consequently, they may specify that the implementors should be professional therapists and that the personality traits of the therapists should be matched with the prisoners' personality traits.

Evaluation of the Normative Implementation Environment

After the normative implementation environment has been specified, empirical data must be gathered for evaluating congruence between the normative implementation environment and the actual implementation environment. There are two general data-gathering methods for evaluating the implementation processes: monitoring and scanning.

"Implementation environment monitoring" is defined here as the use of formal, standardized instruments to systematically gather program data, with the focus upon the pertinent dimensions of the normative implementation environment, for the purpose of detecting problems in the implementation processes. This definition is broader and more general than the current use of the term, which emphasizes issues relating to only a few dimensions of the implementation environment (e.g., see Grant, 1978; Rossi and Freeman, 1985; Posavac and Carey, 1989).

In monitoring, data are gathered systematically and uniformly across all of the times and/or sites related to a program. For example, schools usually maintain ongoing, formal record-keeping systems for tracking data such as student and teacher attendance, curriculum progress, student grades and achievement, and so forth. The advantage of this type of approach is that the standardized and generally quantitative data gathered allow stakeholders to systematically analyze and compare aspects of an implementation across different times and sites. The techniques and data collection procedures for monitoring, such as using observation, records, interviews, surveys, and so on, have been extensively discussed by Rossi and Freeman (1985). The application of monitoring techniques will be illustrated by a number of research examples discussed in the next section.

Windle and Sharfstein (1978, p. 46) observed that, in terms of the implementation organization, monitoring can serve the following three related purposes:

> To ensure the agencies comply with requirements imposed by the sponsoring or funding sources and by law and regulations. To obtain information about the program's functioning on which to base future program support and design decisions and to stimulate improvement within local projects.

However, the maintenance of an ongoing monitoring system is costly and laborious. However, monitoring has some weaknesses. Because the items or questions being monitored are standardized and fixed, exclusive attention to these questions might reduce the evaluator's and implementor's awareness of problems in other areas. Scanning is an alternative technique for evaluating the normative implementation environment. Unlike monitoring, scanning is a flexible, nonroutine information-gathering strategy suitable for investigating areas of concern in the implementation environment. Many qualitative methods, such as participant observation and interviewing, are particularly useful for scanning purposes. However, quantitative techniques such as surveys may also be used when appropriate.

Implementation environment scanning is a concerted search for problems, difficulties, or opportunities within the pertinent dimensions of the implementation environment that may either disrupt or facilitate program processes. Implementation environment scanning does not require a formalized or standardized ongoing data-gathering system. Rather, based upon the normative implementation environment, information on pertinent aspects of the implementation environment is gathered through interaction with, or surveys of, program implementors. Participant observation of the setting and the implementation procedure and/or examination of existing documentation or records is also conducted in order to discover processes or events that are problematic either in the normative implementation environment or in the implementation process. As an example, evaluators may interview or survey participants and discover that they are considering withdrawing from the program. Two research examples closely resembling the use of implementation environment scanning are studied by Shapiro et al. (1983) and Weatherly and Lipsky (1977). These two studies will be discussed in the next section.

It must be remembered that both scanning and monitoring have pros and cons. Due to its inflexibility, scanning gives the evaluator a free hand to investigate any necessary dimension or issue. Scanning may reveal implementation problems that would not be detected in a more structured form of data collection. Furthermore, because it requires less ongoing record keeping, its cost is lower. In contrast to monitoring, however, scanning may not help stakeholders to continuously and systematically track implementation across different sites and times, especially if the program is on a large scale or highly complex.

On the other hand, monitoring allows ongoing and systematic tracking of the implementation processes across different sites and times, but it is more expensive because it necessitates coding, filing, and administrative maintenance. In addition, because attention is paid only to standardized questions and pieces of information, monitoring can neglect significant developments in the implementation dimension that may disrupt the program.

Although it is beneficial to use both monitoring and scanning in program evaluation, in practice, an evaluator may have to choose one over the other because of resource constraints. Generally speaking, this choice depends on how well the implementation of a particular program is understood. If the implementation process is well understood from past study and experience and the likely issues in relevant dimensions can be identified in a formal data-gathering process, monitoring may have advantages over scanning. On the other hand, if the implementation process is new or ill-understood and the evaluator needs to keep options open in case of unexpected events, scanning may be more appropriate. For example, the implementation process of an emergency medical service at a new general hospital is better understood than that of a community antidrug program, and the monitoring system may, therefore, be more appropriate.

Another factor influencing the choice of strategy is the scale of the program. The larger the program, the more program managers and decision makers will require standardized and systematized information to track and compare progress at different sites or at different times. Under these conditions, monitoring may be more useful than scanning. This is perhaps the reason why monitoring has been used frequently by the federal government to track the implementation of regulations or programs by state and local agencies (Grant, 1978).

APPLICATIONS OF NORMATIVE IMPLEMENTATION ENVIRONMENT EVALUATIONS

The conceptual framework of the implementation environment discussed in the previous section facilitates the discussion of the application of the normative implementation environment evaluation. After the pertinent dimension or dimensions have been identified, a normative implementation environment evaluation can be applied to that particular dimension or dimensions. As discussed in the previous section of this chapter, this application involves, first, a specification of the normative theory of the pertinent dimension or dimensions. Empirical data then are gathered to assess the congruency between the normative and actual environments. The application of the normative implementation environment evaluation to each domain is discussed in detail in the following section.

Normative Participant Evaluation

A normative participant evaluation involves an assessment of congruency between the normative and actual participant dimensions, which requires an identification of the normative participant dimension. This includes a specification of issues such as these: Who should be the target group? What kind of characteristics should they have? How should they behave during treatment implementation? And so on. Program designers and other key stakeholders usually have clear ideas on the normative participant dimension. If they do not, then the evaluators have to help them to clarify or identify the crucial issues in the normative participant dimension.

After the normative participant dimension has been specified, the evaluator needs to use either monitoring or scanning techniques to gather empirical information on the actual participant dimensions that correspond to the issues raised. After the information has been collected, the evaluator then assesses the congruency between the normative and actual participant dimensions.

For example, the purpose of enacting medicare was to remove financial barriers to adequate medical care for the elderly and enable them to seek medical attention commensurate with their needs. Davis and Reynolds (1975) carried out a one-shot monitoring study to assess whether or not medicare enables the aged to seek medical care primarily on the basis of need. They found out that high-income elderly persons received much greater medicare benefits than low-income elderly persons. Furthermore, elderly whites also received higher payments than elderly blacks. Similarly, one of the central points in the legislation of the Comprehensive Employment and Training Act of 1973 (CETA) was to serve low-income groups and those most in need of manpower services. A monitoring study by Baumer et al. (1979) mainly focused on the appropriateness of participants covered by this program. It was found that the poor and women received proportionately fewer benefits from CETA.

The normative participant dimension evaluation provides immediate information on whether the participants of the program are appropriate. If the results of the evaluation indicate an incongruence between the normative and actual implementor dimensions, the program may be regarded by key stakeholders as wasteful of resources or even a total failure. Early feedback from the evaluation information is useful for helping the key stakeholders to recognize problems in the participant dimension and develop strategies to cope with them.

Normative Implementor Evaluation

A normative implementor evaluation involves an assessment of congruency between the normative and actual implementor dimensions, which requires the identification of the normative implementor dimension. The following issues are important in this stage: Who should be the implementors? What attributes should they have? What kind of relationships should they have with the participants? Again, if the key stakeholders are vague or unclear regarding the normative implementor, the evaluators have to help them to clarify or identify the crucial issues in this dimension.

Based upon the normative implementor dimension, the evaluator can then proceed to gather data on the actual implementor dimension. With the information on the normative and actual implementor dimension at hand, the evaluator then assesses the congruency between the normative and actual implementor dimensions. For example, in a prison rehabilitation program, if group leaders ought to be professional personnel, then incongruence exists if it is found that untrained prison guards are the actual group leaders (e.g., Kassebaum et al., 1971). Early feedback from information on the implementors from the normative implementor evaluation can be very useful to help key stakeholders improve program implementation.

A good example to illustrate the normative implementor evaluation is Weatherly and Lipsky's (1977) use of the scanning technique to study the implementation of the State of Massachusetts Comprehensive Special Education Law (Chapter 766). Their study showed how implementors overburdened by new legislation without additional funds may develop many undesirable coping behaviors that eventually will undermine program goals. The Comprehensive Special Education Law was intended to provide a "flexible and uniform system of special education opportunities for all children requiring special education" (Weatherly and Lipsky, 1977, p. 174). In terms of the normative implementor dimension, the law made local teachers and educational experts the normative implementors responsible for educating handicapped persons between the ages of 3 and 21, regardless of handicap, and for providing a wide number of medical and social services for the child, as well as offering counseling to parents. Children had to be assessed by an interdisciplinary team, and standardized tests had to be used with all due caution and care.

Weatherly and Lipsky were particularly interested in how this act would actually be implemented at the local level, by "street-level bureaucrats." They believed that the teachers and educational specialists who had to put Chapter 766 into practice in their classrooms and offices would be the ones who determined what the law actually meant, and their determinations might be substantially different from the lawmakers' intentions.

To examine the actual implementor dimension, Weatherly and Lipsky employed qualitative methods: interviewing various officials, attending meetings, especially evaluation team settings, and reviewing records. They discovered that the major factor undercutting the intended impact of the law was the amount of work it required. Teachers, principals, and other specialists made substantial and sincere efforts to comply with the new law's imperatives, but there were simply not enough resources available for them to do it. The new law made more demands on the educational system's time and energy but added no resources.

Accordingly, education personnel developed coping mechanisms. Instead of impartially conducting assessments of all handicapped children, assessments were rationed among students who had behavioral problems and were not likely to be sources of expense or to those under the care of a specialist. They also emphasized group treatment, used specialists-in-training rather than experienced specialists, and put pressure on parents to go along with staff recommendations. The implementation problem, in this case, was not lack of concern, motivation, or enthusiasm. In fact, as pointed out by Weatherly and Lipsky, concern for the well-being of the children was the foremost consideration for the majority of school personnel. School administrators and specialists put forth extraordinary amounts of time and effort while attempting to implement the law. However, a program of this complexity could not be handled by local school systems. School personnel had to develop various coping mechanisms that actually subverted or distorted the intent of the special education reforms. In showing this, Weatherly and Lipsky's study provides suggestive, useful information that decision makers can immediately act upon.

Normative Delivery Mode Evaluation

The normative delivery mode evaluation is an assessment of congruence between the normative delivery mode dimension and the actual delivery mode dimension. This evaluation requires, first, identification of the normative delivery mode. Issues such as what the structural and administrative arrangement should be or what the social climates should be, along with the treatment implementation, are important concerns in this stage. Based upon the normative delivery mode, the corresponding information on the actual delivery mode dimension is gathered. Then, the evaluator assesses the congruence between the normative and actual delivery mode dimensions.

Measurement instruments such as MEAP (Moos, 1988) provide useful tools for carrying out normative delivery mode evaluations in different ways. For example, the instrument can be used by the evaluator to ask the participants (or implementors) to describe the normative or ideal delivery mode they prefer and to report the actual delivery mode they perceive. Then the evaluator can assess the congruence between the normative and actual delivery modes. The evaluation results not only provide a good understanding of the delivery mode but also indicate the area needing further improvement (Moos and Trickett, 1987).

Another application is to use a scale such as MEAP to assess the congruence between the implementor's and the participant's assessment of the delivery mode. For example, Thompson and Swisher (1983) applied MEAP to carry out a normative evaluation of a Rural Life-Care Residential Center for Elderly. They found incongruence between the staff's and the client's assessment of the delivery mode. They report that the staff demonstrated highly positive views of the delivery mode, but the elderly residents judged the delivery mode as only average or below average on a majority of the scales.

Moos's work represents a use of the monitoring method to assess delivery mode. Shapiro et al.'s (1983) study of a leadership and management training program for women employed in higher education provides an example of using the scanning method in evaluating the delivery mode. The purpose of this program was to help develop a positive self-concept and thus encourage women to move up into administrative positions. Program participants were specifically invited, and many came from support staff, entry-level administration, mid-level administration, and faculty. Program treatments consisted of a Case Study Workshop, Leadership and Management Clinic, and a series of Brown Bag Seminars.

Because it was a new program, the evaluator and program staff anticipated that the mode of delivery in the normative implementation environment would be problematic and in need of change. The evaluators applied the scanning technique to track the implementation processes to find any problems relating to the mode of delivery. The evaluators applied various flexible data collection techniques, such as field observation and interviews, to track problems in the mode of delivery. Some problems in the mode of delivery were detected and this information was promptly fed back to program staff for improving program implementation.

For example, participants were originally divided into groups based on their occupations. After the first meeting, however, participants called this "elitism" and emphatically objected to it. On the basis of this information, the program designer changed the format of the program, changing the mode to one of mixed groups. In a follow-up interview, participants agreed that elitism was no longer an issue.

Normative Implementing Organization Evaluation

The normative implementing organization evaluation involves an assessment of congruence between the normative implementing organization dimension and the actual implementing organization dimension, which requires an identification of the normative implementing organization dimension. This involves a specification of the normative organizational structure and processes that are necessary to implement the program. The evaluator then gathers empirical information on the corresponding actual organizational structure and processes. After that, the evaluator assesses the congruence between the normative and the actual implementing organization dimensions.

A good example of the normative implementing organization evaluation is Fiene and Nixon's (1981) study of Pennsylvania's day-care monitoring system. This normative implementing organization dimension of how day-care centers should operate was developed through intensive joint efforts between the evaluators and officials from the Office of Children and Youth in the Pennsylvania Department of Public Welfare to specify the normative implementation environment.

Following closely the format of the normative implementing organization dimension, a monitoring instrument on the dimension of implementing organization was formulated. This monitoring instrument addresses questions in such areas as health and safety requirements, standards for program activities such as credentials for staff, and the child-to-staff ratio in the day-care centers. All the day-care centers in the State of Pennsylvania are required to periodically provide information contained in the monitoring instrument. This monitoring system provides state officials with useful information for their policy decisions. State officials use this system to assess whether the day-care centers' health, safety, and operations are consistent with the standards specified in the normative implementation environment. This information is then used to determine whether there is a need to intervene at a day-care center to improve its conditions in order to maintain the quality of the treatment implementation.

Normative Interorganizational Relationship Evaluation

The normative interorganizational relationship evaluation involves an assessment of the congruency between the normative and actual interorganizational relationship dimensions, which requires an identification of the normative interorganizational relationship dimension on issues such as how the relevant organizations should relate and cooperate in order to implement the program appropriately. The corresponding information on actual interorganizational relationships is then gathered. The congruency between the normative and actual interorganizational relationships, then, is assessed.

An example to illustrate the interorganizational relationship evaluation is a study of public employment agencies done by Klatzky (1970). According to the Social Security Act, state employment agencies receive a large percentage of their funding from unemployment compensation revenues. Some of this funding, the percentage used to fund unemployment compensation, is given directly to the agency. However, the part used to directly fund the agency's operations is collected by the Bureau of Employment Security and distributed back to the states according to a formula that, Klatzky argues, has never been fully disclosed. Some parts of the formula that have been revealed include (1) the higher overhead of states with scattered populations and thus scattered offices, (2) different unemployment rates, (3) cost of salaries and rents, (4) administrative costs, and (5) special programs targeted for groups such as youth, veterans, minorities, and so forth.

In terms of the normative interorganizational relationship dimension, these factors should work to distribute funds to the areas of greatest need. In terms of the actual interorganizational relationship dimension,

Klatzky found, they work to send the money to the most wealthy states at the expense of those less prosperous. Wealthy states, for example, have higher rents and salary scales and are also more likely to have special programs. One effect of this funding inequality is that the wealthier states emphasize providing unemployment compensation, while the less wealthy concentrate on more cost-effective employment-finding services.

Normative Micro-Context Evaluation

Normative micro-context evaluation assesses congruence between the normative micro-context dimension and the actual micro-context dimension, which requires an identification of the normative micro-context dimension, that is, what the ideal immediate social surroundings during or after the treatment implementation should be. An example would be whether or not the behavior and attitude of people who are closely related to the participant (such as family members, friends, coworkers) are caring or supportive. The evaluators then collect the corresponding empirical information to assess congruence between the normative and actual micro contexts.

Some psychiatrists, such as Bowen (1960) and Minuchin (1974), believe that mental illness does not represent a sick individual but an improperly functioning system, such as a dysfunctional family. In this case, in treating a patient, a psychiatrist may specify the normative micro-context dimension relative to how the family members should behave toward the patient. A normative micro-context evaluation, in this case, requires gathering empirical information on the family members' actual behavior. The evaluator then assesses congruence between the family members' normative and actual behavior as well as attitudes toward the patient.

Normative Macro-Context Evaluation

Normative macro-context evaluation assesses congruence between normative macro-context and actual macro-context dimensions. This requires an identification of the normative macro-context dimension, which includes an identification of pertinent issues regarding what the ideal situations of the larger contextual environment of social, economic, cultural, or political systems toward program implementation processes should be. Then, information on the corresponding issues in the actual macro context are gathered in order to assess its congruence with the normative macro context.

A good example to illustrate normative macro-context evaluation is Cumming and Cumming's (1955) study of an educational program that attempted to alter attitudes about mental illness in a western Canadian community. Program designers set out to develop an educational program that would change residents' knowledge and attitudes toward mental illness, so that they would be more accepting and supportive of discharged psychiatric patients. This, in turn, would lower patient relapse and readmission rates. The educational program consisted of a variety of educational activities, such as presentations at local meetings and articles in the local paper. The normative macro context of the program assumed that hostility toward the mentally ill was rooted in fear, which, in turn, was rooted in ignorance. Education would alleviate the ignorance, diminish the fear, and reduce the hostility. However, the program met with increasing hostility, and postprogram measurements showed that community attitudes about the mentally ill were almost totally unchanged.

The researchers concluded that their original assumption on the normative macro context was incorrect. Information on the actual macro context indicated that the residents' attitudes toward mental health were not based on ignorance but on the need to control deviance. When someone could not abide by community norms, the community responded by isolating itself from the offender and sending him or her away to an asylum. By arguing that those people should be accepted back into the community, the experimenters had threatened the system used by the community to maintain its stability. From this incongruence, it is not surprising that the educational program, which attacked this coping behavior and offered no substitute, was rejected.

ISSUES ON PLANNING AND UTILIZING NORMATIVE IMPLEMENTATION ENVIRONMENT EVALUATION

The previous section demonstrated that the normative implementation environment evaluation can be carried out on each of seven dimensions. The selection of which type of evaluation to focus upon depends on key stakeholders' needs and the nature of the program. Generally speaking, as shown earlier, normative evaluations in the participant dimension, implementor dimension, or micro-context dimensions are highly relevant in labor-intensive programs such as therapy, medical care, and the like. For programs requiring more group activities and administrative coordination, such as psychiatric and educational programs, the delivery mode evaluation becomes more relevant.

Many governmental programs require intensive organizational and interorganizational efforts, and in such programs the implementation organization and interorganizational relationship evaluations are relevant issues. In large-scale community intervention programs directly relating to community structures and processes, the macro-context evaluation becomes relevant.

Furthermore, an evaluator can flexibly combine two or more dimensions of the implementation environment in an evaluation, depending on the situational requirements. For example, delivery mode evaluation can be combined with micro-context evaluation. Similarly, an implementing organization evaluation can be combined with an interorganizational relationship evaluation.

The normative implementation environment evaluation can provide stakeholders with timely information on whether the environment under which the program is being implemented is creating problems. If the evaluation shows that the normative and actual implementation environments are congruent, this means the program is being implemented appropriately. The evaluator makes contributions in clarifying and verifying that the normative implementation environment theory has been put into operation in the field. However, if incongruence is found, it implies problems in the implementation processes. This information enables program staff to immediately take the necessary actions to improve implementation processes in order to develop a better fit between the program and its environment. This evaluation is most useful in the early stages of implementation when a program has not yet become stabilized and routinized. Program managers and administrators often need this early information to find out how they are doing. In fact, the earlier in the program that problems in the implementation environment are identified, the easier and less costly it is to modify the program.

In addition, it should be noted that the normative implementation environment evaluation can also be flexibly integrated with other types of normative evaluation. Brekke's (1987) evaluation of a community support program for the chronically mentally ill represents such an integrated normative evaluation. In this study, normative theories were formulated mainly using the stakeholder approach. The evaluators relied on discussions with program designers and managers as well as on a review of published literature and manuals of the program to develop a monitoring instrument relating to both the normative treatment and the normative implementation environments. Questions or hypotheses relating to the normative treatment, such as the nature of care, or relating to the normative implementation environment, such as mode of the delivery, were asked in the monitoring instrument. Data from this monitoring instrument were collected on an ongoing basis. The information on consistency or discrepancy between the normative patterns and observed patterns were fed back to stakeholders for policy purposes.

Information from the normative implementation environment evaluation also is important for the utilization of the evaluation results. Without the contextual information provided by this kind of evaluation, it may be difficult to interpret the evaluation results because it is unclear under what kind of implementation environment the evaluation results should be applied. Furthermore, information on the implementation environment can be structured into an impact evaluation for enhancing the program effectiveness or generalizability. These issues will be discussed in more detail in Chapters 13 and 11.

PART IV

Causative Evaluations: Basic Types

Part IV presents a detailed discussion of causative evaluation. This category of evaluation deals with causal relationships in a program. Three basic types of causative evaluations are investigated in this part. Impact evaluation is discussed in the next two chapters. Chapter 8 focuses on the assessment of program impact by using a broad evidence base. Chapter 9 examines issues related to the assessment of both intended and unintended plausible outcomes. Intervening mechanism evaluation, discussed in Chapter 10, attempts to assess causal mechanisms underlying a program so that factors in the causal chains that lead to program success or failure can be identified. Generalization evaluation, discussed in Chapter 11, looks at enhancing the generalizability of an evaluation.

8. Impact Evaluation I: Broadening the Evidence Base

The three basic types of normative evaluations discussed in the last three chapters are useful in improving and developing program structure according to the normative theory. When key stakeholders are unclear exactly what specific goals they should pursue, what treatment format should be constructed, or what implementation environment should support the treatment, normative theory may provide stakeholders with information on how to appropriately develop and routinize the program structure.

However, social or intervention programs are created to deal with problems or to provide services. When the program is mature, stakeholders, particularly funding agencies, decision makers, and/or taxpayers, typically want to understand how successful the program is in achieving its purposes and/or through what kinds of causal mechanisms it will operate. Under this condition, causative evaluations such as impact evaluations are needed.

An evaluation that attempts to evaluate whether or not a program attains its designated goals is traditionally labeled a "summative evaluation" (Dunn, 1981) or an "outcome evaluation" (Posavac and Carey, 1989). However, the traditional conceptualization of the summative evaluation or outcome evaluation has two limitations. First, the application of designs in dealing with issues related to trustworthiness, as will be discussed later, has been too passive and rigid (Cordray, 1986). As a consequence, the evidence provided in a summative evaluation to test a causal hypothesis may be too limited. Second, traditional summative evaluations have mainly been based on the goal-attainment model. However, this model has the problem of being insensitive to real impacts or important unintended impacts (Scriven, 1972; Chen and Rossi, 1980).

The concept of the "theory-driven impact evaluation," or simply "impact evaluation," conceptualized in this book attempts to avoid such limitations. The main purpose of the impact evaluation is to assess the impact of the treatment on the outcome. However, unlike the traditional summative evaluation, the impact evaluation has one or both of the following characteristics:

(1) When assessing the impact of the treatment on the outcome, the impact evaluation uses theory-guided strategies to generate a broad evidence base to assess the impact of the treatment on the outcome.

(2) When specifying the outcome in the study, the impact evaluation uses both the stakeholders' views and the existing theory and knowledge related to the program to assess the important intended and unintended impacts.

Issues related to the second characteristic will be the major focus of the next chapter; this chapter concentrates on issues related to the first characteristic.

One of the important concerns in an impact evaluation is how to generate sound evidence for assessing the impact. For the experimental paradigm, the best method is randomized experiments. However, as discussed in Chapter 1, many naturalists are strongly against this view. However, as discussed in Chapter 4, the usefulness of a design or method is contingent on the contextual factors such as evaluation purposes, participants' reactivity, the ability to maintain the integrity of the design, and so on. It is not convincing either to argue for a categorical rejection of the use of randomized experiments or to insist that randomized experiments should be applied in every impact assessment. Rather, this book takes the position that randomized experiments should be regarded as one among a number of good alternatives for carrying out an impact evaluation but not necessarily as the best design for every impact evaluation.

Randomized experiments may be the most powerful designs in terms of ruling out threats to internal validity (Campbell and Stanley, 1963), but they also have some limitations. In addition to ethical and administrative reasons that prevent the use of rigorous designs, Argyris (1980) found insistence on the use of rigorous designs may cause problems in research execution, administrators' resistance, participant reactivity, attrition, and so on, which may disrupt the research purpose or distort the research results. Currently, the views on randomized experiments or other rigorous designs are more sophisticated. Problems related to designing and executing randomization plans for the application of randomized experiments have been identified. Better strategies have been developed in the design and execution of randomized experiments to deal with problems such as participants' rejection or reactivity (Boruch and Wothke, 1985). Ruling out threats to internal validity should be regarded as one of the many important factors to be considered in deciding whether to use rigorous designs in impact evaluation. The evaluator and key stakeholders should also carefully assess other factors, such as the capacity to maintain the integrity of the rigorous design throughout the evaluation. The merits of rigorous designs for impact evaluation may be greatly enhanced after these potential issues and problems have been seriously considered by the evaluator and key stakeholders.

Another important issue related to impact evaluation is the application of the design taxonomy provided by the experimental paradigm. The experimental paradigm has made a highly important contribution in developing a design taxonomy for impact evaluation. This taxonomy describes a list of designs and identifies a checklist of threats to validity that a particular design can or cannot rule out (Campbell and Stanley, 1963; Cook and Campbell, 1979). Because the strengths and weaknesses of a design are clearly identified, this taxonomy is very useful in planning an impact evaluation. Researchers following this tradition usually select a design from this taxonomy that best fits the research conditions and purpose and that will, hopefully, entail the fewest threats in the checklist. If the researcher can select the randomized experiment for the research, he or she may proudly claim that the research employs the strongest design for ensuring a high level of internal validity.

However, under research conditions more suited to a quasi-experimental or preexperimental design, the researcher frequently tolerates the inherent weaknesses associated with the experimental design—though perhaps apologizing for the quality of the research. This sort of use of the design taxonomy tends to be passive and dogmatic. A passive use of research designs in conjunction with a devaluation of other strategies may not only hinder an evaluator from searching for alternative strategies to enhance trustworthiness in an impact evaluation but may also prevent an evaluator from simultaneously dealing with other issues beyond trustworthiness.

This book is not alone in arguing for a more flexible and creative use of research designs. Lately, post-Campbellians such as Cordray (1986), Lipsey (1987), Trochim (1986b), and Cook (1985) have urged evaluators to move from a passive use of designs to an active use, and even to formulate new designs in their evaluations. They propose to cut across or break down the traditional taxonomy of research designs by combining different designs or methods to produce consolidated evidence for causal inference. Similarly, Chen and Rossi (1987) have argued that theory can be integrated with a design to strengthen causal inference. This new conceptualization of design is crucial to expanding and developing the scope of strategies that deal with issues of trustworthiness in impact evaluation based upon the important contributions made by the experimental paradigm.

Based upon the above discussions, it can be construed that impact evaluation shares the same purpose as traditional summative evaluation in assessing the impact of a program. However, unlike a passive application of a design in the traditional summative evaluation, impact evaluation emphasizes the development of a broad evidence base of causal inference by systematically using various strategies such as synthetic designs and causation probing to enhance the quality of impact assessment.

STRATEGIES FOR BROADENING THE TRADITIONAL DESIGN TAXONOMY

There are at least two general strategies in impact evaluation for broadening the design taxonomy provided by the experimental paradigm: synthetic designs and causation probing. As will be seen, the contributions of the experimental paradigm are useful in these new developments.

The Use of Synthetic Designs

This strategy attempts to integrate two or more designs having different strengths, but not sharing the same biases, into a synthetic research design. If the empirical results from such multiple designs are consistent or compatible, the overall synthetic design provides a stronger causal inference than either of the original designs alone. If the empirical results produced by synthetic designs do not converge, the evaluator must then explain or reconcile this contradictory evidence.

A brilliant illustration of combining a set of nonexperimental designs into a powerful synthetic design is the Campbell and McCormack (1957) study of the effect of military training experiences on attitudes toward authority. For simplicity, only part of their design is discussed here. In this study, different classes were admitted for training. Their evaluation started with the first group as a one group posttest-only design, and the second group as a one group pretest and posttest design. The two designs were combined in the following way:

| Class A: | X | O_1 | | (Design 1) |
| Class B: | | O_2 | X | O_3 | (Design 2) |

In these designs, X represents the treatment and 0 the attitudinal measures. Obviously, when these designs are used individually, they suffer many weaknesses. When they are combined, however, one overcomes the weaknesses of the other (see Cordray, 1986).

For example, history is one of the major threats in either Design 1 or Design 2. Yet, as pointed out by Campbell and Stanley (1963), if the treatment has a genuine impact, then O_1 should be larger than O_2. Because both O_1 and O_2 are measured in the same time period, the threat of history is effectively eliminated from the synthetic design. Similarly, if the difference between O_3 and O_2 is the same as the difference between O_1 and O_2, rival hypotheses such as testing and mortality are also ruled out. Again, these threats to validity would be quite problematic if either Design 1 or Design 2 was used alone.

The use of a synthetic design strategy does not mean that we must literally integrate one design with another. Sometimes the inclusion of additional design elements such as observations, control groups, and so on into a design can also enhance causal inference.

The addition of one or more design elements into a traditional design may enhance the power of an evaluation. For example, in their study of the Educational Voucher Demonstration Program, Wortman et al. (1978) showed that the addition of one or more pretest measures into the traditional nonequivalent control group design allowed them to examine the natural growth trend and strengthened their causal inference.

The modern application of synthetic designs to strengthen causal evidence has been exemplified well by an evaluation of the impact of a lottery promotion program by Reynolds and West (1988). This lottery promotion program involved placing signs that read, "Did we ask if you want a Lottery ticket? If not, you get one free," near the point of sale in business establishments. Free tickets were actually given when customers who were not asked the question by the employees then demanded a free ticket.

Reynolds and West (1988) began this study with the application of a nonequivalent control group design for impact assessment. Each treatment store was matched with a control store in the same area. Audited sales data were used as an outcome measure to deal with the potential threat of instrumentation in this design. The results of this evaluation indicated that the program substantially increased the sale of lottery tickets. However, Reynolds and West (1988) pointed out that, in spite of its strengths, the use of the nonequivalent control group design, as above, cannot rule out three threats to internal validity: selection by maturation, differential statistical regression, and local history.

In order to strengthen causal inference, three additional designs were also applied to overcome these weaknesses. A nonequivalent control, dependent variable design was applied in a chain of gasoline stations. In this design, other dependent variables in addition to lottery sales (such as sales of gasoline, taxable groceries, cigarettes, and nontaxable groceries) were included in the investigation. The contribution of adding this design was that it allowed the evaluation to deal with the threat of local history.

A short multiple group time-series design was used to deal with the threats of selection by maturation and differential statistical regression. In this design, multiple observations of the lottery sales before and after the intervention for both the treatment and the control stores were collected. Furthermore, a removed treatment and the repeated treatment design were also applied to further deal with the potential threats to internal validity of selection and maturation, differential statistical regression, and local history.

The analysis of data gathered from these multiple designs indicated a positive impact of the lottery promotion program. Because these multiple designs do not share a common bias and all consistently indicated the positive impact of the promotion program in enhancing lottery sales, the evidence for concluding a positive program impact in this study is very persuasive.

Another good illustration of the use of synthetic designs is a study by Lipsey et al. (1981) in assessing the impact of juvenile diversion programs on reducing juvenile delinquency. In their study, designs such as service-level comparisons, tie-breaking randomization, regression-discontinuity, and matched group design were utilized to gather multiple lines of evidence. The evidence from the findings of these designs allowed Lipsey et al. (1981) to draw conclusions that the juvenile diversion program had a small positive effect in reducing juvenile delinquency for less serious offenders.

The Use of Causation Probing

Causation probing is integration of the theoretical patterns of a program, that is, intervening and contextual patterns, into evaluation processes to enhance the strength of causal inference. Alternative strategies of using either rigorous design or causation probing to strengthen causal inference should not be regarded as incompatible. Chen and Rossi (1987, forthcoming) argue both strategies can be integrated into an evaluation to strengthen the basis for making causal inferences. The use of causation probing combined with a rigorous or synthetic design is the strategy focused upon by the theory-driven perspective.

Using causation probing as a basis for the strengthening of causal inference goes beyond the notion of covariation between cause and effect. This has been one of the major foci in past research. Einhorn and Hogarth (1986) argue that the way people judge causation is, in fact, broader than the traditional notion of covariation. Einhorn and Hogarth insist that the judgment of causation is commonly affected by a causal background or causal field (i.e., contextual factors) and cues-to-causation (e.g., the strength of a causal chain, temporal order, and distinctiveness). Similarly, Cordray (1986) argues that an input-output conception of causal inference, especially in quasi-experiments, is too limited. Instead, he argues for a more comprehensive view of evidence through specifying causal mechanisms and rival hypotheses as evidence for substantiating the treatment as a plausible cause.

From the tradition of pattern matching, Trochim (1985, forthcoming) also argues that the evidence base for causal inference in program evaluation can be expanded by an assessment of the correspondence between the theoretical and observed patterns in terms of program characteristics, implementation, participants, measurements, and causal processes.

Generally speaking, one of the fundamental postulates in causation probing is that there are many clues or factors internal or external to a program that can be used to confirm or disconfirm the causal relationship between the treatment and outcome in addition to the traditional notion of covariation between the treatment and the outcome. Information about these clues or factors is revealed in terms of the patterns of the implemented treatment, extraneous factors, intervening mechanisms, implementation environment, and so on. Strategies for using causation probing to test causal hypotheses or to strengthen causal inference in the impact evaluation will be the focus of the rest of this chapter.

CONSISTENCY OF TREATMENT AND/OR IMPLEMENTATION ENVIRONMENT PATTERNS

In order for a treatment to have the expected impact, a prerequisite is that the treatment be appropriately implemented. Accordingly, an assessment of the normative treatment and/or normative implementation environment, as discussed in Chapters 6 and 7, can contribute to the evidence base for a stronger causal inference regarding program impact.

Consistency of Normative and Observed Treatments

As discussed in Chapter 6, normative theory specifies that the delivered treatment should maintain the strength and/or components required by the normative treatment in order for the treatment to have an impact. Theoretically, the consistency between the normative treatment and observed treatment can be used as part of the evidence base in the impact evaluation for inferring the impact of the program.

If the treatment is found to have an effect in an impact or summative evaluation, the consistent pattern of the treatment provides additional evidence to support the plausibility of the treatment effect. Similarly, if in an impact or summative evaluation the treatment is found to have no impact, and if it is also found that the implemented treatment is substantially inconsistent with the normative treatment, the inconsistent treatment pattern serves as additional evidence as to why the treatment had no impact.

If the treatment is found to have an impact, but the normative and observed treatment patterns display serious inconsistencies, the evidence base for suggesting a treatment effect is mixed. Additional information is required to explain or reconcile the incongruency. Similarly, if the treatment is found to have no impact, but the normative and observed treatment patterns are found to be highly consistent, the evidence base is also mixed. Before it can be claimed that the treatment has no impact, other information may be needed to substantiate the arguments.

Consistency Between the Normative and Observed Implementation Environments

Similarly, consistency between the normative and observed implementation environments may also provide additional evidence to strengthen claims of causal inference regarding the impact of the treatment. If the normative theory of the implementation environment specifies that certain characteristics of the participant dimension (e.g., high motivation) and the implementor dimension (e.g., professional therapists) are required in the implementation processes in order for the treatment to have an impact, then the consistency between the actual implementation environment and the normative implementation environment may provide additional evidence for strengthening the causal inference.

If the treatment effect is found to have impacts in an impact or summative evaluation, a consistent pattern between the normative and actual implementation environments provides additional evidence for the argument that there is a treatment effect. Similarly, if the treatment effect is not found, an inconsistent pattern between the normative and actual implementation environments provides additional evidence for supporting the assertion that there is no treatment effect.

However, when the treatment effect is found, but an inconsistent pattern in the implementation environment is also found, or vice versa, the incongruency suggests a weak causal inference unless additional information can reconcile the difference. For example, an inappropriate implementation environment can lead to the finding of a big treatment effect, or an excellent treatment implementation can lead to no effect or negative effect, but we cannot show a strong causal inference without some additional information to back it up.

CONSISTENCY OF CORRESPONDING PATTERNS
BETWEEN TREATMENT AND OUTCOME

Social science theory and knowledge may be useful to suggest what the theoretically corresponding patterns between the treatment and outcome should be in terms of strength and relationships. When these patterns between the treatment and outcome are actually observed, causal inference of the treatment effect is strong; otherwise, it is weak.

Strength of Congruence Between Treatment and Outcome

It is usually more convincing in causal inference to observe that the strength of treatment matches the strength of the outcome. For example, Cordray (1986) argues that a causal relationship is more convincing when we observe a comparable strength between cause and effect, such as a strong cause producing a strong effect or a weak cause producing a weak effect. Cordray argues that seemingly anomalous relationships, such as a weak cause producing large effects, require that we must specify the additional processes that generate these anomalies.

Multiple Patterns Between Treatment and Outcomes

Theory can be used to derive the multiple relationships between treatment and outcomes. If the observed patterns of relationships match the theoretical patterns, the evidence of treatment effects is confirmed; otherwise, it is not. This strategy has been demonstrated in Cook and Campbell's (1979) formulation of the nonequivalent dependent variable design.

According to Cook and Campbell (1979), the basic structure of this design is similar to the one group, pretest and posttest design. However, in addition to the designated dependent variables in the design, additional matching dependent variables derived from theory and/or knowledge are included for investigation. Cook and Campbell argue that this synthetic design is more powerful than the original design in ensuring internal validity.

The matching dependent variable must have the following characteristics: both the matching and the designated dependent variables must be conceptually similar and be affected by the plausible alternative hypothesis. In addition, the treatment variable theoretically only affects the designated dependent variable but not the matching variable. A simple example provided by Trochim (1985) is that of an educational program designed to improve scores in geometry (the designated dependent variable) but that will presumably have no effect on ability to work fractions (the matching dependent variable). If the program affects the scores on geometry but not on fractions, we may conclude that the program has a positive impact on geometry scores, given that mathematical ability in both geometry and fractions would be equally affected by rival hypotheses such as maturation.   •

Cook and Campbell (1979) use Broadbent and Little's (1960) study, of the effect of noise reduction on the decrease in frequency of momentary lapses in efficacy, to illustrate their point. Broadbent and Little surveyed the literature on industrial production and found matching outcome variables, such as rate of work and absenteeism. In this case, the causal inference was strengthened by the inclusion of matching outcome variables. Because the extraneous influences of temperature, payment, skill level, and so on may affect momentary lapses and the rate of work or absenteeism, the effect of noise reduction was expected to affect only momentary lapses but not absenteeism and the rate of work. This consolidated the evidence of the treatment effect.

Cook and Campbell suggest that this design may be further strengthened by increasing the number of matching outcome variables or by integrating it with other major taxonomic designs.

SPECIFYING EXTRANEOUS PATTERNS

Program treatment often correlates with extraneous factors in affecting program outcomes. The specification and investigation of the theoretical patterns of these extraneous variables can strengthen causal inference. If the theoretical patterns of these extraneous variables are found in empirical observation, then a strong basis for causal inference is established. The use of this theoretical strategy for enhancing causal inference has, so far, been more readily recognized than other strategies.

This strategy has been well illustrated by Kutchinsky (1973) in a study of the effect on sex crimes of the Danish liberalization of pornography laws in 1965 and 1968. The design of this study was basically an interrupted time-series design using time-series data on sex crimes from 1958 to 1978. Police reports indicated a steady decline in sex offenses after the intervention. However, based upon the time-series graphs alone, it is not very convincing to attribute this decline to the change in the pornography laws. Based upon knowledge of the program, Kutchinsky proposed the following list of plausible rival hypotheses for factors that may also be responsible for the decline in sex crimes:

(1) changes in official registration procedures for sex crimes;
(2) changes in the victims' definition of these acts as being criminal or not and/or the tendency to report to the police when they were victimized; and
(3) a change in police reactions to people reporting sex crimes.

In order to assess the plausibility of these rival explanations, Kutchinsky adopted other methods, such as case studies and survey methods, to gather additional information. Data were gathered through examination of the related official registration procedures in past years, from a survey of changes in public attitudes toward sex crimes and experiences of sex crimes, and from interviews of policemen about their past procedures for handling reports of sex crimes. None of these data supported the rival hypotheses above. The convergence of the evidence from these data did, however, allow Kutchinsky to argue that, in at least one type of offense, child molestation, the decline in reported incidents was a result of the more liberal pornography laws.

The same strategy was also used in Ross et al.'s (1970) evaluation of the effect of the British breathalyzer crackdown in 1967 on traffic accidents. The use of a multiple group, interrupted time-series design revealed positive effects from the crackdown. In addition, the authors applied knowledge of the program to devise plausible rival hypotheses that could confound the causal inference, such as publicity over the crackdown, improvement in traffic controls, improvement in traffic law enforcement, and so on. The extra data did not support the rival hypotheses. Again, evaluation of all the evidence enhanced the coherence of the causal inference that the crackdown had a positive impact.

Selection bias modeling (e.g., Achen, 1986; Maddala, 1983; Heckman, 1979; Berk & Ray, 1982), which has been used in dealing with selection bias, also belongs to this strategy. Since quasi-experiments, such as the nonequivalent control group design or pre-experimental designs, usually suffer from the problem of selection bias, selection bias modeling deliberately deals with this problem by including the selection process in the model for investigation.

These methods for correcting selection bias are characterized as two-equation simultaneous systems. The first equation is called the substantive equation; it is designed to estimate the treatment effect. The second equation is the selection equation, and it is designed to model the selection process by means of a proxy variable. The inclusion of the proxy variable captures the selection process and controls for the selection bias. Consequently, the estimation of treatment effect in the substantive equation is unbiased.

However, the application of selection modeling has not been without controversy. For example, Murnane (1985) points out that the use of selection modeling proposed by Heckman (1979) to control selection bias is subject to specification error. Because the residual structure is not known a priori, different assumptions about the model can lead to different results. There is a debate between Heckman et al. (1987) and critics such as Lalonde and Maynard (1987) regarding the appropriateness of using selection modeling for correcting selection bias. Such debates underline the necessity for further refinements in selection modeling, but this should not detract from the usefulness and importance of these techniques.

Even when strong designs such as randomized experiments are used in an evaluation, there are additional benefits from including extraneous factors in a model for statistical analysis. Without controlling for the extraneous variables in the model, these extraneous variables will be incorporated as a portion of the residuals. Consequently, the error variance can be large and can reduce statistical power in detecting the treatment effect. In general, the specification of extraneous or relevant variables within the equation will enhance precision in the statistical test.

SPECIFYING INTERVENING PROCESSES

An evaluator can rely upon existing theory and knowledge to specify the intervening processes that mediate between the treatment and outcomes. The evaluator then gathers qualitative or quantitative information to examine the relationships among treatment, intervening, and outcome variables. If the data support the intervening processes predicted by theory and/or knowledge about the program, inferences regarding a causal relationship between the treatment and outcome are strengthened. Otherwise, if the treatment fails to produce change in the intervening variables, the relationship found between the treatment and the outcome is doubtful.

An example illustrating this strategy is found in a discussion by Miles and Huberman (1984, pp. 226-29) concerning the adoption of innovations. They argue that, in finding out whether a well-funded innovation produces more organizational changes in structures and procedures than a less well-funded innovation, qualitative methods may be inadequate to establish convincing causal relationships between variables. However, the inference of a causal relationship between variables will be strengthened if intervening processes are also observed. For example, funding increases would supposedly lead to heavier implementation requirements, greater support from administrators, and greater success in implementation. When these intervening processes are found, evidence for the relationship between the size of funding and organizational change is also consolidated.

Even where a rigorous design is used in assessing the treatment effect, the specification of intervening mechanisms can strengthen the causal inference. To better illustrate this point, it may be useful to consider a controversial study by McCord (1978). In her study, McCord attempted to evaluate the impacts of the Cambridge Sommerville Youth Study in a 30-year follow-up. When the program began in 1939, 506 boys between the ages of 5 and 13 were randomly assigned to treatment and control groups. Children in the treatment group received services such as tutoring, counseling, medical and psychatric care, and summer camp programs. There was an extraordinary effort by McCord and her research team to trace most of these participants through records and contacts.

Bivariate analysis was used to detect differences between the treatment and control groups. A wide variety of 57 outcome measures was used, including criminal behavior, disease and death rates, occupation, status, and job satisfaction. Only 7 of the 57 variables exhibited differences between the groups. It is surprising that the results showed that the treatment group was more inclined to commit crime and to suffer from alcoholism, mental illness, early death, heart problems, low occupational prestige, and lower job satisfaction. McCord concluded that, after 30 years, the good intentions of the program not only had failed to produce the anticipated benefits but also had tended to create many harmful side effects.

A major basis for McCord's claim that the program had negative effects lies in the use of randomized experiments. Because the treatment and control groups were equivalent in every respect except for the treatment, any differences discovered between the treatment and control groups must have come from the treatment. However, this assumption is questionable. The use of randomized experiments 30 years ago may have made the treatment and control groups equivalent in the initial period, but, after that, changes in many uncontrollable extraneous factors (peer influence, family, background, education, marriage, and so on) can easily upset the comparability of the treatment and control groups. The use of randomized experiments in this case did not provide strong proof for the claim of harmful program effects. In this case, the evidence generated from investigating intervening processes would be vital in order to substantiate McCord's argument.

McCord herself mentioned that perhaps the program created unrealistic expectations and aspirations among the participants in the treatment group. This intervening variable is worthy of investigation, because it is possible that unrealistic expectations or aspirations may have led the participants to experience frustrations in confronting reality, which may, in turn, have generated the negative impacts. If McCord could verify this causal mechanism in her evaluation, her causal inference regarding negative program impacts would be much more persuasive. There is no intention here to deny McCord's contribution. Her efforts to locate the participants after 30 years were remarkable. The conclusion that the program had negative impacts, however, is based in large part on the use of a 30-year-old randomized experimental design, and many extraneous factors could easily have exerted important effects upon the results after so many years.

In addition, the inclusion of intervening mechanisms in an investigation not only strengthens causal inferences but also enhances construct validity. Knowing that the treatment affects the outcome through a theoretically relevant intervening mechanism rather than through some mysterious process will enhance the stakeholder's confidence in the treatment and also enhance the utilization of evaluation results. For example, stakeholders may be more confident in, and likely to adopt, an innovative education program where the effects are achieved through appropriate and clearly specified channels such as student motivation and enhanced self-esteem. A program that is comparably effective, but that cannot clearly explain how program results are generated, is likely to be viewed skeptically by stakeholders. Issues and strategies for evaluating intervening mechanisms will be discussed in detail in Chapter 10.

IDENTIFYING CONTEXTUAL PATTERNS

For the advocates of the experimental paradigm (e.g., Campbell and Stanley, 1963; Cook and Campbell, 1979), preexperimental designs, such as the one group pretest and posttest design, one group posttest-only design, survey research, case study methods, and qualitative methods in general, are unsuitable for program evaluation. Their argument is that these designs are liable to so many threats to internal validity that they do not permit adequate causal inference.

The theory-driven perspective does not share this hard-line position on preexperimental designs in program evaluation. Undoubtedly there are some merits in the argument that preexperimental designs cannot provide valid evidence for causal inferences. However, the problem with such arguments is that they are stated in the manner of a universal truth, which ignores the many contextual situations to which pre-experimental designs are sensitive. This total rejection of preexperimental designs not only gives these designs an unwarranted pejorative label, but also hinders our understanding of the potential contributions that preexperimental designs can make in dealing with issues in the impact evaluation.

There may be some contextual conditions under which the use of preexperimental designs can produce strong causal inference. Instead of universally condemning the weaknesses of the preexperimental designs, perhaps we should investigate carefully the contextual conditions that allow, or do not allow, preexperimental designs to produce valid information on treatment effect. If the contextual conditions can be reasonably specified, an evaluator can make a good argument for obtaining valid information on the treatment effects. Preexperimental designs should be used when they are appropriate and when the researcher is not intimidated by not using randomized experiments. This book has no intention of advocating the use of soft methods in impact evaluation. However, if the contextual patterns permit such use, and the more rigorous designs are not applicable, there is no reason for not considering the preexperimental designs when formulating an evaluation strategy. In order to broaden the scope of causal inference, it is important for us in the future to investigate the contextual conditions that can or cannot allow the generation of strong causal inference. The following section attempts to describe three sets of contextual conditions under which a causal inference can be made when using preexperimental designs.

When a Treatment Directly Acts on the Characteristics of a Problem

Some intervention programs directly change the characteristics of a problem. That is, when the intervention is introduced, the problem is automatically alleviated or solved at least for a period of time. An example would be a food distribution program that provides food for hungry people. As long as food reaches the hungry, the problem of hunger is solved for a period of time. Similarly, a homeless shelter program may provide room and board for the homeless. The problem of a group of homeless people is temporarily solved when they enter the shelter.

These types of direct intervention programs change the problem or an outcome variable directly almost by definition. Usually the effectiveness of this type of program can be evaluated by the one group posttest-only designs. For example, the effectiveness of food distribution programs can be assessed by a counting of how many hungry people or families receive food. Similarly, the effectiveness of a homeless shelter program can be counted by the number of homeless people or families served. The use of the pretest and posttest are even better when stakeholders attempt to compare the relative effectiveness of the present program with the performance of a past one. Similarly, survey research can be used to compare the relative effectiveness of different agencies. In these types of programs, it would be odd for anyone to argue for the use of a randomized experiment or a strong quasi-experiment to assess whether food reduces hunger or the shelter program helps the homeless.

Because this type of program treatment effect can be dealt with by using preexperimental designs, according to the balancing strategy, other evaluation domains become of more concern than the impact domain in the evaluation. This issue can be highlighted in the following example. Suffering a few riots in a prison, the prison warden introduces a new policy to prevent future riots. The new policy is to introduce tighter security including locking up the prisoners in their cells most of the day. This kind of direct intervention program can easily be evaluated by using preexperimental designs such as the one group pretest and posttest design. For example, if the data indicate that there has not been a riot for a year after the intervention, this clearly indicates program effectiveness. The lock-up policy by definition reduces the possibility of riots. Few of us will deny the effectiveness of the new policy and insist on a randomized experiment in order to establish valid causality.

Because the impact evaluation will not be difficult to assess in this type of program, other evaluation domains, in fact, are more salient than the impact domain. In this case, issues in the outcome domain, such as whether to focus on the short-term effect or long-term effect of the program in the evaluation, should be a major concern. Stakeholders may be greatly concerned with whether the new policy of tight control, which prevented a riot in the short term, will later create a "time bomb" effect, which produces a more serious riot resulting in injuries and death.

Or the issue can also be perceived on a humanitarian level. That is, is it justifiable for society to punish the prisoners in such a cruel way in order to prevent riots? A further concern may be whether it is justifiable to adopt the new policy and abandon the goal of rehabilitation in a prison. The consequence of this new policy may be to create a marked imbalance between rehabilitation and punishment, which, in the long term, may encourage continued criminal behavior after release. Evaluation focused on these areas may be more useful to stakeholders.

CLOSURE OF CONTEXTUAL SETTINGS

Sometimes an intervention program attempts to change a social process that operates in a closed context where the intervention program is the only possible source of change. Within such a contextual situation, the treatment effect can be validly inferred through the use of pre-experimental designs.

In order to apply this principle, an evaluator requires good knowledge of the program and its contextual environment in order to rule out alternative causal influences. Furthermore, the use of preexperimental designs will be more persuasive when the treatment effect is large and occurs immediately after the intervention.

An example of this might be an organization that adopts a new computer system. A simple pre- and posttest study finds that there is a dramatic increase in efficiency of information flow right after the new system is installed. If the evaluator can establish that the information process in that organization is closed, then the preexperimental design provides good evidence that the new computer system produced the observed impact. Knowing the context of the organizational processes allows the evaluator to argue that there were no other changes in the organization that could possibly have caused the observed increase in efficiency.

Similarly, in the middle of 1960, the Singapore government launched the Keep Singapore Clean Campaign. One of the major components of this campaign was a fine of about $250 for littering. The program was vigorously enforced by the police. Singaporeans and tourists all regarded the campaign as an effective measure, as the city was much cleaner after the program took effect. In fact, Singapore is now regarded as one of the cleanest cities in south Asia. Again, in this case, the knowledge and familiarity of the situation in Singapore allowed effective judgment to be made regarding the closure of the setting such that no other alternative reasons could be attributed to the city's cleanness aside from the governmental intervention. The effectiveness of the campaign could be validly inferred by the use of a preexperimental design such as the one group pretest and posttest design.

The requirements that the treatment effect must be immediate and large can be further relaxed when the intervention is unique to its contextual setting. The uniqueness of the intervention guarantees that the intervention is the only possible source of the impact. For example, as in other Asian countries, college entrance examinations in Taiwan are highly competitive. Only those who have scores around the top 30th percentile in the examination are admitted to college. Influenced by Confucius's philosophy of emphasizing the value of education, an educational program was started to tutor those juvenile offenders who wanted to take the college entrance examination in the juvenile prisons. Special classes were offered for learning and study. Faculty members for these educational programs were highly educated adult inmates and outside volunteers. In August 1987, the juvenile prison officials announced the success of the program. There are now a few juvenile delinquents in the institute who have participated in the program and passed the tough college entrance exams.

In this case, the claim of program success is convincing even with a one group posttest design. Within the regular juvenile prisons, it is very difficult for delinquents to continue a high-quality education that sufficiently prepares them for passing the college entrance exam. The special education program is unique to its contextual setting and is the only plausible reason for success. Under these conditions, even a one group posttest design is sufficient to prove the program's effectiveness.

The prevalence of situations that allow evaluators to use the closure of a contextual setting for causal inference may be greater than we are aware. This principle can be applied to isolated geographic locations to assess the adoption of new technology such as the telephone, television, and so on or greater development projects such as new dams and highways.

Even when the phenomenon under investigation is not within a closed context, we still can make strong causal inferences by using preexperimental designs when the following two conditions are met:

(A) The regularity or pattern of the movement of the outcome variable under investigation is well understood.

(B) Treatment effect is expected to be immediate and large.

If condition A is met, it implies that when we have a good understanding of the regularity or pattern of movement of the outcome variable under study, we could use this information to reasonably infer what would happen without the intervention of the treatment. If condition B is met, it means that because the chance for treatment effect is immediate and large, it reduces the possibility that alternative sources could be confounded with the treatment in assessing the treatment effect. Furthermore, when the effect is expected to be immediate and large, even if the alternative sources do have effects on the outcome variable, they must be so drastic that evaluators can detect them easily.

A few research examples can illustrate in more detail how, when these conditions are met, the use of nonexperimental methods can produce strong causal inferences. The research design used in the Sanai green manuring (new fertilizer) project, which will be discussed in Chapter 13, is a preexperimental design—the one group pretest and posttest design. When wheat production in the villages was compared before and after the fertilizer program, it was found that wheat production after the use of the new fertilizer had increased by more than 60% over the previous year (before the intervention). The project was deemed successful. Although the evaluation used a preexperimental design, few of us would regard this causal inference as invalid. Why? The social scientists and farmers involved in this project have worked in the field for a considerable time. They are familiar with the normal fluctuations in wheat production, and the wheat production would not increase such a great deal without the new fertilizer. Because no other obvious alternative events that could have drastically decreased the production in the baseline year were observed by those involved in the project, large and immediate increases in the production of wheat must be attributed to the fertilizer.

Similarly, the study by Foxx and Azrin (1973) on the impact of a toilet-training program provides another example of how preexperimental methods are sound when the above two conditions are met. The research design they used in this study was also a one group pretest and posttest design. However, because the regular patterns of the children with difficulty in toilet training were well known and the evaluators expected the training effect to be immediate and large, the use of a one group pretest and posttest design did not weaken the causal inference of this study. Foxx and Azrin (1973) had obtained the children's pattern of accidents from their mothers, and this indicated about six accidents per day per child. In the day after the training, it was found that the accidents had decreased to less than one accident per day per child.

The evidence of treatment effect is convincing in spite of the use of a preexperimental design. Because the regularity of the accidents was well known, and the effect of training was large and immediate following the training, it is difficult for critics to argue that the effect was due to rival hypotheses such as the threats to internal validity identified by Campbell and Stanley (1963) and others. The use of these contextual inferences in preexperimental designs is not unusual in social science literature. For example, many famous experiments carried out by Frederic W. Taylor, the founder of scientific management, in fact used preexperimental designs to study the effect of physiological factors (e.g., fatigue and physical coordination) on productivity (Taylor, 1947). Because Taylor's study met the above two conditions, the use of preexperimental methods does not make his causal inferences less valid than if he had used randomized experiments.

For example, in his famous pig-iron experiment, Taylor knew through previous experience that an average worker could load about 12.5 tons of pig iron per day. The workers carried 82 pounds of pig iron up an incline and dropped it into a railroad car. Taylor believed that productivity could be raised by giving both incentive pay and proper instruction to the workers on motion, pace, and rest. To demonstrate that the intervention would be effective, Taylor asked a worker named Schmidt to carry out the experiment.

Schmidt was told he would have his pay raised from $1.15 to $1.85 per day if he could exactly follow the instructions on when to pick up the bars, carry them, put them down, and return. Schmidt agreed. After following instructions concerning motion, pull, and rest, Schmidt raised his production from 12.5 tons per day to 47.5 tons per day. The treatment effect was well established. Other workers were asked to take part in the new working method and incentive pay scale. Their participation also considerably raised output. It should be noted that in this experiment the research design was a weak, one group (actually individual) posttest-only design and that the evaluation of the results of treatment effect is convincing. The reasons lay mainly in the two pattern conditions mentioned previously:

(A) There was good prior knowledge of the pattern or regularity of loading pig iron bars (about 12.5 tons per man per day).
(B) The treatment effect was immediately observed and was large (3.8 times the original production).

These two conditions together can offset the major threats to internal validity. Although condition B of this strategy requires the treatment effect to be immediate and large, this requirement does not limit the application of this strategy to areas such as development projects, therapy, health, antilittering, construction, and so on. Many programs in this area may require treatment effects to be immediate and large in order to be useful. In such programs, stakeholders may decide that small and gradual treatment effects do not meet their needs. For example, if the toilet-training program could only reduce accidents from six per day to five per day, parents would not be interested in the program and the program designer would not be satisfied. Similarly, if an agricultural program can increase wheat production by only 2%, farmers will not bother to switch to the new fertilizer.

SPECIFYING FUNCTIONAL FORM

A specification of the correct functional form of a relationship between the treatment and the outcome is essential for assessing the impact of a program. For example, if the true relationship between the treatment and the outcome is nonlinear and a linear model is used to assess the impact of the treatment on the outcome, the treatment effect may not be detected. As a consequence, the evaluation may provide the misleading information that the program has no impact. Although the correct functional form is difficult to know, social science theory and knowledge may be useful in suggesting a plausible functional form to serve as the basis for assessing the impact.

For example, beginning from the period of September 1977, three steel mills in sequence were permanently closed in Youngstown, Ohio. Following that, about 10,000 steel workers were laid off. It was hypothesized that this misfortune would have a substantial impact on marital instability in the community. However, without guidance from a theory, this type of impact is difficult to assess, at least as shown in Chen and Lin's (1989) study. During their data analysis, Chen and Lin found that mindless data analysis, such as a mechanical application of a step function (i.e., the preintervention period is coded as 0; the postintervention period, 1) for intervention analysis, the impact of plant closings would not be found.

However, social science theory and knowledge provided a hint to specify a better intervention model. Durkheim's anomie theory (1965), in fact, implies that plant closings may temporarily increase marital instability, but after a readjustment period the incidence will be decreased and stabilized. This hint led Chen and Lin (1989) to specify an alternative intervention function. When the intervention model devised from theory was assessed, the impact of plant closings on marital instability was found.

FURTHER CONSIDERATIONS REGARDING
DESIGNS FOR IMPACT EVALUATION

The experimental paradigm has made the most important contribution in dealing with issues of impact evaluation. However, due to recent efforts to broaden the basis of evidence in making causal inference, some of the experimental paradigm's conceptualizations and applications of designs in impact evaluations may have to be modified or changed. This chapter has shown that the problem does not lie in the experimental and quasi-experimental designs proposed by the experimental paradigm but in the traditionally rigid conceptualization and dogmatic application of these designs. Perhaps it is more useful to view the experimental paradigm's design as an important source that an evaluator can actively and innovatively use to create various strategies for strengthening causal inference. As demonstrated in this chapter, strategies such as the use of causation probing and synthetic designs can enhance the scope and quality of impact evaluation.

Furthermore, the selection of a design for an impact evaluation requires consideration of all of the following factors simultaneously: rigorousness, cost, ethics, and the likelihood of maintaining the integrity of the design in the field. Except for the last factor, the first three factors have already been intensively discussed in the literature (e.g., Reicken and Boruch,

1974). The following discussion will focus on issues related to the last factor.

As discussed in Chapters 6 and 7, due to complexity in execution, generally speaking, the more rigorous a design is, the more difficult it is to maintain the integrity of the design in the field. Serious compromises may have to be made when attempting to carry out a rigorous design in the field. For example, studies such as Crano and Meese (1985) and Cook and Poole (1982) reported that the evaluator had begun with a randomized experimental design. However, after execution in the field, treatment conditions were difficult to maintain, and the executed design came to resemble a quasi-experimental or even a preexperimental design. Furthermore, the situation may be even worse when rigorous designs are rigidly and uncritically applied; it might create implementation problems such as program staff's and participants' rejection, which can eventually jeopardize the feasibility of completing the evaluation (see Shapiro, 1984; Fetterman, 1981). Accordingly, a poorly executed rigorous design may be worse than a well-executed, less rigorous design.

The capability to maintain the integrity of design must be of primary consideration in the choice of a design. Randomized experiments are particularly useful for impact evaluation when it is anticipated that there will be minimal problems in execution, cost, and ethics. Otherwise, other designs are preferred.

The discussion in this chapter has assumed so far that stakeholders mainly want to know whether or not their program has the intended impact. However, in many situations, stakeholders require information beyond the program's intended impact. This issue will be presented in Chapter 9.

9. Impact Evaluation II: Assessing Intended and Unintended Outcomes

Chapter 8 focused on issues related to broadening the evidence base related to the impact evaluation. This chapter will focus on issues related to enhancing the sensitivity of an impact evaluation by assessing major intended and unintended outcomes.

In terms of specifying pertinent outcomes for investigation, the traditional summative evaluation has focused mainly on program goals, especially official goals (e.g., Deutscher, 1977). The theory-driven impact evaluation attempts to broaden this traditional concern. According to Chen and Rossi (1980), outcome specification in an impact evaluation mainly consists of two dimensions: desirability and plausibility. The desirability dimension reflects the anticipated worthiness or benefits generated by the program. The plausibility dimension concerns the broader, more realistic questions of the potential impacts of the program. Most goal statements reflect questions pertaining to the desirability dimension, for example: "What good could this program do?" But, as we will see later, they are weak on plausibility dimension questions, for example: "What outcomes will actually be generated by the program?"

Traditionally, an outcome or summative evaluation using a goal-based model is weighted heavily toward the desirability dimension. As will be discussed in the next section, limiting our attention to desirable goals can be misleading. In order to balance the concerns between desirability and plausibility, the theory-driven perspective argues that the normative outcome theory should be formulated using both the stakeholder and the social science approaches.

Because of their great involvement in planning, formulating, and implementing a program, the stakeholders' perceptions of the normative outcomes of a program tend to be fixed upon the desirability dimension. An evaluator mainly using a stakeholder approach to formulate normative outcome theory may easily encompass the desirability dimension while at the same time failing to adequately assess other outcomes in the plausibility dimension. In contrast, the social science approach emphasizes the use of objective social science theory and knowledge to formulate a normative outcome theory. An evaluator emphasizing the use of the social science approach to construct a normative outcome theory may deal with the plausibility dimension but miss some key concerns of the·stakeholders in the desirability dimension. Only through use of the integrative approach, which integrates both the stakeholder approach and the social science approach to formulate a normative outcome theory in the impact evaluation, can the concerns of both desirability and plausibility be balanced.

Generally speaking, in carrying out an impact evaluation, an evaluator should be concerned not only with assessing whether goals are achieved but also with discovering what actually happened as a result of the program. Critics such as Mushkin (1973) urge that evaluators, in order to enhance policy relevance, broaden the scope of evaluations by investigating both intended and unintended consequences. The following discussion begins with a review of a number of traditional outcome models; then a comprehensive approach is proposed for the impact evaluation.

THE GOAL MODEL

Traditionally, evaluation has approached the question of program effectiveness in terms of the goal model. This model has mainly relied on program goals in the assessment of a program's outcome, and, subsequently, program effectiveness has been defined as the extent to which the program has attained these goals. Many theorists have understood program evaluation principally in these terms. For example, Suchman (1967, 1970) has viewed program evaluation as being mainly an assessment of whether a program has achieved its predetermined goals. Because goals are regarded as the major criteria in assessing program effectiveness, many evaluation research texts often have an entire chapter dealing with goal specification (e.g., Weiss, 1972; Reicken and Boruch, 1974).

Evaluators using the goal model emphasize the idea that intervention programs are simply goal-seeking machines. They assume that the people who design, manage, and administer a program have a general consensus or agreement on a set of program goals, and also that these agreed-upon program goals can be achieved by using available resources in a rational and efficient way.

The goal model has special appeal to evaluators, decision makers, and funding agencies. Intervention programs are created to achieve goals and it is only natural to assess program effectiveness in terms of the attainment of these goals. Furthermore, program goals are usually formally documented in publications such as annual reports, program pamphlets, or brochures, which makes them easily accessible. Because the program goals are at least conceptually agreed upon by everyone involved, evaluators can avoid accusations that they are imposing their personal views on the evaluation or charges that the results of the evaluation are irrelevant to the goals of the program. Finally, the goal model provides a clear guideline for the contract or understanding between the policymakers, funding agency, and evaluators concerning the nature of the evaluation. As long as the goals are identified and agreed upon, evaluators need only supply information on how well the program attains them.

However, despite its popularity, the goal model is not without its shortcomings. One of the major problems encountered in the goal model is that program goals are often nebulous and general (Weiss, 1972). The stated aim of many social programs is to change certain types of individuals, a community, or society for the better, but the exact processes by which they will institute such change and the exact ways that they will implement improvements are not specified. Phrases frequently used in social program goals—such as "to enhance human dignity," "to preserve democratic values," "to improve well-being of minority groups," "to strengthen family life"—signify ideas valued by everyone, but the goals rarely explain exactly what these phrases mean or how they will actually be achieved. In some cases, the realization of a goal is so impractical that it is doubtful whether it can be achieved by the existing resources and technology (Deutscher, 1977).

Another criticism is that a goal model limits the evaluator's views. Scriven (1972) argued that goal attainment models that look only in the direction of the goals may be misleading. This orientation impedes the investigation of the actual program effect by blinding the evaluators to other important impacts of the program that are not specified as program goals. Various system theorists have produced more detailed versions of this criticism (e.g., Etzioni, 1960; Georgopoulous, 1973; Yuchtman and Seashore, 1967). According to system models, a system such as a social program is multifunctional rather than simply a goal-seeking machine. Therefore, in addition to achieving goals, a system must also fulfill other functions such as maintenance, socialization, and adaptation. The important functions of a system are, therefore, interdependent, and if evaluators focus exclusively on goals and ignore other important system activities, they risk being misled in their views of the program.

However, not all goals can be easily identified or measured and the quest for measurable goals further narrows the perspective of the goal model. A goal model requires clear-cut, measurable goals in order to evaluate effectiveness, and the demand for such goals is frequently emphasized in evaluation literature. Weiss (1972, p. 26) advised that, for evaluation purposes, the goal must be clear, specific, and measurable. Similarly, as Reicken (1972, p. 92) indicated:

> It is essential not only that the major objectives of an action program be clearly defined, but also that they be stated in operational terms— that is, in terms of concrete behavior, specific accomplishments, or states of affairs—in order that an evaluator can derive appropriate measuring instruments.

There is nothing wrong with evaluation emphasizing measurable goals. However, the methods of the goal model used in evaluation research to derive measurable goals from vague and ambiguous program goals may tend to further narrow evaluators' views or, even worse, mislead them about the program's real intentions. It is informative to examine how traditional evaluators decide which goals to evaluate. Usually they concentrate on those goals that have a clear context or can be measured easily and ignore those goals that are fuzzy or difficult to measure.

Wholey and associates (1970) went so far as to insist that a social program should not be evaluated if its goals are unmeasurable. In their analysis of the Community Mental Health Center program of the National

Institute of Mental Health, Wholey and his associates (1970) suggested that all 46 branch goals and 5 out of the 6 program goals could not be evaluated "because they were not stated in measurable terms." The sole surviving measurable program goal of the CMHC program, according to Wholey, is the establishment of "economically viable CMHCs, independent of federal support," which is certainly a much narrower focus than the program's original intention.

Urgent pressure to identify measurable goals often renders the evaluation insensitive to a program's real intentions. Even though the program may in many cases have a very broad aim, only a few narrowly focused measurable goals may be targeted for evaluation. For example, the broadly aimed program, Head Start, was evaluated in the Westinghouse-Ohio University Study (Cicirelli, 1969) only in terms of two narrow, measurable goals—reading and arithmetic scores—in spite of the fact that the program served additional purposes in the areas of nutrition, health, interpersonal skills, and so on.

This tendency to narrowly focus upon measurable goals is not a problem exclusive to the Head Start evaluation. Stake (1978) indicated that many evaluations tend to choose easily measured indicators, even when these indicators do not really encompass the most important effects of the intervention. In educational programs, one frequently selected measure is that of standardized test scores. Stake noted that, because these indicators are easy to use, they tend to be employed even when the program is only peripherally aimed at educational improvement.

Similarly, Deutscher (1977) argued that the search for specific and measurable goals for the goal model may lead evaluators into a "goal trap." He (1977, p. 224) described how the goal trap problem occurs:

> In pursuit of a clear-cut evaluation design and the selection of appropriate measuring instruments, the evaluator is relentless in his quest for specific goals . . . he hounds program people: "Is this a goal?" "or this?" "or this?" . . . Program people may resist at first, but eventually be intimidated by the evaluators' relentless pursuit of something he can measure. . . . The end result of this process is that, more often than not, the program is evaluated in terms of marginal goals which are unlikely to be achieved . . . and likely to be denied their legitimacy when the evaluator finally reports that the program does not seem to make any difference.

Because program goals are often formulated to obtain funding rather than to serve as practical guides for program activities, the goal trap, according to Deutscher, traps both the trapper-evaluator and the victims—the funding agencies and program administrators. If the program people have given a phony proposal to funding agencies in order to obtain funds, it is naive to study the program in terms of phony goals that were never intended to be realized.

ALTERNATIVE OUTCOME MODELS

A few alternatives to the goal model, such as the goal-free evaluation and the system models, have been proposed by some evaluators. Unfortunately, in spite of their strengths, there are weaknesses in these models also.

Scriven (1972) has proposed a goal-free model for evaluation. Scriven proposed that evaluation should proceed in such fashion that the evaluators are not exposed to, or contaminated by, knowledge of the program goals. Scriven (1972, p. 2) argued that "the less the external evaluator hears about the goals of the project, the less tunnel vision will develop; the more attention will be paid to looking for actual effects (rather than checking on alleged effects)."

The concept of goal-free evaluation is well known in evaluation circles, but, due to the many difficulties in using it, this approach has not been seriously applied in program evaluation. Therefore, only a few of its shortcomings are discussed here. First, as mentioned above, social programs are created to serve some purpose, and to ignore the program's intention is to ignore a specific dimension of it. It is possible that a goal-free evaluation may bypass the issues that policymakers or program managers want to know about and focus instead on something irrelevant or not useful to program stakeholders. Second, because this approach requires minimum communication between evaluator and administrators in order to avoid goal contamination, it creates much more administrative resistance. As Stufflebeam (1974, p. 4) explains:

> How can program people be protected against the potential arbitrary actions of an inept or unscrupulous goal-free evaluator, especially when he is employed by an external funding agent that may be a bureaucracy with neither a conscience nor a memory?

Chen and Rossi (1980) also question the quality of information provided by goal-free evaluation. They (1980, p. 108) argue that "undisciplined ferretting about for differences between treatment and control groups, for example, might maximize Type I errors, confusing chance-generated differences for program-related ones."

A more sophisticated alternative to the goal model for outcome specification is the system model (e.g., Etzioni, 1960). The system model views a social system such as a social program as a set of interdependent subsystems. If any subsystem performs poorly, the performance of the whole system will eventually be damaged. In order to survive, a system has to maintain its internal stability and cope with its external environment. The system model is not focused on short-term, specific goals. Instead, it is interested in how the system survives and grows, how it acquires scarce resources, deals with conflicts, adapts to environmental change, balances resource allocation to promote internal maintenance, and so on.

The system model may overcome some weaknesses (such as the narrow view) inherent in the goal model, but it too has shortcomings that hinder its use in program evaluation. In the policy-making process, timely feedback from the evaluation regarding program outcomes is crucial (Cronbach et al., 1980). The system model, which focuses on the long-term maintenance, adaptation, and survival of the system, may not meet the time constraints of policy-making. Furthermore, the system model also suffers problems because it is vague. Not only are the concepts of system survival or health unclear and futuristic, they are also difficult to translate into actual practice (Weiss, 1972). Finally, as discussed at the beginning of this chapter, social programs have multiple objectives. Unlike a country club, a social program has to serve its external clients as well as its internal members. Sooner or later, questions relating to the program's intention must be answered, and this remains a problem in the system models.

Evaluators clearly are faced with a dilemma when deciding how best to specify program outcomes. To unquestioningly accept the official goals of a program as valid outcome criteria, as the traditional goal model suggests, can be highly problematic. Conversely, to simply dispense with a program's official goals altogether, as the systems model and goal-free approach imply, is perhaps going too far. An alternative approach is to use the impact evaluation, which may be comprehensive enough to resolve these difficulties.

One of the major features of the impact evaluation is that it provides a conceptual framework for formally dealing with unintended outcomes without ignoring intended program goals. In order to gain a better

understanding of the nature of program goals and use them properly
in program evaluation, we must closely examine both program goals
and program practice.

PROGRAM GOALS AND REAL PROGRAM INTENTIONS

The pursuit of goals leads to the first practical problem for evaluators:
When the officially stated program goals do not reflect the actual program
operation, they may prove a misleading guide to the program's actual
results. It is well recognized in organization theory that there is often
a gap between the organization's announced, official goals and its actual
operative goals. Perrow (1961) made an important distinction between
official goals and operative goals. According to Perrow (1961, p. 855),
official goals are "the general purposes of the organization as put forth
in the charter, annual reports, public statements by key executives, and
other authoritative pronouncements." He defines operative goals as "the
ends sought through the actual operating policies of the organizations;
they tell us what the organization is actually trying to do, regardless
of what the official goals say the aim is" (Perrow, 1961, p. 855). Because
official goals may not reflect the realistic goals to which an organization's
members are committed and may reflect only a *desirable* state of affairs,
Perrow argued that organizational effectiveness can be better understood
by studying operative goals rather than official goals. Etzioni (1960)
also made similar arguments in favor of studying the real goals rather
than the formal goals of an organization.

Perrow's distinction between official goals and operative goals and
Etzioni's distinction between formal goals and real goals both hold true
in evidence not only from profit-oriented organizations but also from
public agencies and social programs. In his study of correctional
institutions, Zald (1963) found that the formally stated goal of such
organizations is rehabilitation, but, in fact, these organizations are mainly
dedicated to custodial care—the operative (real) goal. The emphasis
on rehabilitation in the official or formal goals was to make the
organization more appealing and acceptable. Similarly, Warriner (1965)
noted that a group of community service organizations pursues their
formal goal of providing community services to only a minor extent.
The real or operative goal is to raise funds through club benefits for
community service activities (e.g., a community fireworks program, the
sale of products made by the handicapped).

A typical result of the insensitivity of the goal model to the difference between official and operative goals in program evaluation is well illustrated in the evaluation of the Executive High School Internships program (Crowe, 1977). The major, formal objective of this program was to provide an opportunity for high school juniors and seniors to learn about leadership by serving as interns to executives. As stated in the Memorandum of Understanding of the Program, the official goals were as follows:

> That participating high school students will develop a more accurate understanding of organizations and those who manage and administer them.
> That participating high school students will demonstrate the ability to function effectively in an organizational environment with an executive.

In spite of these two basic official goals, during the research period, Crowe and his associates became aware that the program actually pursued a set of operative goals, which they called the "hidden curriculum." The operative goals were oriented toward personal growth, interpersonal skills, and future educational plans. The evaluators observed that the interns showed more realism about their personal careers and educational plans, recognized that they had more control over their behavior, and became more aware of the range of consequences occurring from specific actions.

Unfortunately, the evaluation was carried out following the traditional goal model, which focused on the official program goals. None of the outcome variables derived from the operative goals was included in the evaluation, perhaps because it was too late to change the research design. The rest of this evaluation story is familiar to many evaluators; the program showed no significant difference between the experimental and control groups in terms of the measurable goals derived from the official goals.

The above example clearly illustrates that program goals, especially those stated officially, may not adequately reflect what the program is actually doing. It also shows how the traditional goal model may easily lead evaluators to look at goals that are not actually pursued by the program and may well address the wrong issues.

The major discrepancies between official and operative program goals cannot simply be attributed to reasons such as bureaucratic inertia, administrators' low motivation, or neglect of official program goals. The problems may be deeply rooted in the art of policy formulation and program implementation (Nakamura and Smallwood, 1980). In order to formulate a more efficient model to assess program purposes, the factors that widen the gap between the official and the operative goals must first be examined.

Program Goals Are Formulated to Build a Coalition

As discussed in Chapter 5, goal formulation is an integral part of the political process. From the decision maker's perspective, the major concern in policy formulation is not how to implement the program or how to evaluate the program after implementation; rather, their basic concern is how to gain enough support from political coalitions in a pluralistic society for approval of a policy or program (Nakamura and Smallwood, 1980). An important strategy to attract support or avoid opposition is to state goals vaguely and idealistically and to address noble causes. Coalitions are easy to form under a vague and noble goal (Weiss, 1972; Quinn, 1978) because each member can find some reason or motive to participate. Conversely, operative goals, involving the details of resource allocations or value trade-offs, only highlight differences among coalitions and enhance the conflicts between them. Therefore, for the purposes of decision makers, neither goal statements containing detailed information on specific strategies to achieve the program's goals (which would be highly desirable to program managers and administrators) nor goals stated clearly, specifically, and unambiguously (which would satisfy evaluators' needs) are desirable in the decision-making process.

This explains why, in goal formulations, it is permissible for a program to have contradictory goals. For example, Hall (1982) reports that juvenile detention centers contain contradictory goals such as "maintaining secure custody" and "providing healthy living arrangements." He noted that these two goals are incompatible, because locking youths into cells may optimize security but is hardly healthy. From the implementation or evaluation point of view, it may seem odd that a program has contradictory goals, but from a policy formulation viewpoint, it is reasonable to have contradictory goals as long as they help bind coalitions. Program goals that are contradictory, or serve only as "window dressing" and do not truly reflect what the program is actually pursuing, are often justifiable on political grounds.

The Discretion of Program Managers and Administrators

When planning a social program, decision makers or funding agencies have high hopes for it. However, they may not know exactly how to translate those hopes, or goals, into actions. The work of defining the target groups, screening the applicants, contacting the clients, allocating the resources, deciding what delivery systems are needed to accomplish the program, and so forth often is not considered to be the responsibility of decision makers or funding agencies, and perhaps not even a matter for them to consider. These problems are usually left to program managers or administrators (Williams and Elmore, 1976). As Lipsky (1980) noted, street-level bureaucrats who take all responsibility for direct contact with clients and who exercise a large degree of discretion in day-to-day decisions on program activities actually shape the direction of the program. Consequently, a gap may exist between the decision makers' and the program managers' or administrators' expectations of a social program. The problem of discrepancy is magnified when the deliverers also have their own interests, values, and incentives (Nakamura and Smallwood, 1980). The program treatments actually delivered are often quite different from those originally conceived and described in official goals.

The slippage between official program goals and operative program goals creates a serious problem in program evaluation. Decision makers may insist upon using official goals to evaluate program effectiveness, while program managers and administrators may argue that program evaluation should focus on what the program really does.

In program evaluation, official goals rather than operative goals are frequently used as criteria, and because evaluators are hired or funded by the decision makers, they will, therefore, usually take the decision makers' viewpoints. Under these conditions, the evaluation findings are often disappointing because the evaluation does not reflect what the program actually accomplishes.

A good example of discrepancies between the different expectations of decision makers and program managers is the Ohio University–Westinghouse evaluation of the Head Start program (Cicirelli, 1969; Smith and Bissell, 1970). The Head Start program was a national preschool program funded by the Office of Economic Opportunity (OEO). The purpose of the program was to prepare children from disadvantaged backgrounds for entrance into formal education in primary

schools. The program had been established as a decentralized program
where local centers were given autonomy in carrying out the program.
However, the directors of the centers and the OEO had conflicting views
regarding the problems of disadvantaged students, the nature of the
program, and how to implement it. The views of local directors led
them to work for growth in all areas of children's lives: physical, social,
and emotional, as well as intellectual. Therefore, their efforts and
resources were directed to all these areas rather than concentrated only
on cognitive development. The OEO did not explicitly express its concept
that the primary goal of the Head Start program was cognitive
development until the formulating stage of evaluation. The evaluation
team from Westinghouse Learning Corporation and Ohio University
took only the OEO's perspective. It is not surprising the evaluation
found that the program had no effect, according to the OEO's standards
of cognitive development. In this case, decision makers and treatment
deliverers lacked mutual agreement about the treatment and the goals.
The Ohio University–Westinghouse evaluation has been criticized for
not measuring the outcome of the treatment that was actually delivered.

Routinization Requirement

Some programs can be easily planned and launched. For example,
a welfare program for mailing benefit checks is relatively straightforward
and this kind of program would not require much time to routinize.
However, many social programs need a period of time operating in the
field to reach maturity, and the necessary field adjustment may result
in programs diverging from the original plan. This change, however,
may not be reflected in statements of program goals.

Frequently, implementation of a program is much more difficult than
anticipated. In the Performance of Contracting experiment (Gramlich
and Koshel, 1975), private firms were contracted to teach students in
school and received pay according to the student's performance. In spite
of the fact that the program would be evaluated one year after delivery,
many firms had difficulties in implementation. They could not supply
their own teaching materials on time, their teaching machines and other
hardware did not function efficiently, some firms failed to pay their
teachers incentive payments, and so on. In addition, program operations
were further hindered by the hostility of regular teachers, unexpected
strikes, and the like.

An example, which illustrates well the necessity of letting the program
operate in the field for a period of time in order to become routinized,

can be found in Birnbaum et al.'s (1986) study of the implementation of the Long Term Home Health Care Program (LTHHCP), a program providing nursing home care to chronically ill patients who need institutional care but live in the community. The purpose of the program was to reduce the cost involved in institutionalizing chronically ill persons while at the same time increasing their quality of life.

In this study, the authors discovered many implementation problems only after the program was started. For example, in the area of eligibility, a few changes in standards had to be made. Originally, eligibility for the LTHHCP was limited to persons "who would otherwise require placement in a hospital or residential health care facility." This eligibility requirement was vague because it is difficult to measure which persons "would otherwise require" institutionalization. Eventually, the eligibility criteria were amended, so that the program would include a person medically eligible for placement in a hospital or residential health care facility according to his or her DMS-1 score, an acceptable measure of eligibility for institutional care. Similarly, the original legislation required screening and assessment of the client by both the local department of social services and a representative of LTHHCP. This reviewing process took time and caused a considerable delay in service delivery. Later, the law was amended to allow the program to service the clients before the joint assessment had been completed, but at its own financial risk. Birnbaum et al. warned against overoptimistic expectations of a rapid start-up period and suggested that this treatment implementation should allow for modifications to the original plan. It took the LTHHCP two and a half years to progress from a concept to an operational program, even though many home care programs were already in place in New York.

The Dynamic of Goals

Program goals are not static; they tend to change due to newly perceived needs, the external environment, or internal structural change. As a consequence, though the official program goals may remain static for years, the program actually pursues different operational goals.

In his study of the District Eleven Adoption Project, Olsen (1981) observed that the original goal of the project was to serve handicapped children. However, after implementation, it was found that a much broader group was in need of service—minority children. Children with minority backgrounds were overrepresented in the backlog of cases. Information from environmental services led to a change in the program goal of serving only handicapped children to the broader goal of serving the needs of minority children. Olsen (1981) made an interesting note that, in spite of the project's expansion of purpose during the project period, the official goals of the program were never changed.

The shift of program goals is not necessarily obvious or explicit. Sometimes even the decision makers, program managers, or administrators do not exactly know the direction in which a program is moving. Kress, Kochler, and Springer (1981) use the term "policy drift" to describe the fact that a social program and its objectives may be fundamentally changed due to cumulative decisions required in responding to the environment during the process of implementation. Originally, the accommodations may be within the guidelines of legislation and regulations. However, as time goes by, these decisions may accumulate and lead to changes in the program format. Decision makers may not be aware of this cumulative change in program activities and objectives, and gradually lose contact with the program as implemented.

Policy drift occurred in the Business Enterprise Program (BEP) of the California Department of Rehabilitation (Kress et al., 1981). The Business Enterprise program is a federally sponsored, state-administered program that "places rehabilitated blind persons as vendors in food-service facilities such as vending stands, snack bars, and caterers that are established and supported by the program." Vendors derive their income from the profits of their local facility. The original legislation in 1945 represented a token effort to help the blind defray economic hardship by providing them with sheltered employment opportunities appropriate to their disability. The legislation did not specify the detailed means for implementing the program. The program began to be transformed because the policy environment shifted from employability as a rehabilitation objective toward a broad concern with the whole person. Program goals experienced a movement from professionalized counseling and support to self-help and mainstreaming into society, and an emphasis on the individual rights of disabled persons. Pressure from interest groups supported and protected the income and advancement of vendors in the program. New amendments to the law required the vendors to elect representatives to the California Vendor's Association in order to participate in the decision making. The service environment shifted from small dry-vending stands to large, full service cafeterias. This change required the BEP to place a higher priority on monitoring effective communications with contractors and on ensuring some means of service quality control. Finally, the management of BEP agreed that the maintenance of existing locations and the use of management resources to enhance their income potential were the operating objectives of highest priority in the program.

This particular policy drift created confusion and conflict among stakeholders of the program. The California Department of Rehabilitation perceived the need for a comprehensive evaluation of the program's objectives, performance, and future. Kress et al. demonstrated that evaluators, using the normative outcome evaluation, can help to clarify the confusion in program activities and program objectives. In this case, they suggested that the BEP be characterized as a state-administered business enterprise rather than as a rehabilitation program. As a business enterprise, the BEP is not intended to prepare blind persons for employment; it is intended to provide opportunity for business enterprise.

In order to deal with the above problems, a comprehensive model for specifying the outcomes in an impact evaluation will be developed in the rest of this chapter. This model will be called the theory-driven model.

THE THEORY-DRIVEN MODEL: STRATEGIES AND PROCEDURES

The above discussion clearly indicates two things. First, at both the theoretical and the practical levels, the traditional goal model is not adequate. An evaluator who relies on this model may risk producing a skewed picture of what the project is actually doing. Second, neither of the major alternative approaches, the goal-free evaluation or systems model, is deemed desirable either. There appears to be a clear need for a new, alternative model.

The theory-driven model is presented as an alternative. It includes strategies for dealing with the two major flaws of the traditional goal model: official program goals that do not reflect the program's real activities and insensitivity to unintended program impacts.

Identifying Plausible Goals and Plausible Outcomes

The theory-driven model requires the evaluator to specify two types of outcomes in any final list of outcome variables. The program's plausible goals, whether official or operative, constitute one type of outcome. Theory-derived plausible outcomes constitute the other.

Plausible Goals

Plausible goals or intended outcomes are those goals valued by stakeholders and actually pursued through program activities. Official program goals, however, may contain some implausible goals that serve important political purposes but were never intended to be pursued (e.g., see Etzioni, 1960; Nakamura and Smallwood, 1980). Unless the stakeholders insist upon it, it is wasted time and effort to assess these implausible goals.

The integrative approach, integrating stakeholder and social science approaches must be used to construct a normative theory of plausible goals. In using the stakeholder approach, an evaluator should work with stakeholders to create an explicit specification of their normative theory of the program goals that are of utmost concern and include it in an impact evaluation. However, because stakeholders tend to emphasize desirability rather than plausibility, the set of goals derived from the stakeholder approach may not necessarily be the plausible goals. The evaluator should use the social science approach to investigate which of these goals are actually attainable. More specifically, an evaluator should examine these stakeholders' goals in terms of the following criteria.

(1) Sufficient resources are allocated to implement program activities toward the goals. Plausible goals can be seen as those goals, whether formally stated or not, that are actually pursued by the program managers and administrators. For a goal to qualify as plausible, the program has to show evidence of time, effort, and money being spent on pursuing it. According to this criterion, in the Title I program (McLaughlin, 1975), the announced goals of helping disadvantaged students to overcome educational deprivation cannot be considered as a plausible goal because few program activities were identified as serving this purpose.

More commonly, and as previously discussed, an agency may claim to have several goals in order to please various coalitions or for other political purposes. In reality though, only a few of them may actually be pursued. An examination of resource allocation or operating activities can provide information for distinguishing from among the official goals those that are plausible and those that are not.

In analyzing the program goals of a local fair housing contact service, Chen (1979) found that a number of official goals related to preventing discrimination in housing were formally stated to be pursued by nine projects: affirmative action and marketing program, evaluation of the housing delivery system, complaint investigation, relocation, metro-outreach, education, interagency coalition, referral and exchange, and home seekers contact program. An investigation of the expenditure allocation showed that, of these nine projects, five received the vast majority of available resources. It was suspected that goals related only to these five projects were actually pursued by the program: affirmative action and marketing program, evaluation of the housing delivery system, complaint investigation, metro-outreach, and education. Other goals, listed for political or other reasons, were not seriously pursued by the agency—at least not at the time of the investigation. Subsequent interviews with program managers and staff, and observation of the program operation, in essence supported this speculation.

(2) The goals are consonant with the current knowledge and understanding of the problem to which the program is directed. This criterion emphasizes that the goal should have at least some connection with prior theory, knowledge, or experience in order to establish a causal link between the program activities or treatment and the goals. For example, President Ford's effort to urge business and labor to hold the line on prices and wages by distributing WIN buttons (Whip Inflation Now) is regarded as a goal that was implausible, given the program treatment, as hardly any current knowledge or theory indicates that button distribution alone provides enough incentive for business and labor to comply with wage and price guidelines. The only thing the program actually accomplished was perhaps to demonstrate Ford's frustration with inflation.

Another example is the Federal Firearms Registration Act of 1968 (Wright et al., 1981). The program designers intended to restrict access to firearms for criminals, the insane, and a few other groups, and believed that this could be done by registering gun dealers and forbidding them to sell to people in these groups. Two assumptions were implicit in this belief: that people in these groups bought most of their weapons from gun dealers and that gun dealers could identify members of these groups. Neither assumption was true, and in fact both were contrary to what was already known.

If the desirable goals meet these two criteria, then they may be regarded to be plausible goals. If they do not, the evaluators should bring the discrepancies to the stakeholders' attention and work with them again to reach consensus on a set of realistic and attainable goals.

The 55 miles per hour speed limit is an excellent example of a goal that meets the criteria of a plausible goal. The purpose of the "double nickel," when first implemented, was to reduce gasoline consumption based upon the clear evidence that most gasoline engines use less fuel at lower speeds. The program designers of the 55 m.p.h. speed limit also used a reasonable strategy to ensure that their program would be implemented; if states did not enact and enforce the new law, their federal highway funds would be cut off.

Another good example of a plausible goal is the official purpose of the food stamp program to improve the nutrition of the poor. The official goal of the program is actually implemented and pursued by assessing the eligibility of clients and by distributing food stamps and welfare checks.

It may be useful at the stage of program formation for program people to emphasize desirable, yet unattainable, goals in order to help create political coalitions. However, at the evaluation stage, the realistic aspects of the program must be emphasized. For example, decision makers or program designers may have high hopes for a social program to eliminate, say, poverty, and such noble causes can attract wide support. But due to the constraints of existing knowledge, resources, and sociopolitical structures, the program may in reality target and implement a more limited goal such as eliminating hunger. An evaluation emphasizing the desirability domain would indicate that the program has failed to achieve its goal of eliminating poverty. In fact, that goal was never attainable under the given circumstances, and the results of such an evaluation could only detract from the positive impacts the program had actually achieved. On the other hand, an evaluation emphasizing the plausibility dimension would show how the program contributes to the plausible goal of eliminating hunger. Program advocates, and support for social reforms as a whole, stand to benefit more from emphasizing plausible goals than from using the traditional goal model.

Plausible Outcomes

As pointed out by some critics, such as system model theorists (e.g., Scriven, 1972; Deutscher, 1977), insensitivity to unintended outcomes is frequently a weakness of the goal model. In practice, the exclusive focus on intended goals makes the goal model very rigid. Although it is possible that talking with program staff or administrators about their daily operations can provide some ideas on the potential unintended outcomes of a program, a normative theory based upon the social science approach is a more thorough way to identify unintended outcomes.

The construction of a normative theory for deriving unintended outcomes is much more difficult than for deriving the intended ones. In specifying the unintended outcomes, although the integrative approach is applied, the emphasis may be more on the social science approach than on the stakeholder approach. In other words, prior theory and knowledge and understanding of the program implementation are required to infer what the potential plausible outcomes could be when the treatment is actually delivered. Those unintended outcomes derived from this procedure are different from plausible goals and are called "plausible outcomes." The strategies used to obtain the plausible outcomes are illustrated below.

(1) Examination of implementation activities. Plausible unofficial or unintended outcome variables can be identified by an examination of how the program is implemented and how the resources are allocated. Data for uncovering significant aspects of the program, such as resource allocation, can be gathered through a variety of research methods such as field observation, interviews, and secondary data analysis. In Zald's (1963) study of correctional institutions for delinquents, information about resource allocation was obtained from both the observation of daily work and interviews with program managers (superintendents, assistant superintendents, and heads of major departments) and administrators. Zald discovered from these data that, although rehabilitation was an officially announced goal, resources were mainly allocated to the custodial aspects of the organizations rather than to professional treatment personnel. This clearly indicated that the operative goals were custodial rather than rehabilitative. In these institutions, custody should be regarded as the unofficial, policy-directed, plausible goal.

Similarly, based upon his observation and personal experiences with program activities in two U.S. prisons (one treatment oriented, the other custody oriented), Cressey (1958) found that, in addition to the official goals of custody, rehabilitation, and so on, both prisons also pursued an unstated goal: the protection of inmates from society. In the treatment-oriented prison, prisoners needed protection from public tours, which tended to disrupt therapy. In the impersonal, custody-oriented prison, inmates needed protection from the ridicule of employees. In these prisons, the protection of inmates was the unofficial policy-directed goal.

Furthermore, Chen and Rossi (1980) argue that the mode of delivery of a program is an especially important area to investigate in order to identify intended outcomes. According to Chen and Rossi, the delivery system required to implement most programs may have effects that the designers of the program never intended. An administrator may add certain administrative conveniences to the delivery of a program, which have nothing to do with the intended treatment and may create unintended effects, as with the Aid to Families with Dependent Children Program. This program's official goal was to relieve economic hardship in female-headed families. In order to target the program for the most needy, the eligibility requirements of the program restricted benefits to female-headed families. Unexpectedly, however, many husbands left home in order for the family to receive benefits. The mode of program delivery created an unintended impact by destabilizing low-income families and actually intensifying the problem that the program was designed to alleviate.

In many types of programs, participants are brought together in a group and interaction among them is facilitated. Unintended results may arise from these interactions. Friendships may develop, and participants may feel less alienated than before. They may exchange job information, for example, and find employment. A negative example of this is when an inexperienced thief learns more sophisticated techniques from more experienced inmates in a prison rehabilitation program, and so becomes a more successful thief.

(2) The use of existing theory and/or knowledge. Plausible outcome variables can also be inferred from existing theory, knowledge, and understanding of the program. Because many evaluators may not be familiar with this procedure, several research examples will be discussed to illustrate the use of prior theory and knowledge about program activities to infer unintended outcomes. The method for obtaining theory-derived outcome variables has been well illustrated in Conybeare's (1980) study of compulsory seat belt legislation in Australia. The explicit and intended goal of this legislation was to reduce automobile occupant casualties. However, as shown by Conybeare, a careful investigation of the programs' causal process, based upon existing theory and knowledge, suggested other important potential impacts of the seat belt legislation. Drivers may respond to the legislation by increasing their level of driving intensity because they perceive an increase in road safety. This intensity may increase the casualty rate among nonoccupants. These hypotheses were supported by the data. If this research had focused on automobile occupant casualties alone, it would have provided only one side of the story. A program evaluation may provide only partial and misleading information when attention is focused exclusively on official program goals without an investigation of plausible outcomes.

Examples of using prior theory and knowledge to derive plausible outcome variables can be found in other areas. For example, Waldo and Chirico (1977) applied several theories from criminology to derive various outcome variables in evaluating a work release program. Based upon several theoretical perspectives in criminology, they argued that the effects of a work release program could not only reduce recidivism but also improve the participants' lives in other areas, such as through the development of a sense of responsibility and self-discipline and increased opportunities for social adjustment. Measuring recidivism alone in assessing the program results could overlook other benefits.

White (1978) also demonstrated how to derive plausible outcomes through the use of existing theory and knowledge. He indicated that the official program goal of state occupational licensure laws is to regulate the quality of service provided by self-employed professionals. White clearly demonstrated that, in addition to the formal goal, two other potential impacts of the laws can be derived from existing theory and knowledge. These unintended impacts concern wages and employment.

The constraints of licensure on entrance into an occupation will increase the entry cost through fees or education and experience requirements. This tends to increase wages through an upward shift in the supply curve. The imposition of licensure constraints requires an industry to substitute licensed personnel for unlicensed personnel, which thus tends to increase the demand for licensed personnel and push up the wages and employment prospects of these personnel. In his data, White found that stringent licensing laws, instead of having the intended impact, served mainly to increase the wages and employment of licensed personnel.

So far, cost-benefit studies seem to have done a better job in terms of outcome specification. The reason perhaps is that it is well recognized in cost-benefit analysis that ignorance of an important effect (cost or benefit) will bias the calculation of a benefit-cost ratio. Clotfelter and Hahn (1978) showed that the original goal of a 55 m.p.h. speed limit was fuel saving in response to the Arab oil embargo and subsequent higher oil prices. However, the benefits of the lower speed limit were not confined to gasoline savings. Prior theory and knowledge suggested it also would increase highway safety, thereby reducing fatalities, injuries, and property damage. Like other cost-benefit analyses, the authors also assess the adverse effects of the speed limit: time cost of compliance and enforcement cost. By analyzing the wider set of important program

effects (both intended and unintended), an evaluation is more likely
to provide insights for decision makers and the public to use in judging
the worthiness of a program.

Applications

The above discussion implies the requirement of using the integrative
approach to identify intended and unintended plausible outcomes for
investigation. As discussed in Chapter 3, the integrative approach needs
dual theorizing processes. On one hand, the evaluator needs to apply
the stakeholder approach to clarify and refine the key stakeholders'
plausible goals. On the other hand, the evaluator needs to apply the
social science approach to sensitize plausible outcomes for evaluation.
As one of the constituents, the evaluator should not only be sensitive
to other constituents' views but also actively communicate and present
her or his own view to other constituents. The evaluators' knowledge,
expertise, and experience may compensate for other constituents' views.
What emerges from this joint effort may be a mutually agreed-upon
set of outcome variables that will reflect both the intended and the
unintended plausible outcomes in the impact evaluation.

If the available resources and time allow for the inclusion of each
of these intended and unintended outcomes, the evaluator can proceed
with the impact evaluation. However, if the resources and time frame
are not sufficient to allow investigating this complete set of plausible
goals and outcomes, and the stakeholders are unable to expand the
resources or time, the evaluator must work to negotiate a final set of
outcomes for evaluation that can fit the resource and time constraints.
A consensus among evaluators and stakeholders must be reached before
impact evaluation is conducted. The negotiation techniques and processes
discussed in Chapter 5 are useful in this regard.

Conducting the impact evaluation is more tedious than traditional
summative evaluations, but it will enhance mutual understanding between
stakeholders and the evaluator in regard to the nature and functions
of the impact evaluation. Because the stakeholders' views on the
normative outcomes are well articulated into the evaluation processes,
and the issues of unintended outcomes are dealt with, the utilization
of results generated from this type of evaluation should be enhanced.
This kind of evaluation process ensures that the stakeholders will not
accuse the evaluator of failing to evaluate what they are really doing
or of not investigating outcome variables that they believe are important.

ARE INTENDED OUTCOMES MORE IMPORTANT
THAN UNINTENDED OUTCOMES?

The discussion of intended and unintended outcomes leads to an important issue: Are policymakers or other stakeholders more interested in information concerning intended outcomes or unintended outcomes?

Some advocates of the goal model may insist that assessment of a program's intended goals must have the foremost priority in program evaluation. However, past policy and evaluation research has clearly indicated that policymakers may be equally or perhaps even more concerned with the unintended outcomes of a program than with the intended ones. For example, it was claimed that Negative Income Tax programs had the following advantages over traditional welfare programs: simplicity of administration, equality in paying all those whose income falls below a certain level, dignity in avoiding indiscriminate investigation, and encouragement of individual initiative because the payments continued as earned income increased (Kershaw, 1972). However, evaluation of this experiment has focused predominantly on work disincentive, a potential unintended impact, because decision makers were highly concerned with this aspect of the program (Rossi and Lyall, 1976). Similarly, after the implementation of school integration programs, policymakers were concerned with the potential impacts of the program on the problem of white flight from the center of the city to the suburbs (Coleman, 1975) no less than with the program's intended goals of equal educational opportunity.

RELATIONSHIP BETWEEN THE THEORY-DRIVEN MODEL
AND OTHER OUTCOME MODELS

Basically, the theory-driven model can be seen as a multiple outcome perspective. In assessing program effect, both plausible goals and plausible outcomes are considered in the model. As a result, a set of both intended and unintended outcomes is derived from prior theory and knowledge of the intervention and the examination of program activities. This emphasis on multiple outcomes in evaluation makes the impact evaluation more sensitive to program effect. Furthermore, a single indicator is incapable of handling measurement errors that may exist in each outcome variable. If measurement error is suspected when implementing the measures of each outcome, multiple indicators for each outcome variable should be used. (Jöreskog and Sörbom, 1979).

A comparison between the theory-driven model and other outcome approaches should be highlighted. The theory-driven model agrees with the goal model that program goals should be considered in evaluations, but it emphasizes that only those program goals realistically pursued by the program should be seriously evaluated. The theory-driven model also agrees with the system and goal-free models in that an evaluator should be aware of impacts other than goals, as long as those impacts are plausible. An impact is plausible if it can be identified from program activities and/or through the framework provided by the existing theory and knowledge.

The theory-driven model agrees with the system model's criterion that it is important to study the means by which the ends are achieved as well as the influence of the environment on the system. But unlike the systems model, which argues that investigation of internal processes or system survival is the alternative to the goal model in studying program effectiveness, the impact evaluation regards these studies as complementary rather than as a substitution for the goal model. Nevertheless, the theory-driven model can be expanded to deal with issues related to internal processes or system survival raised by the system model when the former is integrated with the intervening mechanism evaluation discussed in Chapter 10 or with the generalization evaluation discussed in Chapter 11.

10. Intervening Mechanism Evaluation

CONCEPT AND ISSUES

As discussed in Chapter 2, in addition to a normative theory, a social program also contains a causative theory. This causative theory explains the intervening and contextual factors through which the treatment affects the outcome. The purpose of an intervening mechanism evaluation, which is the main focus of this chapter, is to identify these intervening mechanisms in an impact evaluation. The issues relating to contextual factors will be discussed in the following chapter in the discussion of generalization evaluation.

Unlike traditional black box evaluations, which mainly assess the simple relationship between input and output, intervening mechanism evaluations attempt to expand the evaluation process by identifying the causal processes that theoretically intervene between program treatment and outcome. Generally speaking, the purpose of the intervening mechanism evaluation is to uncover the causal processes underlying a program so that the reason(s) a program does or does not work can be understood. As will be emphasized in the following sections of this chapter, utilization of intervention programs usually requires knowledge of how the program works, and the intervening mechanism evaluation seeks to address this need. Furthermore, because the intervening mechanism evaluation can pinpoint those factors in the causal chain that lead to program success or failure, this kind of diagnostic function can provide useful information for future program improvements.

The intervening mechanism evaluation requires the formulation of a causative theory regarding intervening mechanisms in evaluation processes. Both the stakeholder approach and the social science approach are useful, but the social science approach may be more useful in formulating this causative theory of intervening mechanisms.

Because formulating a causative theory of intervening mechanisms requires some training or knowledge of theory construction, evaluators are usually more familiar with this kind of theorizing process than are stakeholders. Nevertheless, the involvement of stakeholders in this process is still important. If stakeholders have a special interest in and ideas concerning particular causal chains in the program, the evaluators can explicitly construct this theory for investigation. Or if the stakeholders do not have specific ideas on the causal processes underlying the program, evaluators can use their professional training to design a causative theory of the intervening mechanisms. They should then explain the nature and function of this type of evaluation in order to enhance the consensus between the evaluator and stakeholders for the need to carry out this type of theory-driven evaluation.

STRATEGIES AND RATIONALE OF INTERVENING MECHANISM EVALUATION

Strategies

There are three basic stages in intervening mechanism evaluation.

The Theoretical Specification Stage: Specifying Intervening Variables

In this first stage, evaluators have to identify the intervening variables that come between the treatment variable and the outcome variables. These variables can be identified through existing social science theory and knowledge, through examining the implicit causal mechanism underlying the program, and/or through consulting with program designers. For example, the causal mechanism underlying the Head Start program was based mainly on evidence from social science literature that home environment factors and self-esteem play a powerful role in shaping children's future growth and development (e.g., see Shapiro, 1982; Datta et al., 1973). The status of participating in the Head Start program can be conceptualized as the treatment variable (whether the children attend the program), which is intended to affect the intervening variables (the home learning environment and the student's self-esteem), which, in turn, are intended to affect the outcome variables (achievement motivation and academic performance).

Another example of an intervening mechanism evaluation is an innovative antismoking educational program that uses a comic book as educational material (Chen et al., 1988). The underlying causal mechanism of this program is the assumption that the comic book will attract adolescents' interest and attention and that they will read it closely and frequently, and thereby pick up the important antismoking message contained in it. The message will in turn change their attitudes, beliefs, and behavior regarding smoking. The causal structure of this program is that the program treatment variable (exposure to the comic book) attempts to affect the intervening variable (the intensity of reading), which, in turn, will affect the outcome variables (attitudes, beliefs, and behavior toward smoking).

The Measurement Stage: Observing and/or Quantifying Intervening Variables

After the intervening variables have been specified in the evaluation model, evaluators have to observe and/or measure any variation in them to see whether they have been changed by the treatment variable. Various qualitative or quantitative methods, such as participant observation, interviews, surveys, tests, and records, can be used at this point. Which particular method or methods should be used depends partially on the evaluation design chosen, a point elaborated upon further in this section.

For example, in the Head Start program, evaluators could have used participant observation to observe whether the children's home learning environment changed or the children's self-esteem increased. Or, more formally, the evaluators could have used measurement instruments such as pencil-and-paper questionnaires to quantitatively measure changes in children's self-esteem and their home learning environment. Similarly, in the antismoking program, the evaluators could have used self-administered anonymous questionnaires, interviews, or participant observation to examine adolescents' reactions after they received the comic book. In this stage, quantitative and qualitative measures each have their own benefits and drawbacks. Quantitative methods can provide standardized measures based on representative samples, while qualitative methods can provide rich, in-depth information regarding program participants' experiences, opinions, and reactions to the treatment. If resources and personnel allow, it is a good idea to combine both approaches in observing and measuring intervening processes.

The Inference Stage: Inferring Causal Mechanisms Underlying the Program

The specification and measurement of intervening variables in the evaluation model provides an opportunity to examine the causal mechanism underlying the program. When and if the mechanism works as expected, decision makers and other stakeholders will have more confidence about where and how evaluation results can be used. If the program does not work as expected, examination of the intervening process can help to identify the sources of problems for future program improvement. For example, in the hypothetical Head Start evaluation mentioned above, if the evaluators found that the program failed to enhance the children's home learning environment, decision makers and program implementors could strengthen various program components to improve this part of the program. Similarly, if the antismoking program administrators find that the program comic book does attract the students' attention, but fails to change the students' attitudes, beliefs, and behaviors, the content of the comic book will have to be reformulated.

Approaches to Analysis

There are at least two general approaches to analyzing the intervening mechanism, depending on how sophisticated a statistical analysis is required: exploratory causal analysis or structural equation models.[1]

Structural equation models use a set of equations to represent direct, indirect, and reciprocal relationships among the endogenous and exogenous variables and the disturbance terms (see Kmenta, 1986). These models are usually estimated by the use of advanced statistical techniques such as two-stage least squares, three-stage least squares, or LISREL. On the other hand, exploratory causal analysis, in the context of program evaluation, uses a network of variables to represent underlying causal processes among the variables. The assumptions in the causal model, however, are not mathematically or statistically defined as precisely as in structural equation models. Being less mathematically rigorous, exploratory causal models may be analyzed by use of techniques such as multiple regression.

Both structural equation models and exploratory causal analyses have advantages and disadvantages. Structural equation models have the advantage of being methodologically rigorous and precise, but their use and interpretation require a sophisticated statistical background. Exploratory causal analysis, on the other hand, is less rigorous and precise but may be performed by researchers with a general understanding of statistics. The theoretical specification stages of exploratory causal analysis and structural equation model analysis are largely the same, but, as will be discussed later, structural equation analysis requires a closer examination of the assumptions of the model. However, these two approaches are different in the measurement and inference stages of how the data are collected and analyzed.

Exploratory Causal Analysis

In the measurement and inference stage of exploratory causal analysis, the evaluator can use quantitative or qualitative methods to measure, observe, and analyze the intervening processes. If qualitative methods are used, the evaluator may observe the influence of any intervening variables specified in the model and infer the causal process involved. An example of using qualitative methods for exploratory causal analysis can be found in Miles and Huberman (1984). Where quantitative methods are used, the quantified variable can be analyzed by means of standard statistical techniques. Exploratory causal analysis is not the most rigorous model-building procedure. Hence it must be applied cautiously to prevent misleading results. However, it is easily applied and may be intuitively understood by program decision makers and other stakeholders, thereby helping to enhance the utilization of evaluation results.

Structural Equation Models

Alternatively, examination of the intervening process can be carried out under the framework of structural equation models (see, e.g., Duncan, 1975; Kmenta, 1986). Structural equation models have advantages over exploratory causal analysis when estimating causal relationships among variables in complicated situations, such as reciprocal relationships; in attempting to decompose the total effects into direct and indirect effects; or when the magnitudes of causal effects are important.

However, for structural equation models to produce useful results, three conditions must be met: quantitative methods must be used to measure the intervening and other variables, the causal structure of the error terms and variables must be correctly specified, and the evaluator must be skilled in the formulation of structural equation models. This chapter includes a general discussion of structural equation models.

A structural equation model is a set of equations that represents the behavior and interrelations of two or more endogenous variables (commonly called "dependent variables"). Models that do not attempt to address intervening process issues are known as "reduced form models," in which each endogenous variable is determined by the exogenous variable (commonly called "independent variables") and a disturbance term (or an error term). However, in spite of their merits in assessing the underlying causal mechanism, structural equation models are not always easy to estimate. In a recursive model with one-way causality and independent disturbance terms across the equations, parameter estimation is a relatively uncomplicated procedure because the ordinary least-squares procedures can be applied directly in hierarchical order, as in path analysis. However, in a nonrecursive model with reciprocal relationships among endogenous variables or correlated disturbance terms across equations, parameter estimation is somewhat more complicated. First of all, it is necessary to deal with the problem of identification, that is, to determine whether the coefficients of a particular equation can be estimated meaningfully. In a necessary condition (or an order condition), an equation in the nonrecursive model is said to be identified if the number of exogenous variables (or formally determined variables) excluded from the equation is greater than or equal to the number of endogenous variables minus one.[2]

Even though equations in nonrecursive models may be identifiable, the ordinary least-squares procedure cannot be directly applied to estimate the parameters because the reciprocal relationship between endogenous variables implies a correlation between the disturbance term and one of the endogenous variables. This violates the basic assumption of ordinary least squares. Instead, a nonrecursive model has to be estimated by using advanced techniques such as the two-stage least-squares method to obtain consistent estimates or the three-stage least-squares method to obtain consistent and efficient estimates.

Rationale

With all the trouble they can cause, it is reasonable to ask: Why bother to investigate the intervening processes in program evaluation? What kind of benefits does it provide? The answer may depend on what we conceive to be the main purpose of program evaluation. If the major purpose of program evaluation is to obtain an unbiased estimate of treatment effect, or, in other words, if we believe that the emphasis of program evaluation should be on nonspuriousness alone, then the added effort involved in specifying the intervening process results in little gain. In this case a black box evaluation model provides the desired summary information of the total effect of a program without the necessity of an intervening mechanism evaluation.[3]

However, if we think that program evaluation should also emphasize generalizability, or, more generally, usefulness, as the theory-driven perspective argues, then the examination of underlying causal mechanisms is important. Basically, we need to understand in detail the nature and underlying causal mechanism of a program in order to know how to utilize the results of an evaluation. Exploratory causal analysis and structural equation models are superior to single equation models or reduced form models in revealing the underlying mechanism of the program, and this information is crucial in utilizing evaluation results. For example, a drug company might claim that a new drug is effective in dealing with a disease without providing any information about how the new drug works. Physicians, however, would be hesitant to use the drug on patients, because the intervening mechanisms, such as side effects, would not be well known.

The following sections of this chapter attempt to elaborate in detail how intervening mechanism evaluations can be developed and how they are useful in program evaluation.

ACTION THEORY AND CONCEPTUAL THEORY: SUMMATIVELY DIAGNOSING THE INTERVENTION PROGRAM

As discussed in earlier sections, the traditional summative or outcome type of evaluation only provides information on whether a program succeeds or fails. However, this kind of information creates difficulties for policymakers. What does it mean if the program fails? Does it mean the program was implemented inappropriately? Does it mean the conceptualization of the problem was wrong? Does it mean that the theoretical rationale of the program was wrong? Different causes of failure imply different strategies for effective remedies. If the program's weakness comes down to poor implementation, as discussed in Chapters 6 and 7, improvement may be required in implementation procedures. However, if the problem was conceptualized inadequately or the underlying causative theory was wrong, then the rationale of the program must be redesigned. The issues regarding integrity of treatment and implementation have been discussed in Chapters 6 and 7. This chapter attempts to focus on issues related to causal mechanisms underlying a program.

Suchman (1967, 1969) provides an insightful discussion of how the specification of intervening processes in a model can help decision makers or program managers. Suchman (1969) indicates that a social or intervention program is usually based upon a social theory or that there is some other logical reason to believe that the program treatment has some causal connection with the outcome variables. Accordingly, if a program is unsuccessful, the failure may be attributed either to failure to implement the theory in the program or to an incorrect theory. Suchman uses the term "program failure" to denote the inability of the program to activate the causal processes that the theory predicts and the term "theory failure" to denote invalidity of the theory. He believes that an emphasis on understanding why a program succeeds or fails will make program evaluation a strategic source of knowledge about how social programs should be administered.

Suchman's distinction between program failure and theory failure provides an important argument for specifying intervening mechanisms in program evaluation. However, the label "program failure" may easily be confused with the implementation failure discussed in Chapter 7. The term "program failure" seems to imply that program management and administrators are totally responsible for the failure of the program. However, because failure of a program can result from inadequacy of the causative theory, it is important not to assign program managers and administrators total responsibility for program failure unless they committed administrative mistakes in delivering the treatment. For these reasons, I modify and further elaborate Suchman's conceptual framework in the following discussion.

Conceptually speaking, as indicated in Chapter 2, a social or intervention program usually consists of an implicit or explicit causative theory. This theory suggests that a causal variable has some specific effect upon a desired outcome and that the purpose of the treatment is to affect the causal variable so that the specified outcome can be obtained. For example, a job training program may be based upon the human resources theory that education or job skill (causal variable) influences one's ability to obtain employment or a salary increase (desirable outcome). So the job training (treatment variable) offered by the program attempts to enhance the participants' education or job skill, which hopefully, in turn, will lead to their gainful employment or salary increase. This conceptualization of an intervention program implies that intervening mechanism evaluation has, in fact, two theories to test. First, there must be a test of a "conceptual theory" to see whether the causal variable affects the outcome variable as specified by the theory. Then, there must be a test of an "action theory" to examine whether the treatment variable, manipulated through program activities, successfully influences the causal variable of the conceptual theory. To make this distinction between action theory and conceptual theory in a causative theory and show that both should be tested in an intervening mechanism evaluation is, in fact, to argue that program evaluation must make use of a structural equation model rather than a reduced form model. This framework is illustrated in Figure 10.1.

As an aside, it is important to note that in this framework the causal variable of the conceptual theory is an intervening variable in the overall program, mediating between the treatment variable and the ultimate program outcome.

Basic sciences usually have focused their attention on formulating and testing the validity of conceptual theory. For example, some social science theories have suggested that low achievement scores among disadvantaged students have been caused by factors such as lack of motivation and parental apathy. Various empirical studies may be carried out by social scientists to test this theory. On the other hand, the major concern of program designers, planners, and others is how to devise a set of program activities (e.g., counseling) to motivate disadvantaged students or to enhance parents' involvement and concern about their children's classwork. In short, they need to develop an action theory. The framework in Figure 10.1 suggests that a program's overall success requires success in both action theory and conceptual theory. Not only must the program treatment variable succeed in activating the causal variable, as specified in the action theory, but the causal variable must also validly affect the outcome variable, as specified in the conceptual theory.

One of the major differences between evaluation research and basic research, in this framework, is that basic research traditionally primarily involves testing the conceptual theory, while evaluation research involves testing both the action and the conceptual theories. For example, basic research in education may attempt to test a theory that attributes variation of achievement test scores to factors such as parental apathy about children's schoolwork. A main concern of basic research is to verify

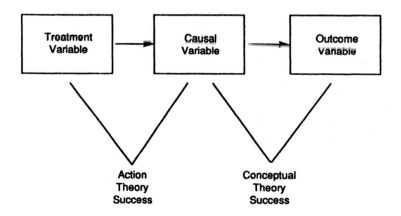

Figure 10.1.

the relationship between parental apathy and children's achievement scores. If this conceptual theory is the basis of an educational program, then our evaluation of this program not only has to test whether the basic theory is valid, it must also test an additional action theory: whether the program successfully changes the causal variable (e.g., parental apathy).

Whatever its degree of maturity, basic science, whether natural science or social science, has systematically developed, tested, and cumulated the core of its conceptual theories. What is less developed is the core of knowledge concerning action theory. Action theory is usually formulated by decision makers, program planners, and/or administrators for a particular program in which they are involved. The success or failure of their action theory is not rigorously tested or documented. However, a good action theory is necessary for successful social reform. The failure of program people and social scientists to clearly specify and assess action theory will reduce their contributions to social reform. Perhaps through proposing a distinction between action theory and conceptual theory in program evaluation, and dealing with both, coupled with the current increasing interest in program implementation, we may systematically accumulate knowledge about action theory.

The immediate advantages of specifying both action and conceptual theories in a causative theory is the assistance it provides in diagnosing sources of program failure or success and in suggesting remedial action. According to this framework, there are three general types of causative theory failure, which are discussed below.

Action Theory Failure

This indicates that the treatment variable fails to affect the causal variable in the conceptual theory, but the basic conceptual theory underlying the program is sound. If program failure comes from this source, it suggests to program advocates that the problem is in the treatment as implemented rather than in the basic conceptualization. Program advocates, such as decision makers, program planners, program managers, and/or evaluators, may have to restructure program activities to effectively activate the conceptual causal variable, but the basic idea is workable.

Conceptual Theory Failure

This implies that program treatment has successfully activated the causal variable in the action theory, but the conceptual theory is invalid. Consequently, the outcome variable is unaffected. This suggests that the underlying concept of the program is fundamentally flawed and that, unless it is redirected by a better replacement theory, it is pointless to implement it.

Double Theory Failure

This is a situation where both the action theory and the conceptual theory are invalid. Program designers have to start over again at the beginning by reconceptualizing the problem, finding an appropriate basic theory, and developing an action theory.

Identifying the type of failure requires analysis of the relationship between the treatment variable, conceptual causal variable, and outcome variable. Research that addresses the issue of the source of failure by using a structural equation model can be found in the study by Chen et al. (1988), which evaluated an antismoking program for young adolescents. The key treatment component of the program was a comic book with a main message that cancer and other diseases are to some extent preventable by not using tobacco.

The action theory underlying this program was that a comic book format may encourage adolescents to keep and read the book voluntarily many times. The conceptual theory of this program assumed that the number of times the comic book was read and the resulting knowledge of the comic book's message would lead adolescents to either consciously or unconsciously receive the antismoking message and change their beliefs, attitudes, and behaviors toward smoking. The action and conceptual theories of the program are diagrammed in Figure 10.2.

The overall assessment of the program indicated that the comic book had no impact on changing students' smoking beliefs, attitudes, and behavior. However, because the intervening mechanisms were included in the analysis, Chen et al. (1988) were able to pinpoint the source of program failure and provide information for program improvement. Their analysis of the intervening processes of the program indicated that the action theory of the program was successful, that is, the program was effective in stimulating students' interests in reading the comic book and in gaining knowledge of the story. However, the problem of the program was in the conceptual theory. Adolescents' interests in reading the comic book did not translate into subsequent changes in their smoking attitudes, beliefs, and behaviors.

On the basis of this information, Chen et al. (1988) indicated the potential difficulties in the conceptual problems and recommended strategies for changes, such as to sharpen the focus on a few primary health-related points and to include some problems immediately related to adolescents' lives, such as bad breath, smelly clothing, stained teeth, and so on.

Another study that addressed the issue of the source of failure by using an exploratory causal analysis can be found in Somers and Stormsdorfer's (1972) study of the In-School and Summer Neighborhood Youth Corps (NYC) Program. The main purpose of the program was to increase the high school graduation rate of students who, for economic causes, were potential dropouts.

The underlying theory was that, if students could earn more money while staying in school, they would be less likely to drop out. The conceptual component of this theory was the belief that low personal and family income is a major factor in the decision to drop out of high school. The action theory was that paid work experience in high school would supplement student's income sufficiently to counteract this influence. The action and conceptual theories of the program are diagrammed in Figure 10.3.

The indicators of economic benefits were average monthly earnings, months of unemployment, and months of voluntary labor force withdrawal. Evaluations/benefits were measured by indicators such as the probability of high school graduation, the number of years of high school completed, the probability of college attendance, and the probability of postsecondary education other than college.

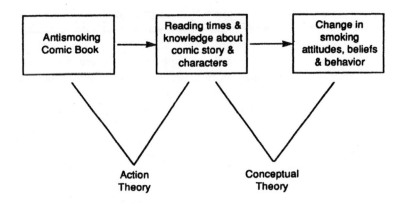

Figure 10.2.

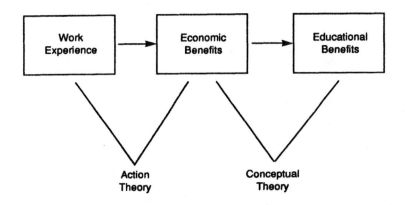

Figure 10.3.

An overall assessment of the relationship between work experience and education benefits revealed that the program failed to achieve its major educational goals, such as increasing the probability of high school graduation or increasing the number of high school years completed, although it did increase the probability of students attending college or acquiring other postsecondary education.

However, Somers and Stormsdorfer's analysis provided some insight into the program's problem. They found that the program's action theory actually worked. The work experience had yielded the postulated economic benefits. However, the conceptual theory was not supported; that is, there was a zero or even negative relation between income per capita per family and graduation from high school. Nevertheless, the authors argued that the income-educational premise upon which the NYC program was based might have been incorrect. They found that the NYC program was justified mainly on economic grounds, not educational ones. Policymakers must modify factors other than family income to reduce the high school dropout rate.

Another program evaluation that partially addressed the issue of diagnosing a failure of theory can be found in a study by Meyer, Borgatta, and Jones (1965), which evaluated the impact of counseling services on a variety of adolescent problems in New York City. The outcome variables of the program were various behavioral measures of academic performance, staying in school, and so on and some indicators of out-of-school behavior such as pregnancy or contacts with authorities and social service agencies. However, the authors argued, the clinical services provided by the program could not be expected to directly affect school continuity and behavior. The implementors hoped that the treatment would cause personality changes leading to better self-image, more satisfactory interpersonal relations, and so on (the action theory) and that these personality changes would be expected to affect school and out-of-school behavior (the conceptual theory). The underlying intervening mechanism of this program is shown in Figure 10.4.

The evaluation results demonstrated that the program treatment produced minimal differences between the experimental and control groups on personality tests. Similarly, it was found that the program had little effect on various behavioral outcome measures. Implicitly, Meyer, Borgatta, and Jones (1965) seem to argue that the failure of the program resulted from the failure of the action theory; that is, the treatment failed to produce personality change, and hence it is logical that no desirable outcomes were achieved. However, it is unclear whether or not the conceptual theory was sound. This issue would have been clarified if the authors had also tested the relationship between personality and behavioral outcomes suggested by the conceptual theory of this program.

FORMATIVE FEEDBACK ON INTERVENING
PROCESSES FOR EARLY IMPROVEMENT

The specification of action theory and conceptual theory in an intervening mechanism evaluation is particularly useful when the evaluation

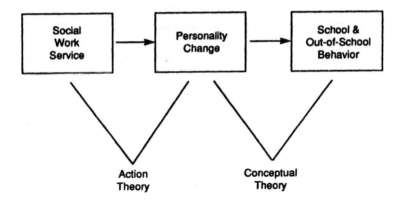

Figure 10.4.

is carried out in the early stages of program implementation. In this case, the resulting feedback can immediately be used for program improvement.

Traditionally, evaluators initially assume that decision makers and program planners have a profound knowledge of the problem they seek to remedy and of the action and conceptual theories involved. In fact, however, the creators and implementors of a program may have incomplete or incorrect information regarding a particular situation and problem and may be guided by incorrect or incomplete theories. If evaluators join the program in the early stages of implementation, they can provide feedback about the realism and effectiveness of both action and conceptual theories, and thus provide information that can be used to guide and strengthen the program through its formulation. Decision makers and funding agencies will find this formative feedback greatly preferable to evaluations that reveal a program's weaknesses long after it has been in operation.

One specific form of early feedback that evaluators can provide is an evaluation of the success of the action theory. For example, the ultimate results of an educational program designed to raise achievement test scores of disadvantaged students by stimulating student motivation and reducing parental apathy might not be measurable until after the program has been in operation for a long time. However, if the program is unable to affect student motivation, the achievement scores will not rise, no matter how long it runs. In other words, the success of the action theory is both a necessary condition for program success and a prior condition for conceptual theory success. By examining the immediate effect of the program on the causal variable of the conceptual theory (i.e., how well the program stimulates student motivation), the evaluator can provide information on the effectiveness of the program long before the intended outcome variable (i.e., achievement scores) becomes measurable.

Because evaluators are continually providing feedback on whether the program works as expected, evaluation can be an ongoing process of program improvement rather than the traditional before and after assessment. This ongoing evaluation provides implementors and evaluators with a means for sharpening program implementation and program theory on a day-to-day basis and hence for enhancing the utilization of evaluation results. Finally, and only after the program treatment is shown to be mature enough to affect the intervening variables, evaluators can proceed to evaluate program effectiveness in affecting the outcome variable.

Klein's (1979; also see Cronbach, 1982) discussion of evaluating the impact of a nutrition program on mothers and children in Guatemalan villages is an example of both the power of quasi-causal analysis and the importance of studying the adequacy of the action theory underlying the program from an early stage of program development. The original purpose of the study was to assess the relationship between a protein-rich supplement (treatment) and the physical and psychological growth of children early in postnatal life. The rationale for supplying protein was the assumption that a shortage of protein is the main reason for the mothers' and children's malnutrition.

Four villages were studied. In two villages, expectant mothers and young children received a high-protein, high-calorie diet supplement, and in the other two, they received supplements with no protein and one-third the calories. The action theory and the conceptual theory underlying the program are shown in Figure 10.5.

However, an early analysis of a group of mothers who gave birth and a study of the regular home diets of villagers immediately challenged the adequacy of the action theory. The villagers were seriously deficient in caloric intake generally but not specifically lacking in protein. As a result of this information, new action and conceptual theories were formed that indicated that caloric intake was the conceptual causal variable and thus the target of the intervention. The evaluation wisely shifted its main focus and efforts to the new treatment variable, caloric supplementation. Klein (1979) reported that caloric supplementation was found to have important effects on children's physical and psychological growth.

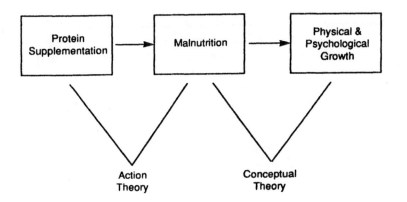

Figure 10.5.

If the evaluators had not questioned the adequacy of the original conceptual theory in the early stages, and had proceeded with a traditional evaluation, the results of the evaluation might have been "no effect" again. Or they might have found an effect, because the protein supplements would have provided more calories for the target population, but they may have attributed the effect to the protein content of the supplement and, as a result, may have drawn and documented false conclusions from program results.

PINPOINT STRENGTHS AND WEAKNESSES OF MULTIPLE UNDERLYING CAUSAL CHANNELS

Frequently the treatment variable is mediated by more than one causal variable, or intervening variable, or, to put it another way, the treatment variable may affect the outcome variable through several different causal channels. In some cases, program planners have a clear idea of the intervening variables they are trying to affect. More often than not, however, this information is not available, and evaluators have to deduce the intervening variables from other social science theory and knowledge as well as from examination of the program as implemented.

Applying terminology from structural equation models, the effect of treatment variables on outcome variables is called an "indirect effect" if it is mediated through intervening variables. If the effect does not result from an intervening variable, it is called a "direct effect." The sum of direct and indirect effects is called the total effect. The total or overall effect of a program is the major focus of traditional evaluation. However, although a report of program effectiveness that only gives total effect has the advantage of providing summary information, it also has the disadvantage of lumping together a variety of positive and negative effects from different causal channels. Knowledge of these multiple causal channels is crucial for the improvement of a program in the future.

Even if the program's overall total effect is positive, there may be some undesirable causal channels within the program that hinder it from achieving even higher effectiveness. Without detailed information about which causal channels lead to which positive or negative results, the evaluation misses an opportunity to strengthen the program.

Furthermore, the diagnosis of strengths and weaknesses of causal channels in an intervening mechanism evaluation is particularly important when the program shows no overall effect. The lack of results may be because positive and negative effects from different causal channels have canceled each other out. In this situation, if the evaluation reports only the total effect, as provided by the reduced form model or single equation model, it may give only a pessimistic report of program failure without pointing out any merits of the program or without identifying sources of weaknesses to help improve it. A structural equation model may be useful at this point in disentangling the obscured program effect and in pinpointing the strengths and/or weaknesses of the program.

This issue has been illustrated in the evaluation of the Transitional Aid Research Project (TARP; Rossi et al., 1980; Berk et al., 1980). The purpose of the TARP experiment was to provide limited financial aid to released prisoners during the period of transition from prison to normal life. It was hoped that this transitional money would provide an incentive for the released prisoners to choose in favor of employment and against crime. A randomized experimental design was used. About 2,000 participants in Texas and Georgia were randomly assigned to one of several treatment groups with different levels of benefits or to a control group. Program treatment conditions were varied in terms of the maximum number of weeks for which unemployment benefits were provided and in terms of the tax on earnings from legitimate employment. The experiment was administered by the staff of the state employment offices in Texas and Georgia. The experiment results were first analyzed by a reduced form model, such as the analysis of variance. The treatment variable in the model involved six groups under varying treatment conditions. The dependent variables were arrests for property crimes and for nonproperty crimes. The reduced form model for this program is illustrated in Figure 10.6.

The findings obtained from the analysis of reduced form equations indicated that the program treatment had no statistically significant overall impact on either property or nonproperty arrests. The scope of this analysis was limited and difficult to translate into policy. For example, was the program totally worthless or could it be improved in the future based upon this research?

Rossi et al. (1980) further specified a structural equation model to evaluate the program, and the results provided much more information for decision makers and other stakeholders. Based on prior theory and knowledge of economic and sociological theories of criminal behavior, the authors constructed a structural equation model that elaborated the underlying causal mechanisms of the program (which is illustrated in Figure 10.7). The exogenous variables in this model contained the treatment variable along with variables of economic need (e.g., savings), human capital (e.g., education variables), past commitment to criminal activity (e.g., number of prior convictions), and so on. The interrelationships among the endogenous variables of this nonrecursive model are presented on the righthand side of Figure 10.7.

The model mainly suggested that TARP payment receivers should both have fewer arrests for property and nonproperty crimes and experience a work disincentive effect. On the bright side, TARP payments

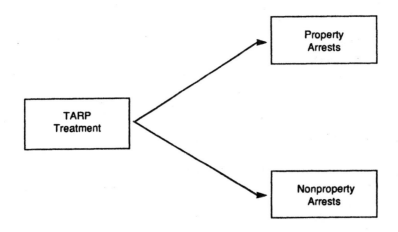

Figure 10.6.

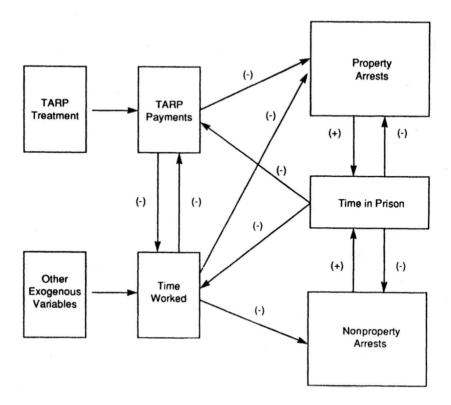

Figure 10.7.

should directly reduce the number of property arrests and nonproperty arrests because, according to the assumption of the diminishing marginal utility of income, TARP payments should reduce the time allocated to income-producing crime. Furthermore, TARP payments increase the opportunity costs of arrests because recipients have more to lose; that is, the recipients of TARP payments will be afraid to commit crime because arrests lead to loss of TARP payments.

On the dark side, TARP payments also have a work disincentive effect. They reduce the necessity for time to be allocated to employment. Furthermore, the work disincentive effect is strengthened by a high tax on earnings from legitimate employment. The TARP experiment placed a 100% tax on TARP payments for the majority of participants. In other words, receivers' payments were reduced dollar for dollar for their earnings received. With such a high tax, the employment opportunities available to TARP participants were poor competition for the TARP payments.

The work disincentive effect, in turn, led to an increase in property and nonproperty arrests, for reasons such as the following: (1) Time was not withdrawn from illegal activities, and (2) the opportunity costs of arrests were not increased due to joblessness, and preferences for legitimate activities were not shaped. In addition, unemployment meant that there was no reliable source of income to reduce the marginal value of earning from illegal activities.

Finally, the model also indicated that, while property and nonproperty arrests would increase time in prison, the time in prison would reduce further nonproperty and property arrests and time in prison would also reduce both TARP payments and time worked.

In general, one of the important implications of the structural equation model was that TARP payments would have both positive and negative impacts on property and nonproperty arrests, through both direct and indirect channels. In terms of direct effect, the model indicated that TARP payments would directly reduce both property and nonproperty arrests. However, in terms of indirect effect, TARP payments reduced the need to work, which, in turn, increased the number of property and nonproperty arrests. This is a counterbalancing model. This model was verified in Texas and also replicated in Georgia.

The results from the analysis of a structural equation model was much more enlightening than the reduced form model. The structural equation model indicated at least the following main implications for the TARP program: First, TARP payments directly reduced the number of property and nonproperty arrests. Second, unemployment increased the number of property and nonproperty arrests, and, third, the TARP payment caused substantial work disincentive. In this sense, the use of a reduced form equation alone, which simply reported that the program had no effect, was superficial and seriously misleading.

The information provided by the structural equation model has important policy implications. Because the major weakness is the work disincentive, the program could be modified to correct this effect. For example, in order to effectively reduce overall recidivism, the unemployment benefit system could be strengthened in the future by disentangling that portion of the program from the portion related to the work disincentive effect resulting from the 100% tax placed on earnings. The authors suggested several possible ways to deal with this problem, such as a generous tax rate or increasing payments for a time if the ex-felon becomes employed.

PROVIDING INFORMATION ON
ALTERNATIVE INTERVENTION STRATEGIES

Another advantage of the intervening mechanism evaluation is the policy information provided on alternative strategies for improving a program's effectiveness. Because the intervening variable links the treatment variable to outcome variables, intervening variables themselves can be regarded as alternative treatment variables, which decision makers or program designers can employ in the future.

Leigh's (1983) study of the impact of education on health illustrates this point. According to Leigh, schooling is usually regarded as one of the important exogenous variables in virtually every study carried out in this field. However, the underlying causal mechanisms through which schooling affects health have not been empirically examined. Past literature has suggested two intervening variables, as follows.

Habits

Habits such as exercise, diet, drinking, and smoking have been regarded in medical literature as important determinants of health. Individuals with a good education may be more willing to exercise healthy habits, and avoid unhealthy ones, than those with a poor education.

Choice of Occupation

Different types of jobs are associated with different risks of injury and illness. Education may influence an individual's choice of and access to healthier jobs. Leigh's model can be presented as a recursive model, as in Figure 10.8. The reduced form model of this study can be illustrated as in Figure 10.9. In these models, "health" is a subjective evaluation of the respondent's health, and "habits" are represented by variables such as smoking and exercise. Job hazards are based upon the respondent's assessment of his or her job situation.

An analysis of the reduced form health equation in Figure 10.9 indicated that schooling had a substantive health advancement effect, based upon the University of Michigan's Quality of Employment Surveys for 1973 and 1977. Leigh (1983) made the point that his analysis of the structural equation model, shown in Figure 10.8, provided him with additional information about the relative effectiveness of the different causal channels affecting the respondent's health. This information is

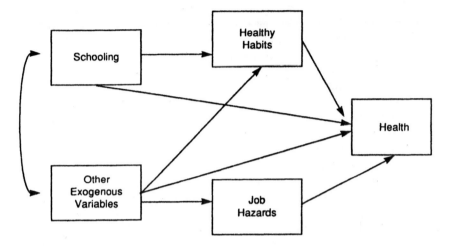

Figure 10.8.

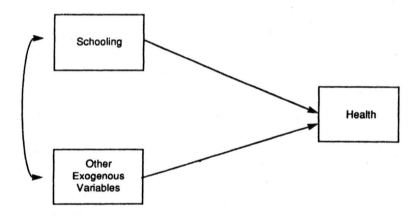

Figure 10.9.

useful for decision makers contemplating alternative intervention strategies, particularly when indirect effects are strong.

The results of his analysis showed that the direct impact from schooling on health was much smaller, in comparison, than the indirect effect through health habits and choice of jobs. In the 1973 survey, the indirect schooling effect of the better educated being more likely to choose a safer job was approximately four times greater than the effect directly from schooling, although the indirect effect via the smoking habit was smaller than the direct effect.

In the 1977 survey, indirect effects were considerably larger than the direct effect. The indirect effect operating through the choice of hazardous or nonhazardous jobs was roughly 10 times and the indirect effect operating through health habits was roughly 18 times the direct effect. Schooling appears to have its greatest impact on health through its intervening effects on health habits and occupational choice. Generally speaking, when assessing the effect of schooling on health, indirect effects proved to be more important than the direct effect.

Leigh argued that previous studies based upon the reduced form model suggest that, from a policy standpoint, years of schooling may be the most important predictor of good health. This reduced form research implies that expenditures for education at the state or national levels should substantially improve the health of the average person. Here again, the results of analyzing a structural equation model provided more comprehensive information. First, education affects health mainly through the encouragement of healthy habits and caution in the choice of jobs. Second, because the intervening variables have strong impacts on health, they can be regarded as targets of alternative intervention strategies. Dollars spent on advertising designed to encourage health habits, or on the improvement of workplace health and safety, may be as important as or more important than dollars spent on education, at least for health purposes.

ASSESSING ISSUES OF REACTIVITY

In an evaluation based upon a reduced form model, even if the data indicate that the treatment effect is substantial, it may still be unclear whether the effect results from the treatment itself or from the participants' reactivity, such as the Hawthorne effect or demand characteristics.

There has been debate about whether participants' reactivity should be treated as a threat to internal or external validity. For example, Kruglanski and Kroy (1976) and Hultsch and Hickey (1978) regard participants' reactivity as a threat to internal validity (nonspuriousness); that is, the treatment is confounded with experimental procedures. On the other hand, Campbell and Stanley (1963) and Cook and Campbell

(1979) argue the opposite—that participants' reactivity should be regarded as a threat to external or construct validity (generalizability) rather than to internal validity. They argue that participants' reactivity will cast doubt on whether the causal relationship between the treatment and the effect can be generalized beyond particular settings (Campbell and Stanley, 1963) and on how the research operations can be generalized to a theoretical construct (Cook and Campbell, 1979). However, these threats do not cast doubts on whether there was a causal relationship between the measured treatment variable and the measured outcome variable.

Joining Campbell and Stanley (1963) and Cook and Campbell (1979), I take the position that participants' reactivity is a threat to generalizability. Reactivity creates difficulties not only in conceptualizing or interpreting the relationship between the treatment variable and the outcome variable, but it also makes it unclear how research outcomes can be applied in the future. Unlike the reduced form equations associated with black box evaluation models (which are insensitive to issues of reactivity), intervening mechanism evaluations can provide some possible ways to differentiate treatment effects from reactivity effects by clarifying the intervening process.

This issue is well illustrated in the exploratory causal studies by Malcolm and Madden (1973) and Malcolm, Madden, and Williams (1974) on the effect of disulfiram, which is reported to create an unpleasant reaction to alcohol, as a deterrent treatment for alcoholics.

As long as patients continue to take oral disulfiram, they may be too afraid to drink. Furthermore, the data also indicate substantial improvements in the marital, occupational, and social adaptation of the patients. Unfortunately, patients often stop taking the drug. Thus a long-acting method of administering disulfiram, such as surgical implantation of disulfiram pellets, would be desirable. Malcolm and Madden (1973) attempted to evaluate the effect of disulfiram implantation on alcoholism. The treatment (disulfiram implantation) was given to 47 alcoholic inpatients, all of whom had experienced the unpleasant reactions to alcohol caused by oral disulfiram. In the surgery, a three-centimeter incision was made in the left lower abdomen at a site corresponding to McBurney's point. Ten 100-milligram tablets of pure sterilized disulfiram were then radially placed deep to the external oblique, and the wound was repaired with catgut and silk sutures. The main outcome variable of this study was alcohol use, although other outcome variables such as improvements in the marital, occupational, and social adaptation of the patients were also included. In their study, Malcolm and Madden (1973) evaluated the effect of the treatment according to a reduced form model, which is shown in Figure 10.10.

Improvements in measures of alcoholism in the patients were found to be satisfactory. The data indicated that the periods of abstinence immediately succeeding the operation were significantly greater than the periods of longest abstinence during the previous two years. Malcolm and Madden's (1973) study revealed that disulfiram implantation effectively reduced alcohol use. The study met the requirements of internal validity. However, in spite of the treatment effect that was found, can we safely conclude that disulfiram implantation alone, without being confounded with other variables, achieved the desired outcome? In other words, the data lead us to believe that disulfiram implantation reduces alcohol use, but is this belief actually true? This is a matter of construct validity that cannot be dealt with by the reduced form equation but that is vital in decision making. Similarly, can we confidently generalize the effect of disulfiram implantation to other situations? Again, this information is vital in policy consideration, but unfortunately the reduced form equation provides little information for such judgment.

A follow-up study by Malcolm et al. (1974) demonstrated to some extent that the use of a structural equation model provides some insightful information on issues of construct and external validity. According to the theory, disulfiram implantation should create pharmacological activities that cause unpleasant reactions to alcohol that, in turn, will deter a patient from consuming any alcohol. The structural equation model suggested by the theory is illustrated in Figure 10.11. It is assumed that disulfiram implantation produces a therapeutic level of the drug in the blood high enough to result in a deterring reaction if the patient drinks.

The study by Malcolm et al. (1974) focused on investigating the relationship between disulfiram implantation and the intervening

Figure 10.10.

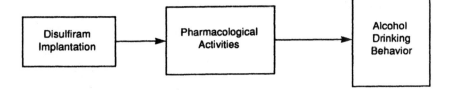

Figure 10.11.

variables (pharmacological activities). Alcoholic patients treated by disulfiram implantation were followed up. Malcolm et al. (1974) found that only three patients described any reaction to drinking. Further, although a blood disulfiram level above 0.1 milligrams is considered therapeutic, it was apparent that the disulfiram implant resulted in therapeutic blood levels for only a brief period after surgery. They argued that the implant usually does not give a level above .01 milligrams. Similarly, a check of exhaled disulfiram in implanted patients only two days after the operation also indicated that the effect was transient.

The examination of pharmacological evidence led Malcolm et al. (1974) to argue that the actual effect of the disulfiram implantation on drinking is through anticipatory fear rather than pharmacological deterrence as suggested by the theory. The results are illustrated in Figure 10.12, which indicates that disulfiram implantation had an impact on alcoholism, but through the wrong causal channel (fear) and not through the causal channel suggested by the theory (pharmacological activities). As a consequence, even though the treatment, no doubt, had an impact, the construct validity of the treatment effect is questionable because the treatment did not work in the way predicted by the theory. Furthermore, the external validity of the treatment effect is also questionable because, as soon as patients learn that disulfiram implantation will not create pharmacological deterrence, they may no longer be afraid to drink alcohol. It is doubtful that the treatment effect revealed in this study can be generalized to any other time or setting. The evaluation using the structural equation model revealed the need for future improvement of the program. An alternative form of surgical implantation of disulfiram must be developed if it is to work.

On the other hand, if the results of the structural equation model evaluation had indicated that disulfiram implantation indeed was effective through the predicted causal channel (pharmacological activities), advocates would have more confidence in arguing that the treatment

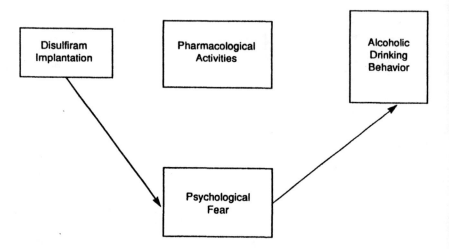

Figure 10.12.

could be applied in other times or settings, because the underlying causal mechanism would have been known.

Even in cases such as this medical research, where the treatment (disulfiram) was surgically implanted in participants' bodies, there was still no guarantee that the treatment would activate the desired intervening process. For intervention programs where the program implementation is less exact and controlled, we cannot simply take for granted that program treatment will follow the theoretical intervening process to create effects as the theory specifies. It is especially important in social programs to include the intervening mechanism in an evaluation.

NOTES

1. Some alternative approaches that may be useful for analyzing intervening mechanisms have been discussed by Lipsey and Pollard (forthcoming).

2. The order condition is only a necessary condition, but it suffices in most cases. A sufficient condition for identification is the rank condition. Interested readers are referred to econometrics textbooks such as Kmenta's (1986).

3. A quantitative analysis, a single equation model, or a reduced form model can ensure an unbiased estimate when rigorous designs such as a randomized experiment or a strong quasi-experiment (e.g., regression-discontinuity designs) are applied.

11. Generalization Evaluation

CONCEPT AND ISSUES

As a practical science, program evaluation cannot be pursued in the same way as pure academic social science. Evaluation results must be responsive to multiple stakeholders' needs and must be applicable to the situations in which stakeholders are interested. Very often evaluators have to deal with issues of generalization when evaluating programs. If generalization is crucial to the stakeholders, but is not formally addressed by the evaluators in the evaluation design, program stakeholders and others interested in evaluation results may not know how relevant or applicable the results are to other programs and situations. When the results of an evaluation are applied without specific knowledge of their generalizability, one of the following errors is likely to be made:

(1) Overgeneralization fallacy. Evaluation results may be unsuitably extended and applied to programs where they do not apply. In the worst cases, decision making based upon this error results in a disappointing failure, where resources and efforts are wasted. Such failure tends to call into question the very usefulness of program evaluation.

(2) Undergeneralization fallacy. Alternatively, a situation could exist in which evaluation results should have been generalized but were not. If sufficient information on when and how the results could be applied is not provided by the evaluator, stakeholders may fail to realize the connection between what was evaluated and their concerns. As a

consequence, evaluation information may not be utilized in situations of interest to stakeholders.

As discussed in Chapter 3, evaluation theorists have different opinions on the priority order of generalizability versus trustworthiness. For example, Campbellians believe internal validity should take precedence over external validity (e.g., Campbell and Stanley, 1963), while Cronbach (1982) insists that external validity should be ahead of internal validity. Nevertheless, all evaluation theorists agree that the ability to make generalizations is essential for a program evaluation.

In spite of its importance, we know much less about generalizability than trustworthiness. Except for a select few, such as Cronbach et al. (1980) and Cronbach (1982), generalization has not been a primary area of focus in program evaluation. Part of the reason may be due to the inherent difficulties of the concept. Campbell and Stanley (1963, p. 5) argued that the question of generalization is "never completely answerable." Part of the reason may be that many of us have followed the Campbellian tradition of devoting more attention and efforts to issues of internal validity.

Nevertheless, avoidance of a difficult area such as generalization will only sustain ignorance of that area. Generalization evaluation attempts to deal systematically with the issue of generalization.

Strategies for Dealing with Generalization

Chapter 3 of this book discussed three general strategies for dealing with multiple values: maximizing, sequential, and balancing. The implications of these three strategies for dealing with generalization and trustworthiness can now be considered.

The decision whether to use a maximizing, sequential, or balancing strategy in a study can be better understood through elaboration on the long and controversial debates between Ronald A. Fisher and William S. Gosset about whether randomized experiments are the best design in agricultural research. Fisher forcefully insisted that, as a science, the results of agricultural research should be valid and accurate and that randomized experiments served best for these purposes. Gosset disagreed. Gosset, an eminent statistician and the inventor of the t-test, who used the pen name "Student" in all his writings, held a balancing view very similar to the theory-driven perspective. In his debates with Fisher, he strongly argued that agricultural research should be designed in such a way that both rigorousness and applicability are balanced.

Gosset (e.g., "Student," 1936a, 1936b) argued that randomized experiments, in spite of their statistical rigor, may not be the best design in agricultural research because they do not deal with real error and provide only limited implications for actual agricultural applications. Instead, he preferred the systematic designs traditional in agricultural research, such as the half-drill strip experiment. In the half-drill strip experiment, plots assigned to the treatment conditions (A and B) are arranged in an ABBAABBAABBA . . . pattern. This design, Gosset argued, not only deals adequately with errors such as a linear trend in the plots but also can be easily accomplished by ordinary farmers. In this method, the seed boxes on the left half of the seed hopper were filled with treatment variety A, and on the right with treatment variety B. Having sown plots AB, the horse or tractor turned at the end, going back to sow BA. The same procedures were repeated again without changing the seed hopper positions. Gosset pointed out that these designs are not as rigorous as the randomized experiments, but certainly can deal with many potential biases. The most important advantage, however, is that these designs use a research procedure similar to a farmer's actual planting practice, and the research results can, therefore, be easily generalized to practical use.

From the statistical viewpoint, Fisher insisted that, without the use of random assignment, the half-drill strip design tends to suffer from all sorts of biases in estimation. Barbacki and Fisher (1936) argued that the estimation of standard error in the half-drill strip experiment is neither valid nor accurate. However, Gosset ("Student," 1936a, 1936b) believed that valid conclusions could be drawn from systematic experiments. He does not deny that the half-drill strip experiment is theoretically not as accurate as the randomized experiment in estimating the standard error, but he claims that the issue of applicability has to be brought into the discussion. Due to artificial arrangement of the plots for fitting the requirements of randomization, the standard error estimated in the randomized experiments tends not to reflect the error in the natural setting. On the contrary, the half-drill strip experiment resembles actual plotting and the standard error tends to be close to the real farming situation. Consequently, the research findings from the half-drill strip experiment are far more applicable than those from the randomized experimental design. During the debates, both Fisher and Gosset were supported by other leading statisticians. Fisher's position has been supported by Yates (1939) and Cochran (1957), while Gosset's position has been supported by Pearson (1937) and Neyman (1952).

In the debates, Fisher's major concern was dealing with biases, and randomized experiments were proposed to maximize trustworthiness. Gosset, however, believed that useful research should pay attention to balancing both trustworthiness and generalizability simultaneously. If the ultimate purpose of an agricultural research project is to benefit actual farmers, then why do we not design a study that has direct implications for the farmer's work and that directly parallels it? In order to enhance generalizability, Gosset argued, the research project should be so designed that the treatment implementation follows the farmer's actual practice in cultivation, uses similar equipment, is carried out on a technical level that the farmer can understand, and so on. Because he considered that randomized experiments have a tendency to prevent the incorporation of these expectations of generalizability into a design, he preferred the half-drill strip experiment. According to Gosset, this method may not be as rigorous as randomized experiments, but it is more flexible in building generalizability into a research project.

Pearson (1970, p. 384) believed that Gosset was satisfied with a highly applicable research design that keeps error as low as possible and that he "did not mind if he was told that the ratio of this [treatment] difference to the estimate of its standard error in a particular experiment could not be referred with mathematical precision to a table of probabilities."

Faced with these two contradictory perspectives, which side we should take may depend on the subject matter and frame of reference. For statisticians who are greatly concerned with rigor and precision, the choice is clearly on Fisher's side, because Fisher's perspective is rigorous in mathematical reasoning and fits well with existing statistical theories. In fact, the great majority of statisticians believe Fisher won the debate (e.g., see Cochran, 1976). This is perhaps one of the reasons Gosset's arguments are rarely discussed these days. Fisher's position can be further strengthened by arguing for the use of the sequential strategy to deal with the issue of generalization, where the same evaluation is replicated a number of times in different populations, settings, and so on.

Many laboratory researchers in areas such as agriculture, biology, and medicine, who usually use the sequential strategy to deal with multiple values, also favor Fisher's position. In these areas, researchers usually have full control of treatment allocation, subjects, and research settings. Experiments can be replicated many times under different conditions. Furthermore, after trustworthiness has been verified, the same research can be extended to different subjects or settings without great difficulty if generalizability is a concern. In other words, like Fisher, these researchers can resolve the paradox of trustworthiness and generalizability by using a sequential strategy: dealing with trustworthiness first, then following it with the enhancement of generalizability. Furthermore, the conflict between scientific and political requirements in these areas is minimal. Decision making in these fields is frequently based more upon scientific merits than upon political merits and researchers are free to concentrate mainly on scientific values. For them, randomized experiments are not only easy to implement in a laboratory setting but they also provide researchers with a powerful weapon to defend their work against the criticism of failing to control for potential extraneous variables. It is natural for these researchers to favor the use of randomized experiments, which can buy them so much for so little.

However, in spite of its rigorousness, in order to apply the sequential strategy to program evaluation, it must be assumed that the evaluation of a program can be replicated a number of times. However, evaluations are usually neither funded sufficiently nor allowed enough time for a series of experiments with different locations, participants, and so on in order to increase generalizability. More often, only one—or at most a few—treatment must provide information within a limited time frame concerning multiple values for policy decision making. Such a major difficulty may prevent as wide a use of the sequential strategy in program evaluation as can be found in the physical sciences. This difficulty is discussed in detail below.

(1) Limitations of evaluator's discretion in implementing programs. Within the limit of available resources, researchers in the physical sciences normally can decide for themselves how many times an experiment will be replicated. Furthermore, subjects in laboratory research are either highly motivated to participate or are nonhuman and have no choice in the matter. Subjects can, therefore, be repeatedly experimented upon without the researcher worrying that they will lose interest and refuse to continue.

In program evaluation, we face an entirely different situation. Program evaluators do not normally have the discretion, authority, or resources to replicate an evaluation. In order to do so, an evaluator must first obtain the support of the stakeholders. They are not likely to appreciate the reasons for a replication, and will frown on the substantial costs involved. The situation is even worse when interorganizational or community cooperation is required. Most evaluations, especially randomized experiments, also tend to disrupt administrative routines. Periodic or continuous disruptions are seldom tolerated by administrators and staff. Participants may also object to being evaluated or tested over and over again unless they are rewarded or highly motivated.

   (2) *Length of time required to implement a program and show impacts.* As discussed in Chapters 6 and 7, program implementation is a complicated organizational effort. The time required to implement an intervention program is usually much longer than the time required for implementing a physical science experiment. Furthermore, after the program has been implemented, it will usually take longer for program impacts to become evident. It takes much longer to detect the treatment effect of an intervention program on social attitudes or behavior patterns than it frequently does to see the physical effect of a drug on a patient. Consequently, while it may take a day or a few weeks to replicate a particular physical science experiment, it may take more than a few years to replicate an intervention program evaluation. Due to the time required, it is doubtful whether a sequential strategy can be frequently used to deal with issues of generalization.

   (3) *Political coalitions.* As pointed out in Chapter 5, many social and intervention programs are the creations of political coalitions. Political processes are characterized by conflict and compromise and tend to be unstable (Weiss, 1975). The political coalition required to implement and/or evaluate a program may exist at one time but not another. In some cases, the program may disappear before a second evaluation can be made. Even if the program is still running, the political climate necessary for repeating the evaluation may no longer exist.

   In addition to the above difficulties, another potential problem of advocating the sequential strategy is that it provides evaluators with an excuse not to pay attention to issues of generalization. An evaluator can always postpone the issue of generalization by arguing that generalization will be dealt with at another time or by other evaluators. Because of these inherent difficulties, such as the long turnover time of a program evaluation, shortages of funding, and changing political climates, the sequential strategy for achieving generalization may often be unrealizable in practice.

   These shortcomings can seriously limit the use of the sequential strategy in program evaluation. Under these conditions, the balancing strategy advocated by Gosset and the theory-driven perspective is a good alternative for simultaneously dealing with issues of generalization and trustworthiness.

However, the balancing strategy carries its own limitations. By dealing with the issues of trustworthiness and generalizability at the same time in a single evaluation, the balancing strategy may sacrifice some precision in causal inference for substantial gains in generalizability. Like Gosset, the theory-driven perspective uses the principle that the loss of some precision or rigor, when necessary, is not serious if there are important gains involved. The gain in generalizability from using the balancing strategy may make the evaluation more relevant and utilizable for the stakeholders. In fact, unless an evaluator can indicate to the stakeholders how the results may be utilized in the future, the evaluation will have little value to them. The evaluation has to provide information about conditions under which the program will or will not work and how the evaluation results can be used. With this contextual information, decision makers and other stakeholders will better know when, where, and how evaluation results can be utilized.

In applying the generalization evaluation, an evaluator has to take into account the issues discussed above and determine with the stakeholders the general strategy that should be used in the evaluation. Nevertheless, regardless of whether the sequential or balancing strategy is utilized, it will require a comprehensive conceptual framework and guidance for applying the generalization evaluation. These will be the major issues in the rest of this chapter.

Traditional Conceptual Frameworks of Generalization

Campbell and Stanley (1963, p. 5) have made an important contribution by proposing a popular definition of external validity (or generalizability). As they put it, external validity asks the question: "To what populations, settings, treatment variables, and measurement variables can this effect be generalized?" In Campbell and Stanley's scheme, external validity consists of four dimensions: populations, settings, treatments, and measurements.

Campbell and Stanley's definition of external validity, however, may be more useful for basic research than it is for program evaluation and other applied social sciences. In program evaluation, the goals of generalization center on anticipated applications indicated by stakeholders. Consequently, the nature and purpose of generalization

226 CAUSATIVE EVALUATIONS: BASIC TYPES

is usually narrower and more specific than Campbell and Stanley's broad and challenging conceptualization.

Alternatively, Kempthorne's (1961) conception of generalization may be more informative and useful for program evaluation. Kempthorne (1961) pointed out that it is important to distinguish between the experimentally accessible population and the target population in research. The "experimentally accessible population" refers to the population of subjects that is actually available to the experimenter for study. The "target population" refers to the total group of subjects about whom the experimenter is interested in learning something. It is this larger group that he or she wishes to better understand and to whom the sample findings will be generalized.

Bracht and Glass (1968) endorse Kempthorne's approach and further indicate that it is difficult to generalize sample findings to target populations because of possible interactions between the treatment and social demographic variables (e.g., age and sex). They caution that treatment effects cannot be assumed to be constant across different groups.

Kempthorne's conceptual framework is very informative, but it focuses only on the population dimension. It would be useful if this scheme could be modified to include other dimensions such as treatment variables, measurement variables, and settings, as mentioned by Campbell and Stanley (1963). This is exactly what Cronbach (1982; Cronbach et al., 1980) has done. His UTOS scheme is intended to expand the dimensions from population alone (U), to include treatment (T), measurement (O), and setting (S). Kempthorne's concept of the "experimentally accessible population" is expanded and redefined by Cronbach as UTOS (i.e., population, treatment, measurement, and setting), and the "target population" dimensions are designated by *UTOS.

Despite the value of Cronbach's contributions, his UTOS scheme may be too broadly abstract to be usefully applied to program evaluation. For example, it is not clear what exactly is meant by the setting (S), and important dimensions such as the implementors and the implementing organization are not specified in his scheme.

Theory-Driven Perspective of Generalization

In further expanding upon the works of Kempthorne, Campbell and Stanley, and Cronbach, this book provides a general conceptual framework for generalization. The concept of generalization is postulated as involving two systems: a research system and a generalizing system. The research system is the system in which an evaluation takes place; it is where a sample is drawn and research is carried out. The generalizing system is the system to which evaluation results will be generalized in the future. The essential issue of generalization is whether the causal processes found in the research system can be validly applied to the generalizing system in the future.

It is important to realize that, strictly speaking, we cannot directly draw samples from the generalizing system or work directly with it, due to its future orientation. Even when the program that is being evaluated is the same program to which the evaluation results will be applied in the future, the evaluator is still not working directly with the generalizing system. Due to the time lag between the conclusion of an evaluation and the application of results, the system may not be exactly identical in clients, resources, implementors, and so on. For example, a child-care center may be different in terms of the size and characteristics of its enrollment, staff, operating procedures, and regulatory policies at the time of its evaluation compared with the time evaluation results will be applied.

The distinction between research and generalizing systems implies that generalization always involves some degree of uncertainty. The best an evaluator can do in generalization is to select a research system that allows plausible inference to the generalizing system. This is not an easy task as it involves a trade-off between trustworthiness and generalizability. Commenting on the population dimensions, Kempthorne (1961, p. 124) observed that

one can attempt to make the experimentally accessible population close, in some intuitive sense, to the target population and then encounter lack of precision. Or one can define the experimentally accessible population rather carefully so that much reduced variability is encountered. One will then have, hopefully, rather precise inferences to this population; but one will have a large gap from it to the target population. There is no clear-cut answer on how one should define the experimental population. Narrowly defined populations tend to dismay the scientific man-in-the-street and the statistical novice. There is the almost irresistible desire to have conclusions of wide generality, but in many cases a broad definition of experimental population will lead to average conclusions which are not only very imprecise but also essentially meaningless because of interactions. Scientific life is no different from life in general in requiring compromises which turn out to be good.

Although he mentions only the population dimension, Kempthorne's argument is applicable to other dimensions. In dealing with the dilemma of trustworthiness versus generalizability, he obviously takes a position similar to that of the theory-driven perspective in arguing for a balance between trustworthiness and generalizability when choosing the research system.

Both research and generalizing systems contain corresponding elements of both the treatment structure (discussed in Chapter 6) and the major dimensions of the implementation environment, such as the participants, implementors, delivery modes, implementing organizations, interorganizational relationships, micro context, and macro context (discussed in Chapter 7). If an evaluation is to be useful, an evaluator cannot focus exclusively on the evaluation of program processes and outcomes in a research system. He or she has to foresee and develop a strategy in which the treatment structure and implementation environment in the research system allow extrapolation to the generalizing system. For example, in an evaluation of an alcoholism program, the evaluator has to be concerned with whether the treatment structure (such as group therapy and individual therapy) and implementation environment (such as group size and therapists' quality) in the research system can be extrapolated to the treatment structure and implementation environment in a generalizing system in the future.

The same principle should also apply to utilization, where stakeholders or users attempt to implement evaluation results. Stakeholders or users should be concerned not just with the processes and outcomes found in the research system but also with how the treatment structure and implementation environment of the research system will be relevant to the generalizing system. For example, in utilizing the evaluation results of a delinquency treatment program, the stakeholders or users should be concerned not only with the treatment effect but also with the relevance of the treatment structure (e.g., length of treatment) and implementation environment (e.g., intensive family and peer support) in the research system for their generalizing system.

In general, to develop a generalizable evaluation requires both evaluators and stakeholders to understand the relationship between research and generalizing systems in terms of treatment structure and implementation environment. This is necessary to prevent the problems of over- and undergeneralization.

Both evaluators and stakeholders have to ask such questions as whether or not the quality of implementors and participants in the research system can be maintained in the generalizing system, or whether the delivery mode and implementing organization will be drastically different. Will the influence of macro and micro contexts be a problem in the generalizing system? Can the same treatment structure used in the research system be maintained in the generalizing system?

PITFALLS OF IGNORING GENERALIZATION

"Generalization evaluation" is formally defined as *the selection and/ or design of an evaluation with a research system that allows evaluation results to be applied to or used in the generalizing system.* More specifically, in order to enhance generalization in research, the evaluator must select or design an implementation environment and treatment structure relevant to the generalizing system.

Because the ultimate purpose of a program evaluation is to apply the evaluation results from a research system to a generalizing system, an evaluator must recognize that the evaluation carried out in the research system is only a means for achieving its utilization in the generalizing system. This recognition will prevent an evaluator from committing the fallacy of means-ends reversal, where the evaluator has consciously or unconsciously considered an evaluation in the research system to be the final end in itself and ignored the ultimate purpose of applying the results in the generalizing system.

Taking generalization into account, an evaluator should purposely avoid deliberately manipulating and controlling the research system in a way that may distort the relevancy of the research system for the generalizing system. The evaluator should also avoid deliberately maximizing the treatment effect in the research system in a way that is irrelevant to the generalizing system.

Problems of Deliberate Manipulation and Control of the Research System

In following the experimental paradigm tradition in order to maximize internal validity, an evaluator may deliberately manipulate and control the research system in order to rule out extraneous sources of variation that may be confounded with the treatment effect. Although it is not wrong in many situations for an evaluation to ensure nonspuriousness through control and manipulation, this control and manipulation can often make the research system irrelevant to the generalizing system because these conditions do not exist in the generalizing system. However, because both evaluator and stakeholders are not aware of the problem, evaluation results from the research are directly applied to the generalizing system. Utilizing evaluation results in this way, without paying careful attention to the issues of generalization, may produce disappointing and confusing results, which may eventually undermine further efforts in social reforms in general.

The problem is that the manipulation and control of research systems can lead to confusion when the evaluation results are applied to the generalizing system. This has been clearly demonstrated by an informative study carried out by Diaz-Guerrero et al. (1976) in evaluating *Plaza Sesamo*. In 1971 a completely new production of *Sesame Street*, called *Plaza Sesamo*, adapted especially for the Latin American culture was developed in Mexico (Diaz-Guerrero et al., 1976). Program planners and specialists such as educators and psychologists decided to launch a pilot program and use this evaluation as a basis for implementing a national program.

The first pilot program was carried out with preschool children in day-care centers in Mexico City. Following the experimental paradigm tradition, Diaz-Guerrero et al.'s evaluation emphasized nonspuriousness. A classic randomized experimental design was adopted. A total of 221 3- to 5-year-old children from varying lower-class day-care centers were divided by age and sex into groups and randomly assigned to experimental and control groups. For the purpose of accurately assessing the treatment effect, six children were selected each day, separated from the other children, and taken into a special room where they viewed *Plaza Sesamo* on television. Trained observers made daily ratings of these six children on the degree of attention they exhibited.

However, because the experimental paradigm is limited in dealing with issues of generalization, nonspuriousness in this case was achieved at the expense of generalization. The artificial manipulation and the mode of delivery in the pilot program created a discrepancy between the research system and the generalizing system.

The research system for the pilot evaluation was characterized by a tightly controlled setting and a great deal of adult attention. However, the generalizing system of the large-scale project, which was expected to benefit from the information provided by the pilot evaluation, was a situation with little control or adult attention. Consequently, there was a great difference in terms of the mode of delivery and micro context of the pilot program and that of the large-scale program.

The results of the pilot program showed significant gains in a number of cognitive and perceptual areas among the preschool children in the treatment group. The evaluation results in the research system were high in nonspuriousness because of the use of a powerful and rigorous design. However, the indisputable treatment effect of the pilot program in the research system was disappointing when applied to the generalizing system.

In 1974, 1,113 4- and 5-year-old children were randomly assigned to experimental and control groups in 12 day-care centers in rural and urban settings. Unlike in the pilot study, the viewing conditions in this large field experiment were not rigorously controlled and the number of children was greatly increased. The experimental groups viewed *Plaza Sesamo*, while the control group watched cartoons for a period of either six or twelve months.

The results of the large-scale experiment were disappointing. The exposure of children to *Plaza Sesamo*, some for up to a year, resulted in no significant gains in their cognitive and perceptual areas when compared with the control group children, who watched cartoons for the same length of time. The evaluators suspected that the delivery mode of the implementation environment may have caused the different results of these two studies. Because the mode of delivery and micro context in the pilot study were characterized by more adult attention from the monitors and research staff than in the large-scale experiments, attention or encouragement might be essential to facilitate the effects of *Plaza Sesamo*.

The study of *Plaza Sesamo* provides some indications that the design of program evaluation in a research system must keep the future generalizing system in mind. The purpose of a pilot study is not simply to test a relationship between program treatment and outcome; it must also pay attention to the issues of generalization.

Problems of Excessive Efforts to Unnaturally Maximize the Treatment Effect in the Research System

The case of *Plaza Sesamo* provides some support for a truism that the use of manipulation and control by an evaluator to ensure the internal validity of a program evaluation in the research system can lead to artificiality that hinders the generalizability of the evaluation results to the generalizing system. However, a less discussed issue is that the intentional efforts of the program staff to do the best they can to enhance the treatment effect may unintentionally move the research system further away from the generalizing system and make generalization more difficult.

As was illustrated in the previous section, a proposed social reform is frequently tried out in a pilot project in a research system with the results of an evaluation of the pilot used as a basis for launching a national program, or at least used to argue for the implementation of large-scale reform. Whether deliberately or not, there is a tendency for stakeholders such as program staff (and perhaps the evaluators as well) to exert extra effort in the hope of generating significant treatment effects in the pilot study in the research system. This is often referred to as the phenomenon of program "creaming."

The tendency of program creaming is that stakeholders have vested interests in the program, and they tend to put forth their best efforts in the research system to make the program look good. The positive impacts of the program help to enhance decision makers' reputations and also satisfy the coalitions involved. The positive impacts may also ensure job security for program managers and administrators.

By the same token, program staff may be highly motivated and concerned for their clients' welfare. This type of dedication to the success of the program is admirable but may mask what could be serious shortcomings in the design of the program. If the same efforts and dedication of program staff in the research system cannot be maintained in the generalizing system, the shortcomings of a program will later emerge.

This tendency of program creaming to press for desirable outcomes in the research system creates a problem in generalization when the evaluation results are applied to the generalizing system. This tendency may create circumstances that are highly irrelevant to and, therefore, difficult to use in the generalizing system. Gavin and O'Toole's (1975) evaluation of a "Basic Skills Training Program" for the hard-core unemployed has demonstrated this problem. This training program was administered to 295 hard-core unemployed who had been recently hired by an airline. The purpose of the training program was to upgrade the basic skills of these unemployed and increase their job longevity.

A barrage of measures involving verbal skills and arithmetic aptitude tests was administered to the trainees before and after the training.

Results of data analysis indicated that the program substantially enhanced both verbal and arithmetic skills.

These trainees, obviously, did well in the training classes. However, a follow-up study of the trainees' class performances and their later job performances is intriguing. The trainees who had scored high in the basic skills tests had shorter job tenure and were more likely to terminate their jobs than those who scored low. Similarly, the high-scoring trainees were more likely to come in late or call off work than those who scored low. Why should the trainees who were most successful in the training program be less successful on the job? The researchers proposed an explanation in terms of the discrepancy between research and generalizing systems. The training classes (research systems) created an "ego-enhancing atmosphere." Trainees with high test scores were often singled out by instructors and company representatives and they were more likely to experience enhanced self-esteem. Obviously though, this ego-enhancing atmosphere was not present in the actual job situation (generalizing system). On the job, the high-scoring trainees were not likely to be praised or supported. The transition from the ego-enhancing program atmosphere to the cold reality of the work world did not elicit continued good job behavior.

Sometimes even the participants are proud to participate in a pilot program and make special efforts to demonstrate that they are "good" participants. This process has been vividly described in the Relay Assembly Test Room Study, which is one of the famous Hawthorne studies (Roethlisberger and Dickson, 1939). The purpose of this experiment was to test whether physical conditions such as rest periods, length of working hours, and free lunches have an impact on productivity.

Six female workers were selected for the experiment. However, the special attention they received from top officials and researchers during the experiment introduced an unanticipated factor. The friendly and supportive atmosphere created within this small working group by the attention and interest of others soon raised the productivity of the workers regardless of changes in the actual physical conditions. As a result, the research system demonstrated an impressive increase in productivity that was clearly irrelevant to the normal work settings of the generalizing system.

The above discussions indicate the serious problems that can result from ignoring issues of generalization in a study. These issues are complicated, but, in general, selecting a research system relevant to the generalization system will always enhance the generalizability of an evaluation.

APPROACHES TO GENERALIZATION EVALUATION

Depending on whether the sequential strategy or the balancing strategy is used, different approaches can be applied to generalization evaluation. If the sequential strategy is proposed, an evaluator can apply the replication approach in generalization evaluation. The replication approach involves systematically repeating an evaluation a number of times in different dimensions of the generalizing system, such as participants and mode of delivery, that are of interest to key stakeholders to see whether or not the same evaluation results are obtained. The replication approach provides a direct answer to the issue of generalization. However, as discussed in the previous sections, the replication approach often requires heroic political support and a great amount of resources, time, and effort to carry it out.

Alternatively, the balancing strategy is less demanding in application. However, because the balancing strategy is based upon inferences drawn from existing information about the research system, generally speaking, it involves some uncertainty regarding the future state of the generalizing system. Approaches for extrapolating evaluation results from the research system to the generalizing system have to be developed and refined in order to reduce the uncertainty in policy-making processes. Four such approaches are discussed below.

Sampling Approach

The traditional view of how generalization can be enhanced is through sampling, and this has been briefly elaborated by Cook and Campbell (1979). Based upon the sampling approach, Cook and Campbell (1979) argue that three sampling models can be used to enhance generalizability:

(1) Random sampling for representativeness model. This traditional technique attempts to draw at random a sample from the potential target population of the generalizing system. According to Cook and Campbell, this random sample will be most representative of the target population.

(2) Deliberate sampling for heterogeneity model. This technique attempts to select a sample of persons from a wide range of classes, settings, and times. For example, a general educational experiment might be designed to include boys and girls from cities, towns, and rural settings who differ widely in aptitude and in the value placed on achievement

in the home settings. Cook and Campbell believe that this approach provides purposive quotas of persons with specified attributes, but the sample may not necessarily be representative of the target population.

(3) Impressionistic modal instance model. This technique attempts to select at least one modal instance that, on the average, represents the kinds of persons, settings, or times that typify the target population. For example, if the target population consists of a number of schools, then the modal school that most closely represents the other schools in size, achievement level, expenditures, and so on can be selected.

As noted by Cook and Campbell, these three techniques of sampling each suffer weaknesses. Random sampling for representativeness, though no doubt the most powerful model for generalizing, is the least feasible in research. The model of impressionistic modal instances, along with being the least powerful model, has the difficulty of determining what the actual modal instance is. Cook and Campbell argue in favor of the impressionistic modal instance model, though it is difficult when using this approach to determine which factors should be considered most relevant in selecting a modal instance. In addition, the other major problem of these sampling approaches is that each has a very restrictive scope. Techniques such as random sampling concentrate mainly on one dimension in the implementation environment—participants. Other dimensions, such as implementing organization and mode of delivery, are difficult to utilize without using more complicated and expensive sampling techniques.

Meta-Analysis

Another approach for dealing with generalization is meta-analysis. The primary purpose of meta-analysis is to calculate effect size from a number of studies that have focused on the same topic (Glass et al., 1981). Because these studies have often focused on the same topic in different settings and with different types of people, it may be argued that, in general, the effect size presents a generalizable result of the treatment effect.

However, the application of meta-analysis in generalization evaluation is hindered by at least two limitations. In order to do meta-analysis, the preexistence of a number of evaluations that deal with the same topic is required. If there exists no or few evaluations studies that directly tie the topic or issue of interest to key stakeholders, obviously, it is difficult to apply meta-analysis for the generalization purpose.

Furthermore, even if there are a number of studies on the topic or issues in which key stakeholders are interested, there are also no guarantees that meta-analysis will be helpful in dealing with issues in generalization. The research system focused on by the existing studies may be different from the generalizing system of interest to key stakeholders. For example, the existing studies may have been carried out by using dimensions of the research system such as the suburban middle class, but the key stakeholders' concern is with the dimensions of the generalizing system that affect the poor in the ghetto. These two limitations need to be overcome to use meta-analysis effectively in generalization evaluation.

Theoretical Abstraction Approach

Cornfield and Tukey (1956) argue that there are two types of generalization. The first is *statistical generalization*, which is achieved through random sampling. The second is *nonstatistical generalization*, which is achieved through knowledge of a research area. As Cornfield and Tukey (1956, pp. 912-13) put it:

> In almost any practical situation where analytical statistics is applied the inference from the observations to the real conclusion has two parts, only the first of which is statistical. A genetic experiment on Drosophila will usually involve flies on a certain race of a certain species. The statistically based conclusion cannot extend beyond the race, yet the geneticist will usually, and often wisely, extend the conclusion to (a) the whole species, (b) all Drosophila, or (c) a larger group of insects. This wider extension may be implicit or explicit, but it is almost always present.

Cornfield and Tukey's idea of nonstatistical generalization is labeled as the "theoretical abstraction approach" and is defined and elaborated as follows: The theoretical abstraction approach extrapolates from the evaluation results obtained in the research system to a lawlike theory or proposition that can be applied to the generalizing system. Mook (1983) points out that, in many basic studies, the generalizability of a research system is achieved through theoretical abstraction rather than representative sampling. Mook uses the Harlow and Harlow (1962) wire and cloth experiment to illustrate his point. In this experiment, infant monkeys were placed in cages with artificial mothers constructed of wire mesh with wooden heads and equipped with nipplelike feeding tubes. Monkeys placed in this isolation were subsequently found to be unable to interact with other monkeys. However, when the wire-mother was covered with soft terry cloth, the infant monkeys clung to it and appeared to derive some emotional satisfaction from the closeness. As a result, the negative effects of their social isolation were lessened.

Mook makes the argument that the baby monkeys used in Harlow's experiment were obviously not representative of the population. However, the results of the study have been used by many social scientists to generalize not only to monkeys but to human beings in their interpersonal socialization. Mook observed that social scientists usually do not dismiss these findings on the grounds that the experiment must first be replicated in the jungle with a random sample of baby monkeys. Mook argues that the generalizability of this study was established through the use of theoretical knowledge.

Yin (1984) also makes the same argument that generalization can be achieved through case studies—not through statistical representation but through some broader theory. Yin (1984) cited Jacob's (1961) study of urban planning, which is based mostly on experiences from New York City. Using this case study, Jacob abstracted the basic elements common to urban settings and formulated a general theory. Nonetheless, the theory she abstracted from her New York study is generalizable and allows many planners in other cities to deal with various issues in urban planning.

The theoretical abstraction approach broadens the traditional thinking on generalization. In addition, it helps broaden the range of useful research designs and provides a promising strategy for case studies and other types of research using nonrepresentative samples. However, the use of the theoretical abstraction approach obviously requires a thorough knowledge of the research area. The specific strategies for, and implications of, using this approach are in need of further development.

Dimension Resemblance Approach

Another approach proposed by the theory-driven perspective, which is perhaps more applicable to program evaluation, is the dimension resemblance approach. This approach postulates that the relationships among treatments, program processes, and outcomes are conditioned by the treatment structure and implementation environment. Accordingly, the generalizability of a program evaluation depends on whether its research system shares an essential resemblance to the implementation environment and treatment structure of the generalizing system. The research system has a high generalizability to the generalizing system if there is a high resemblance between the two systems in terms of the dimensions of the implementation environment and the treatment structure; otherwise, the generalizability of the research system is low.

For example, where the program implementors of rehabilitation programs for juvenile delinquents in the research system are professional, but the implementors of the future program will be community volunteers or paraprofessionals, the generalizability of the evaluation results is low. However, if the program will be carried out by professionals in the generalizing system as well, then generalizability will be high. This principle can be applied to other relevant dimensions of the implementation environment. In other words, the dimensions of the implementation environment provide a framework that evaluators and other program stakeholders can use to plan a highly generalizable program or to assess the generalizability of other program evaluations.

The conceptual framework of the dimension resemblance approach is also general enough to incorporate other approaches. If the particular dimensions permit the use of sampling approaches or theoretical abstraction approaches, these other approaches can be used in the framework of the dimension resemblance approach to further enhance generalizability.

There are three techniques for specifying generalization in the dimension resemblance approaches: explicit generalization, implicit generalization, and dimension test approaches. These techniques are discussed in detail in the following sections.

EXPLICIT GENERALIZATION

This strategy entails investigation of the relevant implementation environments and treatment structure in the generalizing system and systematic incorporation of their features into the evaluation design in a research system. More specifically, explicit generalization requires an evaluator to examine the generalizing system in terms of its treatment structure and other relevant dimensions of the implementation environment, such as participants, implementors, delivery mode, implementing organization, interorganizational relationships, micro context, and macro context. When planning the research system, these features can then be systematically incorporated.

The application of the explicit generalization strategy will be easier to understand by comparing two research projects that focus on similar social programs: one that deals with issues of generalization and one that does not. Luckily, two such pairs of studies are available for this purpose.

The LIFE and TARP Experiments

The first pair of studies for discussion consists of the LIFE experiment (Lenihan, 1977) and the TARP experiment (Rossi et al., 1980). Both of these studies attempted to evaluate programs designed to help ex-convicts make successful transitions to civilian life by providing limited financial aid in the form of unemployment benefits for short periods. Both studies utilized a strong randomized experimental design.

The major concern of the LIFE experiment was nonspuriousness in the research system, and the design and strategies of this study were intended to address this issue. The randomized experiment was utilized to eliminate possible confounding sources. The sample for this study, 500 ex-prisoners, was deliberately selected from a high-risk group of males under the age of 45 with multiple convictions and at least one arrest for a property crime. The rationale for selecting this sample was that the use of a high-risk group was more likely to detect a strong treatment effect. The program was implemented by an energetic and dedicated research team. The results of this study indicated that financial aid decreased arrests on charges of theft but had no impact on employment.

Despite the merits of the LIFE experiment's research design, the results were ambiguous for generalization. One of the major problems was the participant dimension. The selection of a high-risk group for the sample excluded a large proportion of prison inmates who have important implications for policy interests in the generalizing system. Further, the program was run by a committed research team, whose efforts and enthusiasm were difficult to match by regular administrators in state and federal agencies. The evaluation results provided by the LIFE experiment alone were difficult to utilize due to this uncertainty in generalizability.

The TARP experiment also used the randomized experiment model to deal with nonspuriousness. However, this did not hinder the evaluators from using explicit generalization to enhance further generalization. With the generalizing system in mind, the TARP experiment expanded the sample selection of participants to cover the full range of released prisoners and not just the high-risk group.

Also, because the TARP evaluators anticipated that the program would be carried out by one of the federal or state agencies and not by a social science research group, the implementors were selected from regular administrative staff. As the program was to deal with unemployment insurance benefits covering released prisoners, the most likely implementing organization in the future would be the state employment service. To enhance generalization in the implementing organization dimension, the TARP treatment was delivered by state employment services under the existing rules and regulations of the unemployment insurance program. In this sense, because of the researcher's concern with explicit generalization, the TARP experiment was able to deal with issues of generalizability in addition to issues of trustworthiness.

Studies of Psychotherapy Versus Behavior Therapy

Another informative pair of studies that illustrates the issues of explicit generalization are Paul's (1966) and Sloane et al.'s (1975) studies of psychotherapy versus behavior therapy.

Paul (1966) argues that research that compares alternative approaches to therapy is subject to many disturbances from extraneous factors such as differences in patients' characteristics, therapists' characteristics, therapeutic circumstances, therapist and patient interaction, and the external environment. In emphasizing nonspuriousness, Paul indicates that a tightly controlled laboratory experiment and clear criteria for selecting the sample and for assessing the outcome are required in order to assess the relative effectiveness of psychotherapy and behavior therapy.

In his study, he deliberately manipulated and controlled the treatment structure and implementation environment in the laboratory setting in the following ways to ensure nonspuriousness in the research system:

(1) Outcome variable. Paul decided to focus only on speech anxiety, as this problem is widespread enough to make recruitment of a large research sample possible. More important, it can easily be defined in terms of observable and measurable behavior, and improvement can also be objectively assessed.

(2) Participants. Among 710 students enrolled in a public speaking class, Paul deliberately selected a highly homogeneous group of 97 students as the sample for study. They were similar in terms of age,

class backgrounds, and intelligence. Paul indicated that the selected subjects were "good bets" for the research purpose.

(3) Research design. These subjects were randomly assigned to one of five groups: (a) psychotherapy, (b) behavior therapy, (c) attention placebo (given nontreatment activities such as attention, care, warmth, faith, and so on for dealing with the subjects' problem), (d) no treatment (this group received an interview and a promise for treatment later), or (e) no contact (this group never received any communication from the project at all).

(4) Implementation. The treatments were delivered by five of the area's most highly regarded psychotherapists. In addition to their specialty, these psychotherapists were also briefly trained by Paul in the use of behavior therapy.

(5) Treatment structure and mode of delivery. Each therapist in Paul's study was required to use various treatment modalities with the patients. This is unusual in clinical settings.

With Sloane et al. (1975), the therapists were allowed to practice one type of treatment (behavior therapy or psychotherapy) persistent with their expertise in actual clinical settings. Furthermore, because different patients came to the therapists with different problems, treatments were not strictly standardized to an identical procedure.

At the end of four months, all of the experimental subjects were evaluated by Sloane et al., using a variety of instruments and assessors, including the patients themselves and people close to them. All three treatment groups had improved, but the psychotherapy and behavior therapy groups had improved more than the waiting list control group. Basically, no significant difference between the outcome of psychotherapy and behavioral therapy was found.

Approximately one year after the initial assessment, most of the participants in the research sample were reevaluated. All of the patients had had the opportunity of receiving additional therapy, and many of them had done so, which made the comparisons less certain. Generally, the results were similar to the previous conclusions.

The above comparison indicates that there is certainly a discrepancy between the studies of Paul and Sloane et al. Paul's study shows that behavior therapy is more effective than psychotherapy, while Sloane et al.'s study finds no such difference. The answer to the question of which of these evaluation results should be used will depend on the nature of the generalizing system in question.

For academic interests, Paul's study is rigorous and provocative in the development of theory. However, when clinical settings constitute the generalizing system, Paul's study is difficult to utilize. Its treatment structure, outcome, and implementation environment were manipulated and controlled and too far removed from clinical practice to allow extrapolation of the evaluation results. In contrast, Sloane et al.'s study applies explicit generalization to outcome generalizability by using actual outpatients with regular treatment procedures, therapists, mode of delivery, outcomes, and so on that resemble the generalizing system. It should be noted that the enhancement of generalizability in Sloane et al.'s study did not mean that nonspuriousness was greatly sacrificed. Although their study is not as tightly controlled as Paul's, the overall quality of their study in terms of design, measurement, and data analysis certainly makes it a credible example of evaluation research.

IMPLICIT GENERALIZATION

In spite of the high desirability of the explicit generalization approach, an evaluation frequently cannot duplicate the major dimensions of treatment structure and implementation environment in the generalizing system because of ethical, administrative, time, or resource constraints. For example, a program may be created to help the hard-core poor. However, the hard-core poor are difficult to locate and to recruit for a program in time to meet the deadline for a policy decision. The program may have to be tested on the more accessible and cooperative poor, whether they are hard core or not, and on the basis of those results decisions may have to be made as to whether it would be effective with the hard-core unemployed. This type of generalization may be thought of as implicit generalization.

Implicit generalization occurs when a researcher cannot select or formulate the treatment structure or some other relevant dimension of the implementation environment of the generalizing system in the research system. In these circumstances, evaluators may draw from their existing knowledge and experience and provide stakeholders with information about how, given the difference in treatment modality or various implementation environment dimensions, the results of program evaluation in the research system can be applied to the generalizing system. The extrapolation process in implicit generalization requires some use of the theoretical abstraction approach discussed in a previous section.

Consequently, the power of implicit generalization depends on how well we know the subject matter in terms of the treatment and implementation environment in order to extrapolate conclusions. For example, Harlow and Harlow's (1962) work with monkeys showed that, when raised in isolation, they developed abnormal behavior. The generalization of these findings to human behavior must, of course, be done with caution. However, all the existing theories and knowledge of human development suggest that human potential depends even more on social integration than is the case with monkeys, so the application of Harlow's findings to human beings can be made—although cautiously.

However, for many intervention programs, there may not be any relevant existing theory or knowledge to support a strong argument in favor of implicit generalization. Nevertheless, evaluators should not focus solely on the research system, leaving the stakeholders to decide for themselves what the implications of the evaluation results may be for the generalizing system. Using existing knowledge or experience, evaluators should point out the potential problems, limitations, or issues that should be considered in generalizing the evaluation results. In other words, evaluators should use their expertise to provide audiences with information on how to use or apply evaluation results.

This issue is well illustrated in a study by St. Clair et al. (1975) in their discussion of the use of the Daily Staff Log. The Staff Log, a monitoring instrument designed to improve efficiency and effectiveness, is a self-reporting instrument describing staff hours spent in direct patient and collateral contact, clinical backtime, consultation, education, and administration. This monitoring instrument was used daily in a mental health center for one year. A before-and-after comparison of the center using this monitoring system revealed that program efficiency was increasing in the following three areas: (1) The number of therapy sessions increased by 49%, (2) the amount of staff time available for clinical activities for paraprofessionals increased from 72% to 79%, and (3) the amount of money billable to the state's medical assistance program increased by 17%.

The successful application of this program may have depended on the special implementation environment of the generalizing system. St. Clair et al., using implicit generalization based upon their knowledge of and experience with the program, pointed out that the relevant dimensions of the implementation environment have to be considered when applying the program to the generalizing system. There must be a deep commitment at the highest administrative level to the value of logging staff time or the result will be the "garbage-in/garbage-out" phenomenon. Unless the program's top administrators seriously enforce the program, valid data are difficult to obtain. The authors caution that the results of log data must be fed back frequently to staff so that they can improve their performance. More important, the log data should also be used to provide positive reinforcement for staff who are doing well, rather than only to punish those who are doing poorly.

In terms of the participant dimension, St. Clair et al. point out that the success of the program is proportional to the degree to which the staff realizes that their contributions to the log are valuable in improving the delivery of care in their own clinics. To win the professional staff's trust and cooperation, it is necessary to have in-service training on the value of such data for decision making and for improving the quality of patient care.

DIMENSION TEST APPROACH

A particular dimension in the implementation environment may involve different alternatives. Sometimes program stakeholders' interest is to understand the relative pros and cons or consequences among variations or alternatives in a dimension. In the participant dimension, for example, a participant could be young or old, male or female, highly educated or uneducated, and so on. In the implementor's dimension, the implementor can be professional or a volunteer, experienced or inexperienced, highly motivated or poorly motivated, and so on. Sometimes the program treatment effect may be contingent on certain alternatives or types of the dimensions. That is, a program may only work for young people and not for old people. Or a program may be implemented effectively by either professionals or volunteers.

The dimension test approach involves deliberately varying the alternatives within a dimension of the implementation environment and/or the treatment structure in question and testing which alternative facilitates or hinders program effectiveness. The information obtained from the dimension test is valuable in the future application of evaluation results in the generalizing system. It allows program stakeholders to know the viable options and alternative strategies for constructing the treatment and for managing the implementation environment. This approach begins with an identification of relevant dimensions in the implementation environment that are of concern to stakeholders or that are regarded by evaluators as essential for further investigation. Then the alternatives within each dimension are systematically varied to test whether program processes and outcomes are affected. For example, if stakeholders feel it is important to know the relative differences between using regular teachers or trained volunteers in tutoring disadvantaged students, then both types of implementors can be included in the evaluation in order to compare their performances.

The dimension test approach usually involves extra effort from the evaluator and stakeholders. It requires variations in the implementation environment dimension. This means that the same program treatment must be implemented for each of the alternatives, that is, different types of participants, implementors, modes of delivery, and the like. The inclusion of two or more alternative dimensions will require more resources, efforts, and cost in implementing and evaluating a program. However, as will be shown in the following discussion, the dimension test provides information useful in understanding the ingredients in the implementation environment. This type of knowledge is specifically necessary for enhancing the effectiveness of the program treatment.

The dimension test requires the formal examination of those implementation environments that may provide the optimum in program processes and outcomes. Such information is also particularly useful for avoiding errors of over- or undergeneralization.

The quantitative analysis of the dimension test is exactly the same procedure as that used for detecting interaction effects. We wish to see whether the effects of the program treatment depend upon particular types of, or variations in, modes of the implementation environment. In qualitative analysis, the research procedure involves the observation of comparable program activities across two or more modes of the implementation environment.

The detailed procedures for applying the dimension test and dealing with issues of generalization may be more easily grasped by discussing actual research examples in each dimension of the implementation environment.

Participant Dimension

If stakeholders and evaluators are concerned about how program processes and outcomes may be contingent upon the type of participant, a dimension test of the pertinent subgroups in the participant dimension would be useful for future planning and improvement of the program.

A study by Crano and Messe (1985) evaluating the effect of an electric rate demonstration experiment provides an excellent example with which to illustrate a dimension test of the participant dimension. In this experiment, the treatment was an innovative electric rate in which the cost of electricity to consumers varied as a function of the time of day during which it was used. The treatment groups received different versions of the innovative electric rates, while the control groups received either a standard flat rate or a seasonal rate. However, because of the complexity of the treatment, Crano and Messe believed that the treatment effect might be contingent on the participants' knowledge of the complex features of the treatment. Information on participants' knowledge of the treatment was also collected.

A standard statistical analysis assessing consumption differences between treatment and control groups showed the treatment had no influence on the participants' usage behavior. However, when information on the participants' knowledge of the treatment was added into the analysis, it was found that the treatment had a substantial impact on those participants who had understood the complex features of the treatment. A similar finding has also been reported in Nicholson and Wright's study (1977). When the treatment of an intervention program is complex, participants' comprehension of the treatment should perhaps be an important participant dimension factor for consideration in program planning and/or evaluation.

A study by Quinn et al. (1984) on the cost-effectiveness of a mathematical instructional program provides another example to illustrate a test of the participant dimension. Quinn et al. suspected that different types of instruction may have different impacts on different types of students in terms of benefits or costs. Usually pupils differ in their ability to benefit from particular types of instruction. For elementary grade pupils, a significant portion of any difference in ability might be attributed to the home environment, particularly the interaction between adults and children in the home. This, in turn, may be partly a function of the family's social status. In their evaluation of instructional programs, Quinn et al. formally examined the interaction between pupils' socioeconomic status (SES) and program treatment (instructional program).

Two math instruction programs for fifth-graders were compared: a traditional text-oriented approach (called Text-Math) and the Goal-Based Educational Management System Proficiency Mathematics approach (GEMS Math). GEMS is an innovative program that heavily emphasizes individual instruction. Unlike the traditional approaches, GEMS Math introduces new math concepts by means of pictorial representations before presenting them in an abstract form. The pupils also generate stories and pictures to demonstrate their understanding of the concepts. The outcome variable of math achievement was measured by the Iowa Test of Basic Skills (ITBS) and a locally developed District Math Test (DMT).

The overall analysis of the programs found that GEMS Math was more cost-effective than Text-Math. However, when the cost-effectiveness of the two approaches was examined for pupils at different SES levels, some interesting qualifications appeared. For high-SES groups, Text-Math was moderately more cost-effective for both mathematical achievement measures. Furthermore, high-SES groups did well with both methods. For lower-SES groups though, there was a dramatic shift in favor of GEMS Math. Text-Math had little or no positive impact on the achievement scores of these pupils. The results of structuring the dimension test into this evaluation provided decision makers and potential implementors with valuable information about where and how different instructional approaches can be most effectively implemented.

Implementor Dimension

A program may be more effectively implemented by certain types of implementors than others. A dimension test on the implementor dimension can provide information on relative effectiveness of different types of implementors.

The extent to which the success of a program is conditioned by the characteristics of its counselors or therapists is illustrated by Valle's (1981) study. Valle set out to discover the relation of a counselor's interpersonal skill to the success of an alcoholism treatment program. A group of 247 patients, all first admissions to an inpatient hospital-based alcoholism treatment program, were randomly distributed among eight counselors. The patients were "recovering alcoholics" between the ages of 37 and 58 and represented a wide range of education, training, and life experience. The eight counselors were considered the primary therapists and spent the most time with patients as well as coordinating other treatment services. The counselors were tested in four areas of interpersonal functioning: empathy, genuineness, respect, and concreteness. Concreteness if the ability to be specific, direct, and on target in counseling response. Respect, or positive regard, is the ability to convey to listeners that they are persons of worth. This is usually communicated through warmth and understanding. Genuineness is similar to sincerity and opposed to role-playing and phoniness. Empathy, which builds on these three qualities, is the ability to respond to feelings and to the reason for feelings in a manner that communicates understanding. It includes the concepts of reflection of feelings and of diagnostic insight and understanding and is considered the most important of the four areas.

The counselors' scores in these areas were combined into a global score between 1.0 (effectively nonfunctional) and 5.0 (optimally functional). The rate of their patients' relapses were evaluated according to the counselors' scores after 6, 12, 18, and 24 months. The patients of counselors with high scores had much lower relapse rates than the patients of counselors with low scores. At 24 months, the patients of low-scoring counselors relapsed much more frequently than the high-scoring counselors' patients.

Valle's study provides strong evidence that the characteristics of implementors, such as their level of interpersonal functioning, make a great deal of difference in treatment outcomes in an alcoholism treatment program. This information may be useful for the therapist for self-improvement or for decision makers to know how to improve programs in the future.

Delivery Mode

In many situations, the delivery mode of the program treatment can be structured in different ways that can directly or indirectly cause varying program results. It is beneficial for the users of evaluation results to know whether or not the effectiveness of the program treatment is contingent upon a particular delivery mode.

A study of a smoking cessation program by Best et al. (1977) illustrates the importance of the delivery mode dimension. The program's treatment sessions included oversmoking techniques, to create a conditioned adverse reaction to smoking cigarettes, and the development of coping techniques by the use of various behavioral self-management strategies. However, based upon the previous literature, Best et al. (1977) argued that program effectiveness in a smoking cessation program may be conditioned by structural variables related to the mode of delivery: the size of the treatment group and the availability of phone support between sessions.

To test these hypotheses, their evaluation design was systematically varied in terms of group size and phone support.

An overall analysis of the program found that the program treatment was successful. Further analysis of the data indicated that group size conditioned the treatment effect. The smaller the size of the group, the greater the reduction in cigarette smoking. But, surprisingly, phone support tended to increase the relapse rate. As self-control is the basis of this treatment, Best et al. (1977) speculated that phone support might undermine or discourage self-control. Information on delivery mode such as group size and phone support can be used in the future planning of a smoking cessation program.

Another informative study to illustrate the importance of considering delivery modes when evaluating a program is Bently et al.'s (1983) evaluation of the Rural Dental Health Program (RDHP). This study was designed to investigate the effect of enriched dental health programs on children's utilization of dental services. However, the evaluators believed that the effect of the dental education program may depend on delivery modes, that is, how the dental services were provided. Three delivery modes based upon accessibility were included in their study: team, solo, and community. Children assigned to team and solo dental treatments were provided with services from a school-based mobile dental care unit that visited each school annually. The dentist assigned some children to expanded-function dental assistants in the team mode, while giving another group of students the solo mode of care with a chairside assistant. The parents of children in the community group were responsible for making appointments and taking their children to participating dentists, although the care was free of cost. Each delivery mode contained a treatment group that participated in an enriched dental health program and a control group without the treatment. The children were randomly assigned to the different treatment conditions.

Evaluation of the RDHP found that the effectiveness of dental health education programs depends on the delivery modes. Children receiving enriched dental health with delivery modes such as team and solo care were more likely to visit a dentist frequently. In contrast, the positive effect of dental health education did not show up when the delivery mode was community. The above finding provides very useful information on how to design this type of program. Clearly, mere encouragement of students to place high values on dental care is not enough. In the community mode, the parents may not have had the time or interest to bring these children to have dental care even when it was free. Similarly, merely making dental care available to children did not ensure its utilization if children were unconcerned about their dental health. The program was effective only when dental health education was coupled with the school-based dental care delivery mode.

Based upon the discussion of the research examples above, the relationship between the dimension test and generalization can be more clearly seen. If treatment processes and outcomes are found to be contingent upon a particular type of implementation environment, then the generalizability of these processes and outcomes is narrow and restricted. That is, the treatment processes will only be effective in one particular mode of the implementation environment. However, if the treatment processes and outcomes do not depend upon a specific implementation environment, then it is possible to generalize across alternative implementation environments. This means that the treatment processes will be effective within a broad range of alternative implementation environments.

This is well illustrated by a study of alternative telecommunication systems as tools for improving primary medical care (Dunn et al., 1977). Modern communication technology has been suggested as one way to improve access to medical care in areas with few physicians per capita. Moreover, there are a number of technologies available: two-way color television, two-way black-and-white television, two-way frame television, and a hands-free telephone. Each has advantages and disadvantages in terms of cost, convenience, and audiovisual capacity.

It was important for hospitals to determine whether the use of one or another communication mode would have an effect upon treatment results. Dunn et al. (1977) set out to provide this information. Their test sample included patients who had sought help at a community health center and had received additional examinations by means of remote communication technology. The physicians were rotated from system to system so that each had equal time on the different systems. Outcomes were evaluated in terms of diagnosis, number of tests required, length of diagnostic interviews, and type of patient management proposed.

The researchers' analysis showed no significant differences between the systems in terms of the quality of primary care. They also found that the patients expressed no real preference for any particular system. Dunn et al. concluded that the advanced communications were no more effective than a simple telephone. Because the treatment processes and outcomes are not contingent upon the mode of communication, it is not necessary for hospitals to invest in high-cost communication technology to improve access to medical care.

Implementing Organization

The effect of program treatment may depend on characteristics of the implementing organization. Different structures and processes within an implementing organization may influence program processes and outcomes. If decision makers have an option of designing or choosing different types of implementing organizations, the use of dimension tests to assess which type is more effective will be useful for stakeholders in making program improvements in the future.

A study by Trites et al. (1969) on designing nursing units provides a good illustration of how to apply dimension test approaches to assess alternative implementing organizations. Nursing units in hospitals have traditionally been constructed as linear designs such as single corridor or double corridor. However, because radial-shaped designs have become popular and are used in intensive care units, there have been intensive debates among stakeholders regarding the applicability of the radial design to nursing units for general care. Radial-shaped units are designed with a nurses' station in the center area and are arranged so that patients' rooms circle the station. In theory, the radial design has the following advantages over linear designs for making nursing tasks easier: reducing travel time and fatigue of the nursing staff, permitting ongoing direct observation of the patients from the nurses' station at a minimum effort, and enhancing more bedside care of patients by nurses. These improvements on spatial, physical, and organizational designs may, in turn, improve nursing functions and service. A new hospital facility with three physical designs (radial, single corridor, and double corridor) was constructed to provide an opportunity to evaluate these different designs.

It was found that the staff nurses assigned to the double corridor unit spent a total of 9.2 hours more time in travel each 24-hour period than did the nurses in the radial unit. In the single corridor unit, 9.7 hours more time was spent in travel compared with the radial unit. Furthermore, in terms of the total number of hours spent with patients during a 24-hour period, nurses on the double corridor unit spent 7.7 hours less time with patients compared with the radial unit, and those on the single corridor unit spent 11.2 hours less time with patients. It

was also found that the radial units had lower absenteeism, fewer
accidents, and fewer complaints from patients, relatives, and physicians.
This information has proved to be useful in designing new nursing units.

Interorganizational Relationship

A program may be more effective when carried out through one
type of interorganizational relationship than through others. If the
interorganizational relationship is pertinent to a program, the use of
the dimension test can provide useful information as to which type is
desirable for future program improvement. One good example to
illustrate this is Marvel's (1982) analysis of the implementation of the
Occupational Safety and Health Act of 1970.

Marvel's analysis focuses on implementation because the act permits
implementation to occur in two ways: federal operation of the program
(in 28 states) and state operation (in 22 states). Problems in the
implementation of federal programs are well known: goal discrepancies,
differences in influence and authority, and conflicts relating to resources
and communications. These tendencies toward noncompliance increase
as the complexity of the relation between implementing agencies
increases. Lack of direct authority channels between the federal
government and a state agency also adds problems. Effective implementation is less likely when the program has been formulated at a
different level of government from the level that must implement it.

Marvel's study is an empirical measure of the relative effectiveness
of the states and the federal government in implementing the same
federally formulated program. The first mode of implementation possible
under OSHA is entirely federal; ten regional offices have the power
to investigate, issue citations, and propose penalties. The second mode
of implementation is a state-developed and operated program that must
be "at least as effective" as the federal one. For the purposes of the
study, effective implementation was measured by the volume of
enforcement activity, inspections, violations, citations, and penalties.
Marvel found the federal programs to be more effective on this basis
than their state counterparts.

In evaluating the differences, Marvel focused on the nature of
intergovernmental relations. The data supported the hypothesis that
states make relatively fewer inspections of industries important to them,
showing a relationship between economic structure and political power.
State operators are thus more susceptible to forces working against the

full implementation of the program. Marvel concluded that consideration of the forces that will impinge upon local officials must be a part of program formulation. If the economic structure of a state forces local officials to weaken, then only federal implementation can be effective. Yet federal implementation of all programs is impossible. Implementation problems, therefore, must be considered and allowed for in the early stages of the policy process.

Micro Context

Although it is not directly part of the treatment environment, the micro context is the setting where the participants interact and, therefore, may affect program treatment. Applying the dimension test to the micro context should provide program stakeholders, decision makers, and program staff with information as to which would be most effective.

Ward's (1961) study illustrates this. Ward investigated the relationship between the family environments of participants in an alcoholism program and treatment outcomes. He expected that participants who experience satisfaction with and gain meaning from their family relationships would do better than those who do not.

The study sample consisted of the patients who reported that they were living with their families at the time of admission and who indicated some degree of residential and occupational stability. The quality of family relationships was evaluated by surveying the participants' general satisfaction with their family roles and, specifically, their relationship with their spouses and children, if any. The outcome was measured by a 44-item survey of psychological and behavioral functioning, which was administered five months after discharge. These 44 items were split into five categories: affective state, interpersonal attitudes, life satisfaction, drinking behavior, and predictions about future drinking.

Data analysis showed that patients who were satisfied with their family role drank significantly less during the three months immediately prior to follow-up than other patients. They also scored significantly higher on interpersonal attitudes. Relationships with spouses seemed to be more significant than relationships with children. Ward speculated that this is because parent-child relationships are more involuntary than spousal relationships and thus are less rewarding. Overall, however, it is clear that satisfaction with family roles is a significant predictor of favorable treatment outcomes.

Macro Context

Information on the macro environment provided by the dimension test reveals to which communities or societies evaluation results may or may not be generalized. McCrone and Hardy (1978) show that treatment effect may vary in different regions of the country, and therefore success of a national program must still be analyzed separately for use in each major area. McCrone and Hardy (1978) studied the ratio of black income to white income with respect to economic cycles in the United States and also with respect to the Civil Rights Act of 1964. The only relevant statistic regularly reported by the federal government is income for both white and nonwhite males, 14 years and older. As 90% of nonwhites are black, this statistic was used to show the economic status of blacks for the purposes of the study. McCrone and Hardy found that on a national basis improvement in the economic condition of blacks was not due simply to general economic conditions but was related to the Civil Rights Act. But several characteristics of this act made it seem appropriate to break down this result by region.

The Civil Rights Act of 1964 represented the first commitment by the federal government toward racial equality. It has a major influence on the South, because the primary focus of this program was on reducing overt, purposeful racial discrimination, which, though present in other regions, was greatest in the South. Inequality in incomes was also greatest in the South, and implementation of the program's civil rights policies was most vigorous there. McCrone and Hardy found that the apparent national improvement in the nonwhite income ratio was due to improvement in the South alone. While roughly half of the black population does reside in the South, improvement in the economic condition of blacks nationally will depend on additional efforts. The Civil Rights Act of 1964 has not affected the ratio of white to nonwhite income in the other regions of the country.

PART V

Composite Types

Normative and causative evaluations are neither antagonistic to nor incompatible with each other. Part V demonstrates that these two categories of evaluations can be integrated into composite types of evaluation, which are particularly useful when the basic types are not able to satisfy stakeholders' needs. Three composite types of evaluation are covered in this part. Normative treatment-impact evaluation, discussed in Chapter 12, integrates both impact evaluation and normative treatment evaluation. Normative implementation environment-impact evaluation, discussed in Chapter 13, integrates impact evaluation with the normative implementation environment evaluation.

12. Normative Treatment-Impact Evaluation

CONCEPT AND ISSUES

As discussed in Chapters 2 and 6, treatment is the essential force for generating changes in a program. For better understanding of the relationship between the nature of treatment and its effect, it is useful to integrate normative treatment evaluation and the impact evaluation to form a composite type of evaluation.

There are at least two strategies for integrating the two types of evaluation. The first strategy is called the "structural elaboration strategy." This strategy requires the evaluator and key stakeholders to systematically elaborate the normative treatment theory so that treatment components, treatment strength, or alternative treatment formats can be systematically examined. This can provide information indicating what treatment components or treatment strengths are essential to program effectiveness or what treatment formats are more effective than others. Thus the relative effectiveness of these patterns can be systematically examined. This strategy indicates that an evaluation can go beyond the traditional categorical assessment of program success or failure. The traditional evaluation tends to lump all the treatment and/or implementation elements together as a package. The results from such a package approach may be difficult to use. This approach fails to pinpoint aspects of the program responsible for success or failure, so one cannot generate suggestions for improvement. Traditional evaluation also fails to demonstrate the applicability of evaluation results to similar programs in the future. In contrast, in the structural elaboration strategy, the effective aspects of the program are pinpointed. This strategy indicates which parts of the program are relevant for future applications and which parts are not.

However, in spite of its merits, the structural elaboration approach is more expensive to carry out than the package approach. The elaboration of treatment components, treatment strengths, or alternative treatment formats in an evaluation implies the need to increase sample size, program staff, cost of treatment, and so on. In applying the structural elaboration strategy, it is useful for the evaluator both to provide alternative treatment structures or formats and to explain the merits and different costs of each type of evaluation from which key stakeholders may choose.

The second strategy is to incorporate the information on the treatment measured in the normative treatment evaluation into an impact evaluation. As discussed in Chapter 6, the normative treatment is not necessarily the treatment implemented in the field. If there is a discrepancy between the normative treatment and the implemented treatment, as will be discussed later in this chapter, it would be misleading to regard the normative treatment as the treatment variable proposed in the original plan. Under this condition, information on the implemented treatment is essential for understanding and assessing the treatment effect. This strategy provides a post hoc adjustment of those treatments that are not delivered appropriately during the implementation.

Bearing these two strategies in mind, the rest of this chapter will discuss the major types of normative treatment-impact evaluations and elaborate their implications.

TREATMENT STRENGTH-IMPACT EVALUATION

As discussed in Chapter 6, the effect of a treatment or an intervention on an outcome depends, in general, on the strength of the treatment or intervention. The strength of the treatment may have to reach a threshold level before its impacts will appear.

For example, the Giles (1978) study of school desegregation and the tendency of white families to move away from an integrated school district shows this threshold effect. Giles reports that the relationship between these two variables is far from linear. His analysis shows that, when white school districts have a black enrollment of under 30%, the white enrollment remains stable. But when black enrollment rises above 30%, the rate of withdrawal of white students increases exponentially. Without reaching some threshold level, the treatment impacts, whether positive or negative, will not appear.

Similarly, an alcoholism treatment program may be effective as a three-month program but not as a one-month program. In the same way, just because we know that three hours of counseling per week can help a client does not mean that one hour per week will simply be one-third as helpful. Specifying appropriate treatment strength is one of the most important issues in designing an effective program. An appropriate analogy might be the prescribed dosage of a drug in treating an illness. The correct quantity of the drug is crucial for the patient's recovery; too little may not be enough to have an effect, while too much may cost too much or even have negative effects. However, it is frequently the case that normative theory suggests that the treatment will have impacts but cannot specifically indicate the threshold level.

Evaluators and program stakeholders can jointly design alternative treatment levels in order to assess their relative effectiveness. For example, one of the major concerns of the Negative Income Tax Experiment (NIT) was to avoid harmful effects on family stability. The Aid For Dependent Children program tends to encourage marital dissolution due to its requirement that there be no male head of household present. Even without this requirement, NIT program designers were uncertain as to what level of transfer payments would be sufficient to have a positive effect on family stability.

The Seattle and Denver Income Maintenance Experiments (SIME/DIME) provided some possible answers to this problem (Groeneveld et al., 1980). In these experiments, the payments were designed on three levels, with the highest level being 140% above the poverty line. Evaluation showed that only the highest payment level evinced marital stability. Groeneveld et al. suggest that, for a national implementation of NIT, a generous payment level would probably have a major, positive effect on marital stability.

TREATMENT COMPONENT-IMPACT EVALUATION

As mentioned in Chapter 6, program treatment usually consists of a set of components. The normative theory may suggest that each of these components is useful but it is not clear how to effectively combine these components in the overall treatment structure. Some combination patterns may be highly selective, but others may not. A systematic assessment of these treatment patterns can show which treatment patterns are more effective than others.

There are two basic strategies for incorporating treatment component patterns into an evaluation: the package approach and the component approaches. Each strategy has its pros and cons. The strategy that is actually adopted may depend on the stakeholders' needs and the evaluators' judgment of how the evaluation results will be used.

Package Approach

The package approach includes all of the treatment components together as a package for those participating in the treatment group. If the design involves a control group (or comparison group), the control group receives either alternative treatment components or none at all. This strategy has been popular in designing program treatments. For example, in a study of the effectiveness of a Youth Consultation Services program designed to improve school performance (Borgatta and Jones, 1965), the program treatment consisted of a treatment package that included therapy and caseworker contact for the treatment group. The control group received none of the components of the treatment package. Similarly, in Foxx and Azrin's (1973) study of the effectiveness of an innovative program for toilet training, the package of treatment components included a distraction-free environment, manual guidance, and a variety of reinforcements for the young children. The integral package approach can also be found in many other program evaluations, such as the first-year evaluation of *Sesame Street* (Ball and Bogatz, 1970), the Performance Contracting Experiment (Gramlich and Koshel, 1975), and so on.

Because stakeholders such as program designers and program staff want to enhance program success, they often design and implement a package strategy to be able to add as many treatment components as they feel are necessary to maximize program success. The package strategy for designing program treatment has great appeal for them. Evaluators also prefer the package approach because it simplifies measurement of the treatment variable in the analysis. For example, a treatment variable can be a simple contrast between the treatment group and the control group in an analysis of variance or a dummy variable in regression analysis.

For example, in the Cambridge Somerville Youth Study (Power and Witmer, 1951), participants in the treatment group received diversified treatment components (such as psychiatric or medical attention, summer camp, and/or contact with various community services programs), but not all participants received the same components. For simplification of the analysis, despite their diversified treatment experiences, the treatment group was regarded in the analysis of treatment impacts as having received the same package.

In spite of its appeal to some stakeholders and evaluators, the package approach has its limitations. First of all, if the treatment package is found to be unsuccessful, it may be difficult to interpret or use the evaluation results. For example, do the failures imply that every component is useless or are some of the treatment components problematic and other components effective? Should we abandon the entire program? Would the correction of the problematic components effectively improve the program? Much useful information of interest to stakeholders may be unobtainable using the integral package approach. Even if the treatment package is successful, it may also cause some confusion in its future usage. Because it is not clear what the essential components are, it is unclear whether the evaluation results imply that a future application has to duplicate exactly every component in the program in order to create similar program success. It may be possible that some of the components are not useful or necessary and an exact duplication may waste resources.

The problems of the package approach can be avoided if the program evaluation is carried out two or more times to disentangle component effects. The package is tried first to find out whether it is effective. If it has the intended effect, then a sequential evaluation can be applied to identify the exact components that are essential for this effectiveness. Similarly, if the stakeholders' interest is mainly in the overall success of the program effectiveness rather than in program improvement, the integral package approach may be sufficient.

Component Approaches

Unlike the package approach, component approaches attempt to enhance the generalizability and usefulness of an evaluation study by pinpointing the essential, or problematic, components of a program. Generally, there are three component approaches. Each is based upon different assumptions about how the program treatment works.

Component Combination Approach

The component combination approach initially identifies a set of crucial treatment components. It then tests two or more combinations of these components, called "treatment modalities," to examine which treatment modalities are more effective than others in affecting program outcomes. This approach assumes that there is a minimum number of interactive components that must be combined in order to have the desired effect. The purpose of this approach is to examine these essential interactive components.

The Seaver and Patterson (1976) study of the impact of a fuel-oil-saving program illustrates the use of this approach in detecting the appropriate treatment modality. In response to the energy crisis in the winter of 1973-74, the government's strategies for requesting voluntary conservation (an information campaign and the mailing of letters to apartment dwellers) were not effective. Seaver and Patterson proposed alternative programs for reducing fuel-oil consumption. Two components were identified in the program treatment. The first component was the feedback of information to consumers as to their rate of oil use. In addition to the traditional delivery tickets that provide information on consumption rate, this treatment component provided an additional slip that contained three kinds of information: the rate of use during the current delivery period and during the same period of the previous winter, the percentage of increase or decrease in consumption rate and the resulting dollar savings or loss, and the resulting dollar savings or loss compared with what the customer would have paid if he or she had continued to use oil at the previous year's rate. The second component consisted of a commendation for reducing oil consumption. This component consisted of a decal saying, "WE ARE SAVING OIL" for those households that had reduced their rate of consumption.

To examine the minimum set of components for program treatment that were necessary to produce program impacts, three treatment modalities were designed:

Treatment Modality 1: A control group received the regular delivery ticket from the fuel-oil distributor.

Treatment Modality 2: In addition to the regular delivery ticket, a first treatment group received the information feedback component on their rate of fuel-oil consumption.

Treatment Modality 3: In addition to the regular delivery ticket, this second treatment group received both information feedback and the commendation for those who reduced consumption.

This study was carried out from February through May 1974, during an acute oil shortage when the government had requested all households to turn down their thermostats to 60 degrees. It was found that the group that received only the information feedback component (treatment modality 2) did not differ from the control group in terms of oil consumption. However, members of the group receiving information feedback and the commendation decal (treatment modality 3) significantly reduced their oil consumption compared with that of the other two groups. These findings indicate that in this program the information feedback alone was not enough to promote oil conservation. Information feedback and the commendation for reduced consumption had to be combined in order to be effective. Seaver and Patterson argued that the decal, added to the information feedback, may have provided the incentive of social recognition for consumers' efforts to save oil.

Another use of the component combination approach in program treatment design can be found in the study by Chen et al. (1988) of an antismoking program for changing adolescents' smoking attitudes, beliefs, and behaviors. This program consisted of three treatment components: a colorful comic book with an antismoking message, a video version of the comic book, and the comic book and video along with a letter given to the adolescents' parents in order to encourage discussions with their children about the problem of smoking. To detect which combinations of treatment components were most effective, four treatment modalities were utilized:

Treatment Modality 1 (control group): Members of this group did not receive the comic book, but they were given the before and after tests.

Treatment Modality 2 (comic book only group): Members of this group received the comic book and were asked to read it.

Treatment Modality 3 (comic book and discussion group): Members of this group were given the comic book and were asked to read it. In addition, they viewed the videotape and participated in a short discussion of smoking and health.

Treatment Modality 4 (comic book, discussion, and parental notification group): This group received the same treatment as the third group, but in addition they were given a letter about the comic book and asked to give it to their parents. The letter encouraged parents to help their child analyze the message presented in the comic book.

In general, Chen et al. found that the intensive treatment modalities, especially treatment modality four, attracted more of the students' interest and attention to the antismoking message.

The component combination approach provides information that can identify the necessary sets of components in order to affect program processes and impact. In the traditional treatment package approach, many components are arbitrarily added to the program packages without any empirical information regarding the usefulness of the additional components. The component combination approach can provide stakeholders with information on how to construct program treatment more efficiently and effectively.

However, the component combination approach also has its weaknesses. This treatment requires a drastic increase in the sample size because more groups are required for each modality. For example, there are six possible combinations in a treatment construct modality for investigating three treatment components. With a control group, this means a total of at least seven groups for testing all of the treatment modalities. This requires a much larger sample compared with the traditional package approach, which usually requires only two groups: one treatment and one control group. One way to alleviate part of this problem is to concentrate on those few treatment modalities that are most relevant to the stakeholders or have been shown to be important through experience and knowledge or on those that have been indicated by theory to be most viable.

Furthermore, although the cost of carrying out a component combination approach is higher than that of carrying out a regular impact evaluation, the component combination approach can detect some treatment components that are inexpensive to add but crucial to program effects. This information can lower the costs of running an effective program in the future. For example, in Seaver and Patterson's (1976) fuel-oil consumption study, the key to the success of the program was to add an inexpensive commendation decal to the information feedback.

Similarly, in Chen et al.'s (1988) study, a letter sent to parents turned out to be very effective in increasing teenagers' attention to the antismoking message. Again, there was minimal cost for adding this item to the program treatment. Through the use of the component combination approach, we may learn more about how to create an effective program treatment without greatly increasing the cost of the program. Identification of the necessary components for program efficiency or effectiveness enhances the generalizability of evaluation results. Future applications can focus attention on the major relevant interactive components but need not duplicate every aspect of the program.

Component Additivity Approach

Unlike the component combination approach, the component additivity approach assumes that treatment components act on the outcome variables in an additive fashion. That is, each component can have independent and separate effects on an outcome variable. A component can be added or left out without affecting the other components. Except for the assumption of additivity rather than interaction among components, the additivity approach shares the same advantage as the component combination approach in identifying the individual treatment components that are vital for program success or failure and in enhancing the generalizabliity of evaluation results.

The evaluation of paramedic programs by Eisenberg et al. (1979) is an excellent illustration of using the component additivity approach to design program treatment. The purpose of this study was to evaluate the effect of paramedic services on mortality from out-of-hospital cardiac arrest in comparison with existing emergency medical technician (EMT) services. Paramedic programs are emergency services whereby highly trained individuals can administer definitive procedures, such as defibrillation, endotracheal intubation, and perineal cardiac medications for out-of-hospital cardiac arrests. Paramedics receive up to 170 hours of training. On the other hand, EMTs are trained in a standard 20-hour course. They perform only basic life support techniques, such as cardiopulmonary resuscitation (CPR); they cannot provide definitive care.

A bivariate analysis of the data indicated that paramedic programs were superior to EMT services in terms of hospital admission and discharge rates. The findings suggested, generally speaking, that paramedic programs, as a whole, are more effective than traditional EMT programs.

Because no information was provided concerning which components were responsible for the effects, the interpretation rested entirely on speculation. The research would have been a package approach if the analysis had stopped here. Instead, Eisenberg et al. went further in identifying a set of crucial components and discovering which program components were essential and which were not in creating the desired effects. Some major components of the program treatment included in the analysis were the time lapse before initiation of CPR, the person or agency initiating CPR, the duration of CPR, the response time of the emergency agency, the time from collapse to definitive care, ECG rhythm (recording cardiac rhythm), and so on. A multivariate analysis of the treatment components was illuminating. First, the effect of the general experimental conditions (paramedic versus EMT services) disappeared after treatment components were controlled in the equation. Second, after holding other variables constant, only two essential components—time for definitive care and time lapse before initiating CPR—had substantial impact on admission and discharge.

Eisenberg et al. argued that paramedic programs are far superior to EMT services in terms of time to definitive care: the average time to initiate definitive care was 27 minutes for EMT compared with 8 minutes for paramedics. Paramedics take definitive care to the scene while EMT services have to transport the patient to the hospital for definitive care. In addition, the time lapse for initiating CPR was an important factor influencing program outcome. Eisenberg et al. indicated that new paramedic programs were not likely to succeed unless CPR could be initiated within 4 minutes. This example shows how treatment specification provides direct information regarding the exact components that are responsible for program effects. The interpretation of components essential for treatment effect, then, does not have to rely on speculation as it does in the integral package approach.

Identification of essential program components also provides important policy information for strengthening or improving programs whether they are proposed, new, or currently established. As shown in the Eisenberg et al. study, traditional EMT programs could be improved by training the EMT in defibrillation—even without certification—and in other definitive procedures. Additionally, because it was found that paramedic programs are not likely to succeed without the initiation of CPR within 4 minutes, the authors suggested that new EMT programs be improved through citizen training in CPR.

In spite of its usefulness in identifying crucial treatment components, the component additivity approach also has limitations. In order to test the additivity model, it is necessary to have sufficient variation in each of the treatment components. This normally requires a larger sample size than that required by the integral package approach. Furthermore, if there are high correlations among the components (multicollinearity), estimates of treatment effect will be biased.

Component Composite Approach

The component composite approach attempts to combine both the component combination and the component additivity approaches. This approach assumes that some components are interactive with each other while others are independent of each other. As a consequence, both interactive components and independent components are included in the evaluation equation. For example, an alcoholism treatment program may consist of three major components: role-playing, behavior counseling, and alcohol education. However, the evaluator and program stakeholders, based upon past experience or knowledge, might believe that role-playing interacts with behavioral counseling, thereby increasing the effects of both, while alcohol education acts independently in treating alcoholism. Both the interactive components and the independent components can be included in the same evaluation equation in order to evaluate the relative impact of each on the outcome variables.

TREATMENT VARIATION-IMPACT EVALUATION

A normative treatment evaluation can demonstrate the consistency or incongruency between the normative and the implemented treatment. If there is inconsistency, the information can be formatively fed back for improving implementation processes, as indicated in Chapter 7. However, due to circumstances such as timeliness or stakeholders' lack of interest, it is likely that the information obtained from the normative treatment evaluation may not be able to be used formatively. Nevertheless, under this condition, it is still crucial to integrate the information into the impact evaluation. If this is not done, the evaluation results will be misleading because of the variation between planned treatment processes and what participants actually received. The generalizability of the evaluation will also be jeopardized. Because the treatment measures do not reflect the actual treatment, it is likely that evaluation results and conclusions will be off the mark. This is a problem of construct validity; we may not have evaluated what we believed we were evaluating. Consequently, the evaluation will not be serving the needs of program stakeholders.

Furthermore, ignoring possible discrepancies between the planned and the implemented treatment will also aggravate problems related to spurious associations between variables. Such problems are easier to detect where the treatment design specifies the use of treatment and control groups. The treatment is then assumed to be a dummy variable where participants receive either the full planned treatment or none at all. For those who receive the treatment, it is assumed that all will receive the same strength and type of treatment.

However, if this assumption of uniform treatment is violated during the course of implementation, then the dichotomous measure of the treatment variable will not be a precise measure of the implemented treatment. In this situation, treatment strength becomes an important issue, even though the program designers may have originally intended that the treatment be uniform. Because the dichotomous measure of the treatment does not accurately reflect variation in treatment strength, the standard error of the estimate will increase, and this will reduce the statistical significance of the results.

Even the use of a strong research design such as the randomized experiment cannot eliminate the discrepancy between designed and implemented treatment and the problem of estimation of treatment effect. A good example is found in Dobson and Cook's (1980) study of ex-convicts in a job placement program. In their study, the control group consisted of ex-offenders who were in a regular job placement program called DARE (staffed by job coaches and developers). The treatment group was also provided with services, including the regular ones, along with an assigned need-specific resource person to help them. It was hoped that these specific services would increase the probabilities of job acquisition, extend job retention, and affect residential stability while at the same time decreasing the probability of recidivism.

There were three treatment groups distinguished by three different types of resource persons: citizen volunteer, worker, and VISTA paraprofessional. Clients were randomly assigned to treatment or control groups. However, examination of treatment implementation revealed that the strength of treatment received by the clients varied drastically within the treatment groups. About 41% of the clients in the treatment groups never received any of the services that were to have been provided by the program. Just over 30% of the treatment clients matched with a staff worker had had treatment initiated but had stayed less than the appropriate amount of time and did not have a sufficient number of hours with staff workers. In fact, only 5% of the clients received full program treatment. Dobson and Cook (1980) demonstrated in their research that a 10% increase in statistical power was obtained when the treatment was measured as a continuous variable instead of dichotomously as the program design intended.

When such variation exists in the strength of treatment received, and when treatment variables are measured by the traditional scheme (treatment versus control groups), the dichotomous measure will ignore the variation of treatment levels within treatment groups. Imprecise measurement of the treatment variable will lead us to obtain a greater standard error of estimate, thus decreasing the strength of the test. As a result, a Type II error (false negative) is likely to be committed in the test for significance. This is shown by Dobson and Cook's (1980) study. When the treatment variable was measured as the traditional, categorical variable (treatment versus control group), treatment had no effect on job acquisition. The outcome of the analysis implied that the program had failed. However, when the treatment variable was measured against the treatment strength received by the clients, some evidence of treatment effects emerged—the three treatment groups were superior to DARE in job acquisition.

The functional form of treatment strength can also be an issue in the treatment variation-impact evaluation. In evaluating a court-sponsored wife-abuser treatment program, Chen et al. (1988) found that the abusers in the treatment group had participated in the program differentially. Using a traditional dichotomous measure of the treatment variable (treatment versus control group) in the evaluation, the treatment failed to demonstrate any desirable impact. However, further analysis indicated that a relationship did exist between program attendance and recidivism, although this relationship was not linear. Only those defendants who attended 75% or more of the treatment sessions had decreased recidivism; others showed no impact.

As discussed in Chapter 6, control group participants may sometimes receive the program treatment or an equivalent. When this happens, using the traditional categorical measure to compare the treatment and control groups will create measurement error that biases the estimate of treatment effect (see Kmenta, 1986).

In evaluating the Individually Guided Education (IGE) program, Hall and Loucks (1979) discovered that this had happened. The purpose of IGE was the instructional reorganization of schools to facilitate individualized study. The treatment groups comprised 22 schools that had implemented the IGE organizational format. The same number of schools that had not adopted the IGE format were used as controls. These were matched with the treatment schools in terms of geographic location, socioeconomic factors, ethnic composition, and size.

Hall and Loucks reported that, when they used the planned treatment measure (IGE versus non-IGE schools) in their analysis, the program was found to have no significant effects on reading and mathematics. However, they found that individual teachers in the IGE schools implemented the IGE format at different levels. For instance, in some of the schools the teachers individualized their instruction, while in others they did not. Furthermore, the teachers in many non-IGE schools did individualize their instructions.

In substituting the implemented treatment variable for the planned treatment, and using a continuous measure of IGE implementation rather than a dichotomous measure, Hall and Loucks found that the program treatment did indeed have significant effects on the reading scores of second-graders and the mathematical scores of fourth-graders. These findings suggest that using the conventional measure for treatment and control group comparisons may be misleading.

The above discussion indicates that the treatment variation-impact evaluation attempts to solve the problem of treatment that was not maintained with integrity during implementation. However, because this is an ad hoc adjustment of treatment variation, selection bias may be a potential problem in this type of evaluation. Participants in the treatment group may self-select into various treatment levels, which, in turn, may be confounded with the estimation of treatment effect (Mark, 1983). This problem needs to be solved for better application of this type of evaluation. Nonetheless, the treatment variation-impact evaluation is an important but understudied area that deserves greater attention in the future.

TREATMENT VARIATION-IMPACT EVALUATION FOR DECENTRALIZED PROGRAMS

Program treatment as discussed in the previous sections is normally standardized. That is, program designers and/or decision makers design a standardized program treatment and formally ask the implementors in different locations to implement the same standardized treatment. However, in some federal programs, program treatment is deliberately unstandardized.

Some federal agencies provide only general guidelines and procedures, while the local managers and implementors are encouraged to select the relevant treatment components and treatment strengths they feel are appropriate for their local situations. This kind of program is called a "decentralized" program, because program treatment on the local level is varied in terms of program components and strengths.

This sort of planned variation has been used in the Follow-Through programs, which give local managers and administrators the authority to develop their own formats and implementation strategies. From the federal government's, program designers', and decision makers' viewpoints, decentralized programs have merits such as more responsiveness to the interests and needs of the local area, more flexibility in adjusting treatment implementation strategies to fit local requirements, and generally better ability to meet clients' needs. From the local agencies' viewpoints, Edwards et al. (1980) argue, the decentralized program is also attractive for the following reasons:

(1) Funding for local programs may be allocated to a jurisdiction according to needs.
(2) Local interpretation of program objectives may vary widely.
(3) Target populations are locally differentiated.
(4) Administrative organizations and strategies for service delivery vary at the local level.

In spite of its merits, the decentralized program may create disagreement between the federal government and the local agency regarding the nature of the program. For example, Head Start programs were national preschool programs and, as we have noted, were funded by the Office of Economics and Development (OED) and established as decentralized programs. Local centers were allowed great latitude in carrying out their programs (Smith and Bissell, 1970). The purpose of Head Start was to prepare children from disadvantaged backgrounds for entrance into formal education in primary schools. However, no specific treatment or techniques were required of local centers by OED to achieve the objectives. Each center differed not only in structure and curriculum but also in areas of emphasis, such as cognitive development, physical and mental health, and self-esteem.

Decentralized programs create great difficulty in their evaluations. Treatment components vary from one agency to another. For example, in the Head Start program, program treatments in local centers were diversified in terms of class instruction, medical attention, nutrition, interpersonal communication, community visits, and so on. One method traditionally applied with comparative ease to such a problem is to adopt the integral package approach discussed in a previous section— if a control group can be found. Here, all the local agencies involved in program treatment are assembled as the treatment group, and the others are regarded as the control group, as in the Head Start evaluation by Westinghouse-Ohio University (Cicirelli, 1969). However, it is doubtful if the application of the integral package approach to decentralized programs can deal with the great diversification of local government characteristics and efforts in treatment implementation. Program effects, in such an evaluation, are likely to be obscured by poor measurement of program treatment.

Treatment variation-impact evaluation must be applied to identify and measure the essential treatment components and their strengths or local variations. This approach first identifies and measures the crucial components that vary among the local agencies. These variations of treatment components and strengths, in fact, offer an opportunity for identifying and measuring combinations of treatment variables among local agencies. These sets of treatment variables can be included in the evaluation equation to evaluate their relative effect on the outcome variables. Information on the differential effects of treatment components of decentralized programs not only increases precision in estimating treatment effect but also provides valuable information on identifying the important treatment components and their required strengths. Implemented treatment specification can be applied to decentralized programs even without control groups. This is useful because many federal programs are mandated to provide services to all persons who are eligible. There may be no existing control group or equivalent comparison group available for evaluation.

In their study of a federally subsidized small farm program that attempted to upgrade small farm operations, Edwards et al. (1980) provide a useful example for illustrating the implemented treatment specification of a decentralized program without control groups. Although the common program goal was to increase the yearly agricultural sales of small farmers, local administrators and program leaders emphasized different program activities in order to achieve the program goal. Some identified improvement in production and management practices as their most important objective, some emphasized marketing, and still others focused on the improvement of gardening and food production.

Furthermore, local authorities were different in terms of qualifications, education, farm experience, commitments, and so on. Strategies employed in implementation also varied. They included activities, such as meetings, demonstrations, and tours, as well as individual assistance, which for a specific farmer might consist of marketing, production assistance, or planning.

Edwards et al. included these treatment components along with other relevant variables in a multiple regression analysis. The results showed that several treatment components, such as the type of farmers participating, intervention strategies, and field staff characteristics, had substantial effects on raising farmers' sales volumes. Additionally, some interaction effects were found between treatment components and level of farmers' resources.

13. Normative Implementation Environment-Impact Evaluation

CONCEPT AND ISSUES

Evaluation results found in an impact evaluation may provide no hint of which sources in the implementation environment affect program failure or success. If key stakeholders are interested in understanding the relationship between the implementation environment and program effectiveness, then an impact evaluation has to be integrated with a normative implementation environment evaluation to form a composite type of evaluation that, in this book, is named "the normative implementation environment-impact evaluation."

The purpose of this type of evaluation is to apply the normative implementation environment evaluation either to strengthen program structure before an impact evaluation or to explain the findings of an impact evaluation. More specifically, there are two types of normative implementation environment-impact evaluations: summative and formative. In the summative type, information generated from the normative implementation environment evaluation is utilized not to improve the same program but to explain the failure or successes of the program found in the impact evaluation. Accordingly, the normative implementation environment is carried out along with or after the impact evaluation. To some extent, many classic implementation studies belong to this category. For example, Derthick's (1972) study of the New Town-in-Town program and Pressman and Wildavsky's (1973) study of the

Oakland manpower program showed, among other things, how the jurisdictional and coordinative requirements of multiagency programs can create uncertainty, confusion, delay, and eventually undermine the program.

However, a more creative application of the normative implementation environment-impact evaluation is a formative type. In the formative type, although the normative implementation environment evaluation is carried out in conjunction with the impact evaluation, the information obtained from the implementation environment is utilized for program improvement.

An important strategy for constructing the formative type requires an application of a strategy that, in this book, is called a "flow linkage strategy." This strategy refers to the carrying out of an impact evaluation and a normative implementation environment evaluation for the same program in alternating order so that problems in the implementation environment can be dealt with. The application of the flow linkage strategy emphasizes the evaluation as a continuous process rather than a one-shot study.

Ideally, in applying the flow linkage strategy, an evaluation can first carry out a normative implementation environment evaluation to provide feedback information on implementation in order to promote program improvement. After the program has been implemented appropriately according to the normative implementation environment evaluation, then an impact evaluation can be carried out to assess program impact. If the program is found to have no impact, then a normative implementation environment evaluation is applied again to diagnose the problems in order to allow for program improvement. Alternatively, the program may be found to have the planned impact. However, if key stakeholders want to understand how the implementation environment operates to further strengthen the program, then a normative implementation environment evaluation can also be carried out for this purpose. If needed, the evaluations can be repeated through two or more cycles.

However, many programs start out without any concern for issues related to evaluation (Nakamura and Smallwood, 1980). The evaluator may have no opportunity to plan a normative implementation environment evaluation first. Rather, the evaluator may be brought into the program when program effectiveness becomes a concern. Under this situation, the flow linkage approach can be applied in such a way that an impact evaluation can be carried out first to see whether the program works; if not, the normative implementation environment evaluation can be used to assess what was wrong in the implementation environment and to allow for program improvement. After corrective actions have been taken, an impact evaluation can then assess the improved program. Nevertheless, this composite type of evaluation suggests that the evaluator's task does not have to stop at the impact evaluation; she or he can proceed to the normative implementation environment if the program has no impact.

As will be shown later in this chapter, application of the formative or the summative type of evaluation requires the use of monitoring or scanning techniques discussed in Chapter 7. Furthermore, because the implementation environment of a program, as identified in Chapter 7, comprises seven dimensions, it is easier and perhaps more useful to illustrate the normative implementation environment-impact evaluation in each of these seven dimensions to promote better understanding of its nature and application. However, evaluators can combine two or more of the dimensions if necessary.

PARTICIPANT DIMENSION

Participants are the essential element in a program. If participants are not satisfied, or if they reject the program, the program is jeopardized. In a summative type, the normative participant evaluation is conducted along with an impact evaluation. However, information provided by the normative participant evaluation is used to explain the program failure or success found in the impact evaluation. For example, in the impact evaluation of *Feeling Good* (Mielke and Swinehart, 1976), an educational television program, the program was found not to be effective in motivating adults to engage in preventive health practices. However, the evaluation also covered some information on the participant dimension, which indicated that the program had difficulty in attracting the target groups. Among other things, the problem in this dimension then was used to explain the failure of the program.

For formative purposes, the normative participant-impact evaluation is useful in identifying potential problems in the participant dimension for program improvement. If there is no problem, then an impact evaluation can be instituted. If there are problems in the participant dimension, then normative evaluation results can be fed back to key stakeholders for program improvement. After the problems have been eliminated and the structure in the participant dimension has been made sound, then the impact evaluation can proceed.

For example, assume that key stakeholders of an innovative summer job replacement program for youngsters from low-income families ask an evaluator to perform an impact evaluation. However, both the key stakeholders and the evaluator may be unsure of how the new program can attract the youngsters or what kinds of problems may hinder youngsters from participating. In this case, a normative participant evaluation can be carried out to assess potential problems in the participant dimension. In other words, the normative participant evaluation may find that the youngsters have difficulty in getting to work because they must transfer buses in order to cross town to reach their work destinations, and their parents are really concerned about this problem. Based upon this information, key stakeholders and the evaluator can develop some strategies to solve the transportation problem in order to prevent participants from quitting the program. After the problem has been solved, then an impact evaluation can be carried out later to assess program effectiveness.

Alternatively, the normative participant-impact evaluation can be carried out by conducting an impact evaluation first. If the program is found to be unsuccessful, and if the evaluator and key stakeholders suspect that problems lay in the participant dimension, then evaluators can conduct a normative participant evaluation to understand why the problems happened and to help decide how to solve them. The evaluator can then recommend strategies for key stakeholders to make the necessary change. After program improvement, an impact evaluation can be carried out again for assessing program effectiveness.

This type of application has been illustrated by Lewin's (1947) study. During World War II, a factory in the United States realized the need to have female workers wear safety glasses to protect their eyes. The company put on an intensive campaign for the use of these glasses and announced potential punishment for noncompliance. Despite the company's efforts, an impact evaluation found that female factory workers still would not wear the glasses. Lewin was invited in to deal with the problem. Lewin conducted somewhat of a normative evaluation to understand the reasons for the workers' objections to wearing the safety glasses. Lewin discovered that the workers felt that the program had merits, such as the protection of one's eyes, and that they were willing to cooperate with the company's rule (driving forces), but they objected to the program because they felt that the glasses were too heavy and unattractive (restraining forces). The management of the company proposed to stiffen the penalty up to the point of firing and/ or imposing fines on those who failed to wear the glasses. According to his force-field model, Lewin felt that a more effective strategy would be to reduce restraining forces by using strategies such as substituting lighter frames for the old factory glasses, encouraging each worker to decorate her glasses as she wished, and holding a contest to determine the most attractive glasses. The management adopted and implemented Lewin's suggestions. After these program improvements were implemented, the workers' resistance was effectively removed.

IMPLEMENTOR DIMENSION

Problems in the implementation dimension can determine the outcome of a program. If the implementors do not have the quality or capability, or do not implement a program appropriately, a program will have no impacts. In the summative type of the normative implementor-impact evaluation, the evaluation is carried out along with an impact evaluation. Information obtained from the normative implementor evaluation, then, is used to explain the results of the impact evaluation. For example, the summative type of evaluation is illustrated by a study of a prisoner rehabilitation program conducted by Kassebaum et al. (1971). The result of the impact evaluation of the program indicated that the program had failed. However, the evaluators also carried out somewhat of a normative implementation evaluation and found many problems in the implementor dimension, such as that group leaders were unqualified or lacked training and therapy sessions were carried out inappropriately. The problems found in the implementor dimensions then were used by the evaluators as one of the important factors explaining the failure of the program.

In the formative type of the normative implementor-impact evaluation, information obtained from the normative implementor evaluation is used to improve the program. When the structure of the implementor dimension has been improved and made sound, an impact evaluation is carried out to assess the program's effectiveness. An anthropological study of an agricultural development program by Singh (1952) vividly demonstrates this type of evaluation. Singh describes how the Etawah Pilot Project succeeded in persuading Indian farmers to accept the practice of sanai green manuring when regular Indian government officials had failed.

"Sanai green manuring" is an agricultural practice in which a wheat field is planted with "san-hemp," or "sanai." The sanai is allowed to grow for a period of time then plowed under and allowed to decompose. Singh comments that "it was maintained by one authority that green manuring by turning under a standing crop of san-hemp might very well be considered the most economical way of supplying organic materials to the soil in canal areas" (Singh, 1952, p. 57).

However, for all this program's advantages, Indian farmers were slow to accept it. In order to rescue the program, a small group of American experts were hired to organize an action-oriented team to plan, carry out, and evaluate the program. An initial impact evaluation indicated that the program had failed.

After scanning the program implementation environment, these program planners were convinced that program implementors were a major reason for program failure. The average Indian farmer had a hostile attitude toward his country's government agents. The models most Indians had for citizen/government relationships were their own relationships with police and tax collectors. Naturally, they were skeptical of government officials. For their part, Indian agricultural agents tended to assume a paternalistic attitude toward the villages. Furthermore, the Indian agricultural bureaucracy was centralized, authoritarian, and rigid. Programs were planned at the highest level and implemented by decree, leaving implementors with little or no flexibility.

The program planners were convinced that alternative implementors had to be used in order for the program to work. Instead of involving government officials, they recruited their own program implementors— recent graduates from schools and colleges who were familiar with village life and had interpersonal skills as well as agricultural backgrounds. They were encouraged to build relationships with the farmers, which, in turn, meant that they had to work, eat, and join in social activities with them. The official agricultural agents had never done this, and the farmers had never accepted them. The farmers did, however, accept the Pilot Project workers, and were willing to try the new procedures that they advocated. After the change, the program was again evaluated by an impact evaluation. It was found that wheat production was increased by over 60% and the program was a success. These studies demonstrate that the inclusion of relevant implementation environment dimensions for investigation, such as, in this case, the implementor dimension, provides illuminating information for program improvement and other policy purposes.

DELIVERY MODE DIMENSION

The normative delivery mode evaluation can be integrated with an impact evaluation to deal with issues related to the delivery mode and program effectiveness. In the summative type of the normative delivery-mode-impact evaluation, information obtained from the evaluation is used to explain the findings of the impact evaluation. Alternatively, in the formative type, the information obtained from the normative delivery mode evaluation is used to assess problems in this dimension for program improvement. When the delivery mode has been improved and is sound, an impact evaluation is carried out to evaluate program effectiveness.

An example of the formative type is discussed here. One important influence on the success or failure of voluntary programs is the degree to which the program mode of delivery compromises clients' pride and dignity. This is especially important when the program is being implemented across cultural or subcultural boundaries. Americans, for example, believe in lifelong learning and do not hesitate to attend courses at any age. In other cultures, however, this is not so, and various types of group instruction started by well-meaning Americans have foundered because their intended pupils associated "classes" with childhood, and hence the classes were viewed as demeaning.

An informative example is provided by Foster's (1973) discussion of a health education program for prenatal mothers in Chile. Newly established public health centers attempted to hold prenatal classes for mothers-to-be, as their American model did. However, the program was only partially successful because the expectant mothers refused to attend the classes. The problem in this program was found to be the mode of delivery. The expectant mothers did not like the treatment setting; they objected to being taught in "classes" like children.

Based upon this information from the normative delivery mode evaluation, the health center restructured the classes into temporary "clubs," which met for a prescribed number of weeks, usually in the homes of expectant mothers. The health center provided tea and cakes, and the meeting thereby became a social affair that was incidentally mixed with discussion of prenatal care. In Chile, clubs are associated with middle- and upper-class life, and the women were happy to participate. The program was found to be highly successful after the mode of delivery was changed.

IMPLEMENTING ORGANIZATION DIMENSION

The implementing organization may experience problems in areas concerning coordination, communication, and control, and these problems may upset the program implementation process and the consequences of the program. The normative implementation organization evaluation can be integrated with the impact evaluation to deal with issues related to the implementing organization and program effectiveness.

In the summative type of the normative implementing-organization-impact evaluation, the information obtained from the normative implementing organization can be used to explain the program success or failure found in the impact evaluation. In the formative type, information obtained from the normative implementing organization evaluation provides an opportunity for key stakeholders to strengthen the implementing organization. An impact evaluation, or another impact evaluation, can be carried out after the improvement of the program structure.

A good example to illustrate the normative implementing-organization-impact evaluation is the study by Trist et al. (1963) of the impact of new technology in the British mining industry. Before the intervention, coal mining was operated in the single-working system. Under this form of organization, work was organized around small groups of men. The men in a group worked closely and were paid the same wage, the exact amount being determined by a group piece rate. Workers had the right to select their own teammates. The group had high cohesion and required little supervision from top management. In order to increase productivity and reduce cost, the management introduced the long-wall system. The new system involved a drastic change in the organization of the work team, mechanizing the coal-mining processes and making the coal miners conform to the requirements of the new technology. A large number of workers were spread throughout the working places. Workers were divided into different shifts and assigned to specific functions.

An impact evaluation indicated that the new technological change not only failed to increase productivity but also increased absenteeism and workers' resistance. Trist et al. carried out a normative implementing organization evaluation to assess the problems in the new system. They found that it failed to meet workers' need for a primary working group.

Group cohesion was destroyed by the large unit. The workers lacked autonomy and control over their work and found it difficult to engage in satisfactory relationships with other workers.

Based upon the information from the normative implementing organization evaluation, the researchers suggested a composite system, which was a compromise. Under this system, the new technology was maintained but the production teams were reduced to once again form small work groups. Workers in the groups had the autonomy to organize the work and select group members. After the composite system was adopted, an impact evaluation was applied again. It was found that productivity went up, job satisfaction increased, and absenteeism went down.

INTERORGANIZATIONAL RELATIONSHIP DIMENSION

When a program involves cooperation between two or more organizations, interorganizational processes become complicated and may condition implementation processes and program consequences. The normative interorganizational-relationship-impact evaluation is useful for dealing with issues in this area. In the summative type of the normative interorganizational-relationship-impact evaluation, information obtained from the evaluation is used to explain the findings in the impact evaluation. As mentioned earlier, to some extent, many implementation studies fall in this category. Interested readers are referred to Sabatier and Mazmanian (1982) and Williams et al. (1982).

In the formative type, information obtained from the normative interorganizational relationship is used to strengthen the program. An impact evaluation is carried out after the interorganizational relationship has been made sound. A good example to demonstrate the application and usefulness of the formative type is Naegele's (1955) study of the Human Relations Service. The Human Relations Service (HRS) was a pioneering work in preventive psychiatry, established in a Boston suburb with a population of 20,000, under the auspices of Harvard University. At the time it was established in 1949, the concept of what would later become "mental health centers" was new and, therefore, unfamiliar. The HRS had few precedents to follow and no natural constituency. In order to succeed, the HRS staff knew they had to build good working interorganizational relationships with community institutions such as churches and schools. The HRS staff launched a plan to build interorganizational relationships to ensure the success of the program. The plan was carefully implemented and tracked.

The local clergy was one of the first groups with which the HRS made contact through group meetings. The clergy seem to have been slow and cautious in their acceptance of the HRS, as they wanted to know what kind of values HRS staff would be seeking to support or discourage in patients. The HRS staff, whose attitude toward values was totally different from that of the clergy, generally attempted to evade the question of values and return the meetings to their own agenda.

Progress in this relationship became possible only after the clergy did, in fact, refer some parishioners, whom the HRS was able to help. From this experience a working relationship was established, based on a division of labor. Each side came to recognize that the other had a particular area of competence that should be respected. It was agreed that the clergy would not practice psychiatry, and psychiatrists would not interfere with the clergy's function.

There were similar problems in HRS's relationship with the local school system. The schools did not want simply to hand over problem children to another agency; they were willing to refer but they wanted to know exactly what happened to them after referral. They also wanted a specific, precise instrument for measuring children's "mental health." Finally, though they occasionally denied the need for the HRS, they would very much have liked to have had an equivalent program under the school system's control. The HRS felt that the measuring rod was an impossible request and did not want to be under anyone's authority.

The "mental health measuring instrument" was the initial school-HRS problem, and it was dealt with in two ways. The HRS first ran a seminar for teachers on personality development, which suggested the complexity of assessing "mental health" and provided a forum for discussing problems. Next, they established solid referral policies, which stated that only parents could decide whether or not to bring a child to the HRS, although the schools could encourage them to do so.

Referrals, once in progress, created a new problem: Teachers wanted to know what was happening with referred pupils. In response, the HRS established a consultation service that enabled teachers to discuss either specific children or general problems. The service was designed to allow the HRS to maintain its rules of absolute confidentiality.

This consultation process also helped to clarify some of the conflicts between teachers and HRS staff. The staff claimed to be more competent in correcting children's emotional disorders than the teachers. Again, a recognition of the proper roles for each group was achieved, and a good working relationship was eventually established. From these and other factors, Naegele concluded that one of the main reasons the HRS succeeded was that it could work out a division of labor between itself, the clergy, and the school system.

MICRO-CONTEXT DIMENSION

The micro context, including people closely associated with the participants such as friends and family members, and the immediate environment surrounding the participants, may hinder or facilitate implementation processes or condition program consequences. The normative micro-context-impact evaluation deals with issues relevant to the relationships between micro context, implementation, and program effectiveness. In the formative type of the normative micro-context-impact evaluation, information obtained from the evaluation is used to improve problems in the micro context. After the micro context has been made sound, an impact evaluation can be used to assess program effectiveness.

In the summative type, information obtained from the normative micro-context evaluation is used to explain findings in the impact evaluation. This type of application is illustrated by a study by Apodaca (1952). Apodaca (1952) has described an attempt at agricultural reform that foundered because of micro-contextual factors. In the late 1940s an agricultural extension agent attempted to introduce a new variety of hybrid seed corn in order to improve his area's corn yield. The agent, who had worked in the area for several years and spoke the Spanish dialect of the farmers, consulted with experts and selected a hybrid variety that was known for high yields and had been tested in the same area and proven capable of surviving the climate. He then consulted with the leaders of one village and ensured that they were both aware of the problem of low yields and open to the idea of cultivating a new hybrid corn. After the details had been worked out with the leaders, a community meeting was held, a demonstration plot for showing the hybrid's yield was grown, and special arrangements were made to make the hybrid seed readily available to the farmers. After two years, 60 farmers (constituting more than two-thirds of the farmers in the village) were using the new seed.

The next year, however, only 30 farmers used the new hybrid and the rest went back to the strain they had been using. By the fourth year, only 3 farmers were still using the hybrid.

Why? The normative micro-context evaluation indicated that problems lay in the micro context. As one farmer said, "My wife doesn't like the hybrid, that's all" (Apodaca, 1952, p. 38). In fact, all the wives had complained. Some did not like its texture, it did not hang together well for tortillas, and the tortillas were not the color to which the farmers and their wives were accustomed. A few farmers persisted in planting it after the first year, hoping they would get used to it. However, after three years they were still not accustomed to the flavor or texture, and their wives were up in arms.

This study indicates that the attitude and opinions of the significant other, in this case, the wife—the person who actually cooks produce from the new crop—should be taken seriously. However, the information obtained from scanning came too late to change or modify the program. The sooner the agricultural extension agents learn about problems, the sooner an alternative project can be planned and implemented.

MACRO-CONTEXT DIMENSION

Program implementation and program success may be hindered by the larger contextual environment of social, economic, and political structures, belief systems, and competing organizations. The normative macro-context-impact evaluation attempts to deal with issues related to macro context, implementation processes, and program effectiveness.

In the summative type of the normative macro-context-impact evaluation, information obtained from the evaluation is used to explain program success or failure found in the impact evaluation. For example, Beller's (1980) study of the effectiveness of equal opportunity laws indicated that the success of Title VII of the Civil Rights Act was eroded by the recession of the 1970s. In a recession, new jobs are created more slowly and workers change jobs less frequently. Firms find it harder to increase the female/male employment ratio, unless they fill all job vacancies with women or resort to layoffs. Also, unions will resist any effort to replace their existing male membership either by layoffs or by males not being hired. As a result, the weaker the economy, the more costly it will be for firms to increase the female/male employee ratio.

In the formative type of evaluation, information obtained from the normative macro-context evaluation is used to solve problems in the macro context. Impact evaluation for the same program is conducted after the problems in the macro context have been dealt with. The study by Adams (1955) of the implementation of a nutritional program in rural Guatemala reveals the usefulness of this type of evaluation.

This program, sponsored by the Instituto de Nutricion de Centro American y Panama (INCAP), was intended to help discover what supplemental food elements, if any, were needed to improve the diet of villagers in rural Guatemala. The program treatment consisted of giving schoolchildren either food supplements or placebos on a rotating basis, and monitoring their growth and health by periodic physical examinations. The program also sponsored a variety of community activities and established a small medical clinic in the village Adams subsequently studied.

The program was established in five villages. In four of them, it was implemented with few difficulties. In the village of Magdalene, however, program staff encountered increasing antagonism and an anthropologist was finally sent in to see if the program could be saved. After scanning the implementation environment, largely through case study methods, the anthropologist identified four factors that were contributing to community antagonism and reported this information to the program decision makers. Steps were taken and the problems were subsequently solved.

The first factor was national political tension in Guatemala. At the time of this case study, the government of Guatemala was a constitutional democracy with a liberal government in power. This government gave substantial freedom to communist groups, and this was drawing communists from outside of Guatemala. Gradually, the government became associated in the minds of many Guatemalans with communism, and a wave of antigovernment, anticommunist agitation reached a peak in 1951.

The village of Magdalene felt this tension, but had no means of expressing it until a rumor sprang up that INCAP was a communist organization. This argument was supported by the logic that the government of Guatemala was procommunist, and INCAP worked very closely with the government, so INCAP must be a communist organization. Accordingly, village residents became increasingly antagonistic to the program, and some began to demand its expulsion.

The anthropologist and social worker associated with the program confronted the rumors directly. The social worker visited her friends, and told them that INCAP was a nonpolitical organization and not interested in Guatemalan politics, and that the Americans involved with the project were anticommunist, as was shown by the fact that Americans were fighting communists in Korea. While spreading this information, the social worker began to find out how the rumors were spread and who was behind them. The anthropologist also confronted these people, reiterated the social worker's claims, and added that the rumors were actually helping the communists.

These direct steps were enough to deal with the problem. The community gradually warmed to the project again, and little more was heard of INCAP's alleged communist connections. However, in another village involved in the research project similar rumors arose and, because there was no social worker or anthropologist in the field, the program there had to be abandoned.

The second problem was related to the villagers' traditional beliefs about blood, which created problems in implementation. The villagers believed that a human being had a certain fixed amount of blood, and that, whenever any was lost, it was lost permanently. For more educated program staff, taking blood samples during physical exams was a minor matter, but for the villagers it was much more serious. Why were these people, who were supposed to be out to make children stronger, busily taking away blood, which could only make them weaker? Some parents became so concerned that they began to withdraw their children from the program.

The anthropologist recommended that two steps be taken to deal with this conflict. First, the program staff were encouraged to draw the minimum amount of blood possible, both by taking small samples and making sure that a minimum of retesting was required. Second, a social worker was assigned to explain the need for blood sampling to her contacts in terms that fit with their own ideas: "If a person had sick blood, he needed curing; if he had well blood, this was also important to know" (Adams, 1955, p. 448). This approach was also successful; rumors and hostility died down over a period of time.

The third factor was a persistent rumor that the nutritional program was intended to fatten up the children so that they could be taken to the United States and eaten. This was related to the blood-sampling conflict; blood testing was supposed to enable INCAP to decide whether the children were fat enough to be shipped.

The anthropologist found that the fear of children being eaten was a common fantasy theme among the native population of Guatemala, evidently ancient and deeply ingrained in the culture. Accordingly, a strategy was selected that did not involve denying that Americans ate children but focused instead on detaching that belief from the nutritional research program. One of the influential men of the village was invited to drive into the city with an INCAP staff member and watch the blood being processed. The technicians explained exactly what each step of the processing involved and what it was for. At the same time, the INCAP staff began discussing the issue with their friends in the village, stressing that INCAP was not involved in sending children anywhere. Again, the strategy was apparently successful; after a few months the rumors died away and were not mentioned again.

The fourth problem involved the social organization of the village. The project staff included a social worker, who was in charge of the community projects side of the program. She was a native Guatemalan, but not a local villager. In the course of her work, she had made a number of friends in one section of the village. Unfortunately, she had not been aware that the town was quite sharply divided into two sections, known as the Upper Barrio and the Lower Barrio, with distinct social and political differences and a certain amount of hostility. When the social worker made friends in one barrio, the other became less hospitable, which, of course, meant that she was likely to make more friends in the first barrio and fewer in the other. After the anthropologist pointed out the problem to her, the social worker divided her time equally between the two barrios, and the antagonism decreased somewhat. The program was found to be successful after these problems in the macro context were solved.

This study demonstrates the importance of monitoring or scanning the larger environment within which a program is operating. Timely and relevant information provided by the evaluators can be utilized immediately to solve the problems in the macro context. An impact evaluation can be carried out after it has been established that the macro context does not severely damage the implementation of the program.

PART VI

Conclusions and Discussion

Chapter 14 starts with a brief summary of the limitations of method-oriented perspectives and argues for the more comprehensive theory-driven perspective. Following that, potential barriers for utilizing theory-driven evaluations are identified and strategies for overcoming them are also discussed. Finally, the chapter ends with a discussion of the future trends that are forming or should form within program evaluation.

14. Conclusions and Discussion

The method-oriented evaluation perspectives developed in the last three decades have made many important contributions to the progress of theory and practice in program evaluation. However, there has recently been a growing awareness of the problems and limitations associated with these traditional perspectives if they are applied uncritically and unilaterally (e.g., see Cook and Shadish, 1986; Cordray and Lipsey, 1986; Bickman, 1987a). There are three major problems connected with these method-oriented perspectives, as discussed below.

Narrowness in Scope

One of the limitations of method-oriented perspectives is that they focus principally on those evaluation areas for which the particular method is best suited. For example, the experimental paradigm mainly focuses on issues related to summative evaluation, because experimental and quasi-experimental designs are best equipped to handle this level of inquiry. By contrast, naturalistic approaches concentrate on formative evaluation, which can be effectively dealt with using qualitative methods. Cronbach's approach also relies heavily on qualitative methods and investigates issues mainly connected with external validity. This kind of selective focus may enable the major perspectives to operate effectively in their areas of expertise, but an overly dogmatic adherence to any one of these approaches may cause an evaluator to lose sight of the multiple domains and issues inherent in an evaluation. With a growing consensus among evaluators that effective program evaluation must deal with multiple issues simultaneously, there has been a concomitant dissatisfaction with the necessary limitations of the traditional perspectives.

Incompatibility Among Method-Oriented Perspectives

Another problem arising from traditional method-oriented perspectives is the incompatibility of their research methods and procedures. Because quantitative and qualitative methods were founded upon divergent assumptions in terms of their logic and research procedures, many evaluators who adhere to a particular methodological tradition tend to expend more effort defending the validity of its procedures than they do toward cooperating in evaluation with evaluators from a different methodological tradition. Although there have been growing arguments for the application of multiple methods, the current forms of method-oriented perspectives have not provided a framework or capacity for such an integration.

Neglect of Contextual Factors

The traditional evaluation perspectives, such as the experimental paradigm, also tend to develop evaluation principles and strategies in a context-free fashion. These general principles and strategies have some merits within some contexts. However, to argue that these strategies will hold as universal truths not only may be controversial but may also be misleading. For example, the experimental paradigm's contention of the superiority of randomized experiments, or Cronbach's proposition that external validity is more important than internal validity, may have some truth under certain circumstances. However, without specifying clearly what these circumstances are, these arguments may only serve to confuse the audience.

The recent emergence of the pragmatic view of research methods is an attempt to overcome some of these problems by abandoning the traditionally uncompromising, hard-line positions associated with particular methods. Instead, from this view, it is argued that a method is appropriate only under particular circumstances. This leads to an argument in favor of using multiple methods in an evaluation when the situation allows. Critical multiplism goes even further in arguing that program evaluation should use multiple methods, investigate multiple issues, and consider the views of multiple stakeholders. Critical multiplism's framework is particularly useful in expanding the scope of traditional evaluation perspectives. However, as admitted by its advocates, critical multiplism, at least at the current stage, has not provided the theoretical basis for dealing with trade-offs when multiple issues must be resolved.

The theory-driven perspective shares the same concerns as these recent developments, but it argues that the current problems and limitations of program evaluation lie more with the lack of an adequate conceptual framework than with methodological weaknesses. The theory-driven perspective systematically developed in this book has identified the basic multiple values and dilemmas in program evaluation and proposed a balancing strategy for dealing with these multiple values and dilemmas.

More specifically, the theory-driven perspective identifies and develops various types of theory-driven evaluations that serve different evaluation functions. Six basic types are identified: normative treatment, normative implementation environment, normative outcome, impact, intervening mechanism, and generalization. Furthermore, many composite theory-driven evaluations can be constructed by systematically combining two or more of these basic types of evaluations. These different types of theory-driven evaluations can serve as a pool from which stakeholders and evaluators can draw when selecting the theory-driven evaluation that best serves their evaluation purposes, within their resource and time constraints.

The conceptual framework of the theory-driven perspective is useful for stakeholders and evaluators when working together to identify the crucial issues in a program evaluation and trying to integrate these issues into the evaluation. Strategies and principles on how evaluators can negotiate with stakeholders in planning and actually conducting a theory-driven evaluation have been systematically provided.

OVERCOMING BARRIERS IN PLANNING AND CARRYING OUT THE THEORY-DRIVEN EVALUATION

In spite of their recognition of the usefulness of the theory-driven evaluation, Bickman (forthcoming) and Cordray (forthcoming), contributors to a forthcoming special issue of the journal *Evaluation and Program Planning* on the theory-driven perspective, point out several barriers that they believe have to be surmounted in order for the theory-driven evaluation to gain acceptance. With the developments in this book, the theory-driven perspective is in a better position to deal with these barriers, which are discussed below.

Cost and Time Constraints

Due to its comprehensiveness, Bickman (forthcoming) argues that a theory-driven evaluation will increase costs in areas such as planning, measurement development, and data collection. Similarly, Cordray (forthcoming) raises the concern that, with the constraints of resources and timeliness in the policy context, it may be difficult for the theory-driven evaluation to optimize multiple options, such as simultaneously dealing with various types of validity.

Whether or not resource and time constraints present a problem may depend on what type of theory-driven evaluation is involved. Some theory-driven evaluations are more demanding of resources than others. For example, as pointed out in Chapter 2, a comprehensive theory-driven evaluation that systematically integrates all six basic types of evaluations is rather expensive and time-consuming. However, normative evaluations usually present fewer problems in resource and time constraints. Similarly, as shown in Chapter 10, information on intervening processes could merely involve some extra items in data collection in the traditional outcome evaluation. The cost of an intervening mechanism evaluation is not necessarily much higher than the traditional outcome evaluation.

Furthermore, the theory-driven perspective has proposed various strategies, such as balancing, sequential, and synthetic designs and causation probing for dealing with trade-offs among multiple options within cost and time constraints. The traditional evaluation may put all the resources into a fixed time frame to maximize one particular value. The theory-driven perspective argues that it is better to use the same resources and time for balancing multiple values.

For example, a traditional outcome evaluation may commit the available resources to an expensive randomized experiment in the field in order to concentrate on dealing with trustworthiness in estimating treatment effect. The theory-driven evaluation may use the same resources with a less expensive, synthetic design that can devote some resources to dealing with implementation issues if this is an important concern of the stakeholders. Viewed in this way, a theory-driven evaluation is not necessarily always more expensive than the traditional evaluation.

In the conceptualization stage of an evaluation, it is important that the theory-driven evaluator explain and discuss the implications of the conceptual framework of the evaluation with the stakeholders. This will ensure that both evaluators and stakeholders will have a more systematic and explicit understanding or conceptualization of the program, of the crucial issues that should be examined in the evaluation, and of what it will take to provide a useful evaluation. At this stage, the evaluator can propose alternative evaluation plans to stakeholders and explain the different levels of comprehensiveness that can be achieved by the number of domains included in the evaluation framework. The evaluator can point out the implications in terms of costs and timeliness and help stakeholders make informed decisions and choices among the alternatives in view of what evaluation results they can expect. For example, the cost of the the theory-driven evaluation will be increased considerably if additional variation of treatment components is structured into the impact evaluation. Similarly, the cost of a theory-driven evaluation will increase if the dimension test approach is used to address issues such as mode of delivery or the micro context in the generalization evaluation.

Motivation

Bickman (forthcoming) indicates that many evaluations are conducted as a response to a request for proposals, and unless the request calls for a theory-oriented evaluation, there will be little motivation for the evaluators to request a theory-driven model because the cost of the theory-driven evaluation will reduce its competitiveness with the less expensive input-output type of evaluation. Nevertheless, as argued above, a theory-driven evaluation is not necessarily more expensive than a traditional evaluation model. Even if it is, the higher quality of the theory-driven evaluation is usually an element in competitiveness that will provide strong grounds for its use. Furthermore, the theory-driven evaluation offers stakeholders choices among evaluation plans, including the traditional type of evaluation focusing mainly on the impact domain. In short, the theory-driven evaluation is not necessarily less competitive than traditional evaluation modes.

Furthermore, contrary to Bickman's (forthcoming) opinion, the usefulness of the theory-driven evaluation will appeal to evaluators other than those who are academically based. Perhaps factors such as the usefulness of the theory-driven evaluation, dissatisfaction with traditional evaluation, and the current interest in theory-oriented evaluation, as indicated in Chapter 1, may provide motivation for stakeholders to request, and for evaluators to adopt, the theory-driven evaluation.

Role Confusion

Bickman (forthcoming) also argues that previous work on the theory-driven perspective (Chen and Rossi, 1980, 1983, 1987) does not clearly define the role of the theory-driven evaluator. The role of the theory-driven evaluator has now been clearly defined in Chapter 4 of this book. The theory-driven evaluator presents him- or herself as one among many multiple stakeholders and, therefore, by definition as an interested party with a stake in producing a high-quality and useful evaluation. Not only should the evaluator actively join in discussions and make his or her view on evaluation clear to other stakeholders, but he or she should also actively work to help the stakeholders reach agreement in designing an evaluation.

Nevertheless, the future utility and popularity of the theory-driven or theory-oriented evaluation has to rely upon collective efforts. Bickman (forthcoming) points out the following strategies that can be used to increase the rate of adoption of the theory-driven perspective in the future.

Education and Training

Education and training includes not only evaluation instruction courses or training programs with emphasis on the methods of the theory-driven evaluation but also the need to educate decision makers or other stakeholders about the centrality of methodological and theoretical issues in evaluation.

Journal Policy

This strategy requires that journals maintain an explicit policy that encourages theoretical contributions pertinent to the development of program evaluation.

Specific Techniques and Principles for Theory-Driven Evaluation

It is obvious that, in addition to the current efforts of this book, the theory-driven or theory-oriented evaluation can benefit from more intensive developments in principles and techniques that guide evaluators in conducting high-quality theory-driven evaluations.

LOOKING FORWARD

In the last few years, some evaluators have made serious efforts to liberate program evaluation from the traditional evaluation perspectives and move forward. Instead of uncritical acceptance of the traditional perspectives, evaluators have increasingly begun to challenge their appropriateness and advocate changes such as adopting multiple methods (Mark and Shotland, 1987), abandoning dogmatic views of methods (Williams, 1986a), recognizing the importance of program theory (Cordray and Lipsey, 1986; Bickman, 1987b; Chen and Rossi, 1983; Cook and Shadish, 1986), and so on.

With these current and fundamental changes, it is likely that program evaluation will move in a new direction in the future, and perhaps these current efforts provide indications of what the future trends and patterns in program evaluation will be. Some of these likely trends are discussed below.

Integrating Research Methods into Theory-Driven Evaluations

The conception of evaluation research methods has gone through major changes in the past two decades. Initially, quantitative methods and experimental designs were regarded as the best methods for program evaluation (e.g., see Suchman, 1967; Reicken and Boruch, 1974). Then, a growing number of evaluators proposed qualitative methods as an alternative (see Parlett and Hamilton, 1978; Guba and Lincoln, 1981). Consequently, intensive debates arose between the qualitative and quantitative camps as to which method was best for evaluation (e.g., see Guba and Lincoln, 1981; Cook and Campbell, 1979). Perhaps it will be fruitful to pursue the integration of methods in each of the major theory-driven evaluations rather than to advocate one best method for evaluations in the future.

As demonstrated in the previous chapters, different theory-driven evaluations require the use of different research methods or multiple methods. There is no single best method for all evaluation needs. The usefulness of a particular method depends entirely on the questions to be asked, the stakeholders' needs, the research situation, and the nature of the program. For example, as demonstrated in Chapter 7, the implementation environment can be examined either by using case study methods to detect a wide range of issues or quantitative methods to collect ongoing standardized information. In this case, the evaluation method chosen depends on the stakeholders' needs and the distinctive features of the implementation.

Because each type of theory-driven evaluation has its own unique characteristics, functions, and structure, its methodological requirements must be different from others. Methods have to be elaborated, refined, or developed to fit these requirements. Efforts to systematically integrate research methods into different types of theory-driven evaluations are greatly needed in the future.

Examining Underlying Causal Processes in a Broad Context

The growing disappointment with the traditional input and output type of evaluation has led a number of critics to advocate the investigation of causal mechanisms underlying a program, such as the examination of intervening processes (e.g., see Bickman, 1987b; Lipsey, 1987) and contextual factors (Cordray, 1986; Trochim, 1986b). This new movement toward theory-oriented evaluations may promote future investigation into underlying causal mechanisms. Compared with simply addressing the question of whether the treatment has achieved its predetermined goals, as assessed in the traditional evaluation (e.g., see Reicken and Boruch, 1974; Suchman, 1967), the investigation of causal processes is much broader and more comprehensive. It will be used to consider such questions as these: "Are the causal chains underlying the program working as expected?" "If not, why not?" "What can be done to correct this in the future?" "Do the dimensions of the implementation environment (such as implementors, delivery modes, implementing organization, and so on) hinder or facilitate program implementation and causal processes?" "What is the nature of the treatment after its implementation?" "What outcomes should be investigated?" "Can evaluation results be generalized to the stakeholders' areas of concern?" Future developments in this area can enhance our understanding of the strengths and weaknesses of a program, of how to improve a program, and of how to use and apply evaluation results.

Enhancing Evaluation's Knowledge-Generation Function

Evaluation research can serve two broad functions. The first is to provide stakeholders with relevant and useful information on intervention programs in areas such as health, criminal justice, and poverty. The second function of evaluation research is to contribute to a systematic body of knowledge that will benefit program evaluation as a distinct social science discipline. The first is a program enlightenment function; the second is an evaluation knowledge-generating function.

Although there is no inherent reason why a single evaluation cannot serve both functions simultaneously, evaluators who follow the traditional perspectives in doing evaluations tend to serve primarily the program enlightenment function and provide information relevant to only a particular intervention program. Following the method-oriented perspectives tends to curtail the opportunities for evaluators to address the central issues in program evaluation in general and thereby to contribute to a systematic body of knowledge.

The reason for this is that the method-oriented perspectives heavily emphasize methodology, yet methodological breakthroughs are difficult for many evaluators who are not statisticians or research methods specialists. Consequently, most evaluators are quite familiar with statistics and research designs, but they may not develop new statistical models or research designs that could make a methodological breakthrough in program evaluation. Similarly, many evaluators know how to use qualitative methods in program evaluation well, but very few would seek to devise a new mode of observation or work toward a new breakthrough in qualitative methods for program evaluation. Accordingly, adherence to a method-oriented perspective appears to decrease the opportunity for evaluators to contribute to the knowledge-generating aspect of program evaluation.

However, with the current efforts toward developing theory-oriented evaluation and expanding the scope of program evaluation, it is possible that program evaluation will expand from the methodological to the conceptual level. Because conceptual issues are most directly relevant to those engaged in the practice of evaluation, evaluators who are concerned with them will have greater opportunities to generate important contributions in the course of their activities. Based upon their knowledge, experience, and creative interests, they will have a most important role to play for the knowledge-generating function of program evaluation.

In addition, because the scope of program evaluation is expanding, evaluators now have a greater range of areas in which they can make contributions. For example, the theory-driven perspective provides formal recognition of different theories, domains, and types of theory-driven evaluations, which will help evaluators to identify and focus upon areas that have traditionally been neglected.

Diversifying Efforts in Different Theory-Driven Evaluations

Traditional evaluations usually fall into one of two categories: formative or summative (process or outcome) evaluation. With the new expansion of the scope of program evaluation, evaluators can work more flexibly in a wide range of areas where they can contribute to program improvement or facilitate decision-making processes.

With the comprehensive conceptualization of evaluation processes, evaluators can more effectively either work on one basic theory-driven evaluation or combine two or more basic types in an evaluation, depending on the nature of the program and its contextual environment. With these diversifying efforts, evaluators may be serving the evaluation knowledge-generating function by providing important contributions to the discipline while at the same time fulfilling their traditional program enlightenment function. These contributions can be made through conceptual developments or through addressing problems and issues by empirically testing various theories and strategies.

Toward a Unique Practical Science of Program Evaluation

One of the important arguments made in this new movement of theory-oriented evaluations is that program evaluation does not just consist of the research methods and data collection techniques that have been emphasized in the traditional evaluation. In fact, the dissatisfaction and frustration expressed by evaluators in the past two decades indicates that the application of sophisticated designs and statistical models from other disciplines cannot in itself solve the many problems confronted by evaluators. As Tornatzky and Johnson (1982, pp. 193-194) stated,

> To carry out an evaluation demands organizational dislocations, and the utilization of results from an evaluation means in the most complete

sense that people's lives will be significantly altered. A corollary is that the training and the how-to-do-it literature of the evaluation field would benefit from less emphasis on methodology qua methodology, and more attention to the social processes, politics, and the logistics of conducting evaluation.

What is needed for the future develpoment of program evaluation are not just new methodological advances but also the creation of new concepts and theories. As discussed in Chapter 4, program evaluation deals with social phenomena in a context of political and scientific requirements. This makes program evaluation somewhat unique compared with other disciplines. Program evaluation has demonstrated a concern not only with its essential values of responsiveness, objectivity, trustworthiness, and generalizablility but also with the value dilemmas confronting the evaluators who must deal with them. Other disciplines do not face the same requirements and dilemmas as program evaluation. Thus program evaluation cannot sufficiently understand or deal with these requirements, problems, and dilemmas by simply adapting research methods, concepts, and theories from other disciplines. The relevant concepts and theories must be developed by evaluators who familiarize themselves with the unique nature and problems of program evaluation.

The development of a systematic body of concepts and theories in program evaluation will be a slow and time-consuming process. However, through continuous dual efforts toward conceptual and theoretical development and the empirical assessment of these conceptual tools, a body of systematic knowledge can gradually be accumulated and integrated. As a result, we will hopefully not only be able to guide systematically evaluation practitioners in making better choices among trade-offs and in dealing with practical problems, but we can also make program evaluation a more mature practical science that has its own unique and systematic body of concepts and theories.

References

Achen, C. H. 1986. *The Statistical Analysis of Quasi-Experiments.* Berkeley: University of California Press.

Adams, R. 1955. "On the Effective Use of Anthropology in Public Health Programs." *Human Organization* 13:15-51.

Aldrich, H. E. 1979. *Organizations and Environment.* Englewood Cliffs, NJ: Prentice-Hall.

Allison, G. 1971. *Essence of Decision: Explaining the Cuban Missile Crisis.* Boston: Little, Brown.

Alwin, D. F. and R. C. Tessler. 1974. "Causal Models, Unobserved Variables, and Experimental Data." *American Journal of Sociology* 80:58-86.

Anderson, R. 1975. "Social Factors Influencing Administrators' Use of Research Results." *Inquiry* 12:235-38.

Apodaca, A. 1952. "Corn and Custom: The Introduction of Hybrid Corn to Spanish American Farmers in New Mexico." Pp. 35-39 in *Human Problems in Technological Change*, edited by E. H. Spicer. New York: Russell Sage.

Argyris, Chris. 1980. *Inner Contradictions of Rigorous Research.* New York: Academic Press.

Babbie, E. 1986. *The Practice of Social Research.* 3rd ed. Belmont, CA: Wadsworth.

Ball, S. and G. A. Bogatz. 1970. *The First Year of Sesame Street: An Evaluation.* Princeton, NJ: Educational Testing Service.

Barbacki, S. and R. A. Fisher. 1936. "A Test of the Supposed Precision of Systematic Arrangements." *Annals of Eugenics* 7:189-93.

Bardach, E. 1977. *The Implementation Game.* Cambridge: MIT Press.

Barker, R. G. 1968. *Ecological Psychology: Concepts and Methods for Studying the Environment of Human Behavior.* Stanford, CA: Stanford University Press.

Barnow, B. S., G. G. Cain, and A. S. Goldberger. 1980. "Issues in the Analysis of Selection Bias." In *Evaluation Studies Review Annual.* Vol. 5, edited by E. W. Stromsdorfer and G. Farkas. Beverly Hills, CA: Sage.

Baumer, D., C. E. Van Horn, and M. Marvel. 1979. "Explaining Benefit Distribution in CETA Programs." *Journal of Human Resources* 14(2):171-96.

Beller, A. H. 1980. "The Effects of Economic Conditions on the Success of Equal Employment Opportunity Laws: An Application to the Sex Differential in Earnings." *Review of Economics and Statistics* 62(3):379-87.

Bentley, J. M., P. Cormier, and J. Oler. 1983. "The Rural Dental Health Program: The Effect of a School-Based, Dental Health Education Program on Children's Utilization of Dental Services." *American Journal of Public Health* 73(5):500-505.

Berenson, D. 1976. "Alcohol and the Family System." In *Family Therapy Theory and Practice*, edited by P. J. Guerin, Jr. New York: Gardner.

Berk, R. A., R. F. Boruch, D. L. Chambers, P. H. Rossi, and A. D. Witte. 1985. "Social Policy Experimentation: A Position Paper." *Evaluation Review* 9(4):387-429.

Berk, R. A., K. J. Lenihan, and P. H. Rossi. 1980. "Crime and Poverty: Some Experimental Evidence from Ex-Offenders." *American Sociological Review* 45:766-86.

Berk, R. A. and S. C. Ray. 1982. "Selection Bias in Sociological Data." *Social Science Research* 11:3-40.

Bersani, C. A., H. T. Chen, and R. Denton. 1988. "Spouse Abusers and Court Mandated Treatment." *Journal of Crime and Justice* 11(1):43-60.

Best, J. A., S. Bass, and L. E. Owen. 1977. "Mode of Service Delivery in a Smoking Cessation Program for Public Health." *Canadian Journal of Public Health* 68(November/December):469-73.

Bickman, L. 1985. "Improving Established Statewide Programs: A Component Theory of Evaluation." *Evaluation Review* 9(2):189-208.

———. ed. 1987a. *Using Program Theory in Evaluation. New Directions for Program Evaluation.* San Francisco: Jossey-Bass.

———. 1987b. "The Functions of Program Theory." In *Using Program Theory in Evaluation*, edited by L. Bickman. San Francisco: Jossey-Bass.

———. 1987c. "Editor's Notes." In *Using Program Theory in Evaluation*, edited by L. Bickman. San Francisco: Jossey-Bass.

———. Forthcoming. "Barriers to the Use of Program Theory." *Evaluation and Program Planning*.

Birnbaum, H., R. Burke, C. Swearinger, and B. Dunlop. 1986. "Implementing Community-Based Long-Term Care: Experience of New York's Long Term Home Health Care Program." *Gerontologist* 24(4):380-86.

Borgatta, E. F. and W. C. Jones. 1965. *Girls at Vocational High: An Experiment in Social Work Intervention.* New York: Russell Sage.

Boruch, R. F. and W. Wothke, eds. 1985. *Randomization and Field Experimentation. New Directions for Program Evaluation* (No. 28). San Francisco: Jossey-Bass.

Bowen, M. A. 1960. "A Family Concept of Schizophrenia." Pp. 346-72 in *The Etiology of Schizophrenia*, edited by D. Jackson. New York: Basic Books.

Bracht, G. H. and G. V. Glass. 1968. "The External Validity of Experiments." *American Educational Research Journal* 5:437-74.

Braskamp, L. A., B. C. Brandenburg, and J. C. Ory. 1987. "Lessons About Clients' Expectations." In *Client Perspective on Evaluation. New Directions for Program Evaluation* (No. 36), edited by J. Nawakowski. San Francisco: Jossey-Bass.

Brekke, J. 1987. "The Model-Guided Method for Monitoring Program Implementation." *Evaluation Review* 11(3):281-99.

Broadbent, D. E. and E. A. J. Little. 1960. "Effects of Noise Reduction in a Work Situation." *Occupational Psychology* 34:134-40.

Bronfenbrenner, V. 1977. "Toward an Experimental Ecology of Human Development."
    American Psychologist 32:513-31.
Brown, B. B. 1968. *Delphi Method: A Methodology Used for the Solicitation of Opinion
    of Experts.* Los Angeles: Rand Corporation.
Burns, T. and G. M. Stalker. 1961. *The Management of Innovation.* London: Tavistock.
Campbell, D. T. 1969. "Reforms as Experiments." *American Psychologist* 24(April):409-29.
———. 1986. "Relabeling Internal and External Validity for Applied Social Scientists."
    Pp. 67-77 in *Advances in Quasi-Experimental Design and Analysis. New Directions
    for Program Evaluation* (No. 31), edited by W. M. K. Trochim. San Francisco: Jossey-
    Bass.
Campbell, D. T. and T. H. McCormack. 1957. "Military Experience and Attitudes Toward
    Authority." *American Journal of Sociology* 62:482-90.
Campbell, D. T. and J. C. Stanley. 1963. *Experimental and Quasi-Experimental Designs
    for Research.* Boston: Houghton Mifflin.
Cantanzaro, R. J. and Associates. 1973. "Familialization Therapy: An Alternative to
    Traditional Mental Health Care." *Diseases of the Nervous System* 34:212-18.
Caplan, N. 1977. "Treatment Intervention and the Reciprocal Interaction Effects." P. 98
    in *Evaluation Research: Methods for Assessing Program Evaluation,* edited by C.
    Weiss. Englewood Cliffs, NJ: Prentice-Hall.
Caplan, R. D. 1979. "Social Support, Person-Environment Fit and Coping." Pp. 89-
    137 in *Mental Health and the Economy,* edited by L. A. Ferman and J. P. Gordus.
    Kalamazoo, MI: W. E. Upjohn Institute for Employment Research.
Caro, F. G., ed. 1977. *Readings in Evaluation Research.* 2nd ed. New York: Russell
    Sage.
Chandler, M. J. 1973. "Egocentrism and Antisocial Behavior: The Assessment and Training
    of Social Perspective-Taking Skills." *Developmental Psychology* 9:326-33.
Chelimsky, E. 1977. *A Symposium on the Use of Evaluations by Federal Agencies.*
    Vol. 1. McLean, VA: Mitre Corporation.
Chen, H. T. 1979. "A Proposal to Evaluate Fair Housing Contact Services." Unpublished
    manuscript.
———. 1988. "Validity in Evaluation Research: A Critical Assessment of Current Issues."
    Policy and Politics 16(1):1-16.
———. 1989. "Values, Dilemmas, and Strategies in Program Evaluation." Unpublished
    manuscript.
———. Forthcoming. "The Conceptual Framework of the Theory-Driven Perspective."
    Evaluation and Program Planning.
Chen, H. T. and L. H. Lin. 1989. "Plant Closings and Marital Instability: A Dynamic
    Analysis." Unpublished manuscript.
Chen, H. T., J. Quane, T. N. Garland, and P. Marcin. 1988. "Evaluating an Antismoking
    Program: Diagnostics of Underlying Causal Mechanisms." *Evaluation and the Health
    Professions* 11(4):441-64.
Chen, H. T. and P. H. Rossi. 1980. "The Multi-Goal, Theory-Driven Approach to
    Evaluation: A Model Linking Basic and Applied Social Science." *Social Forces*
    59(September):106-22.
———. 1983. "Evaluating with Sense: The Theory-Driven Approach." *Evaluation Review*
    7:283-302.
———. 1987. "The Theory-Driven Approach to Validity." *Evaluation and Program
    Planning* 10:95-103.

————. Forthcoming. "Issues in the Theory-Driven Perspective." *Evaluation and Program Planning.*

Cicirelli, V. G. 1969. *The Impact of Head Start.* Athens, OH: Westinghouse Learning Corporation and Ohio University.

Clark, A. and M. J. Friedman. 1982. "The Relative Importance of Treatment Outcomes: A Delphi Group Weighting in Mental Health." *Evaluation Review* 6(1):79-93.

Clotfelter, C. T. and J. F. Hahn. 1978. "Assessing the National 55 m.p.h. Speed Limit." *Policy Sciences* 9:281-94.

Cobb, S. 1976. "Social Support as a Moderator of Life Stress." *Psychosomatic Medicine* 38:300-314.

Cochran, W. G. 1957. "Analysis of Covariance: Its Nature and Uses." *Biometrics* 13:261-81.

————. 1976. "Early Development of Techniques in Comparative Experimentation." Pp. 1-25 in *On the History of Statistics and Probability,* edited by D. B. Owen. New York: Marcel Dekker.

Coleman, J. S. 1975. "Problems of Conceptualization and Measurement in Studying Policy Impacts." In *Public Policy Evaluation,* edited by K. M. Dolbeare. Beverly Hills, CA: Sage.

Conrad, K. J. and C. Roberts-Gray. 1988. *Evaluating Program Environments. New Directions for Program Evaluation* (No. 40). San Francisco: Jossey-Bass.

Conrad, K. J. and T. Q. Miller. 1987. "Measuring and Testing Program Philosophy." In *Using Program Theory in Evaluation. New Directions for Program Evaluation* (No. 33), edited by L. Bickman. San Francisco: Jossey-Bass.

Conybeare, J. A. 1980. "Evaluation of Automobile Safety Regulations: The Case of Compulsory Seat Belt Legislation in Australia." *Policy Sciences* 12:27-39.

Cook, T. D. 1985. "Postpositivist Critical Multiplism." In *Social Science and Social Policy,* edited by L. Shotland and M. M. Mark. Beverly Hills, CA: Sage.

Cook, T. D. and D. T. Campbell. 1979. *Quasi-Experimentation: Design and Analysis Issues for Field Settings.* Chicago: Rand McNally.

Cook, T. D. and C. S. Reichardt. 1979. *Qualitative and Quantitative Methods in Evaluation Research.* Beverly Hills, CA: Sage.

Cook T. D. and W. R. Shadish. 1986. "Program Evaluation: The Worldly Science." *Annual Review of Psychology* 37:193-232.

Cook, T. J. and W. K. Poole. 1982. "Treatment Implementation and Statistical Power." *Evaluation Review* 6(3):425-30.

Cordray, D. S. 1986. "Quasi-Experimental Analysis: A Mixture of Methods and Judgment." Pp. 9-27 in *Advances in Quasi-Experimental Design and Analysis. New Directions for Program Evaluation* (No. 31), edited by W. M. K. Trochim. San Francisco: Jossey-Bass.

————. Forthcoming. "Optimizing Validity in Program Evaluation: An Elaboration of Chen and Rossi's Theory-Driven Approach." *Evaluation and Program Planning.*

Cordray, D. S. and M. W. Lipsey. 1986. *Evaluation Studies Review Annual.* Newbury Park, CA: Sage.

Cornfield, J. and J. W. Tukey. 1956. "Average Values of Mean Squares in Factorials." *Annals of Mathematical Statistics* 27:907-49.

Costner, H. L. 1971. "On the Social Psychology of the Psychological Experiment with Particular Reference to the Demand Characteristics and Their Implications." *American Psychologist* 17:776-83.

————. Forthcoming. "The Validity of Conclusions in Evaluation Research: A Further Development of Chen and Rossi's Theory." *Evaluation and Program Planning.*

Crano, William D. and L. A. Messe. 1985. "Assessing and Redressing Comprehension Artifacts in Social Intervention Research." *Evaluation Review* 9(2):145-72.

Cressey, D. 1958. "Achievement of an Unstated Goal." *Pacific Sociological Review* 1(2):43-49.

Cronbach, L. J. 1982. *Designing Evaluations of Educational and Social Programs.* San Francisco: Jossey-Bass.

Cronbach, L. J. and Associates. 1980. *Toward Reform of Program Evaluation.* San Francisco: Jossey-Bass.

Crowe, M. R., J. Rice, and J. P. Walker. 1977. "Evaluation of the Executive High School Internship Program, Final Report." Columbus: Ohio State University Center for Vocational Education.

Cumming, L. J. and E. Cumming. 1955. "Mental Health Education in a Canadian Community." In *Health, Culture, and Community,* edited by B. D. Paul. New York: Russell Sage.

Dalkey, N. C. 1969. *The Delphi Method: An Experimental Study of Group Option* (RM-5888-PR). Santa Monica: Rand Corporation.

Datta, L. et al. 1973. "The Effects of the Head Start Classroom Experience on Some Aspects of Child Development" (A Summary Report of National Evaluation, 1966-1969). Washington, DC: U.S. Department of Health, Education and Welfare.

Davis, B. G., ed. 1982. "Boruch and McLaughlin Debate." *Evaluation News* 3:11-20.

Davis, H. R. and S. E. Salasin. 1975. "The Utilization of Evaluation." In *Handbook of Evaluation Research.* Vol. 1, edited by E. L. Struening and M. Guttentag. Beverly Hills, CA: Sage.

Davis, K. and R. Reynolds. 1975. "Medicare and the Utilization of Health Care Services by the Elderly." *Journal of Human Resources* 10(3):361-76.

Delbecq, A. L. and A. H. Van de Ven. 1971. "A Group Process Model for Problem Identification and Program Planning." *Journal of Applied Behavioral Science* 7(4):466-92.

Delbecq, A. L., A. H. Van de Ven, and D. H. Gustafson. 1975. *Group Techniques for Program Planning.* Glenview, IL: Scott, Foresman.

Derthick, M. 1972. "New Towns in Town." Washington, DC: Urban Institute.

Deutscher, I. 1977. "Toward Avoiding the Goal Trap in Evaluation Research." In *Readings in Evaluation Research,* 2nd ed., edited by F. C. Caro. New York: Russell Sage.

Dewey, J. 1929. *The Quest for Certainty.* New York: Minton, Balch.

———. 1933. *How We Think,* rev. ed. Lexington, MA: D. C. Heath.

Diaz-Guerrero, R., I. Reyes-Lagumes, D. B. Witzke, and W. H. Holtzman. 1976. "Plaza Sésamo in Mexico: An Evaluation." *Journal of Communication* 26:145-54.

Dobson, D. and T. J. Cook. 1980. "Avoiding Type II Errors in Program Evaluation: Results From a Field Experiment." *Evaluation and Program Planning* 3:269-76.

Duncan, O. D. 1975. *Introduction to Structural Equation Models.* New York: Academic Press.

Dunn, E. V., D. W. Conrath, W. G. Bloor, and B. Tanquada. 1977. "An Evaluation of Four Telemedicine Systems for Primary Care." *Children's Health Research* 12(1):19-29.

Dunn, W. 1981. *Public Policy Analysis: An Introduction.* Englewood Cliffs, NJ: Prentice-Hall.

Durkheim, E. 1951. *Suicide: A Study in Sociology.* New York: Free Press.

———. 1965. *The Division of Labor in Society.* New York: Free Press.

Edwards, P. K., D. Orden, and S. T. Buccola. 1980. "Evaluating the Impact of Federal Human Service Programs with Locally Differentiated Constituencies." *Journal of Applied Behavioral Science* 16:13-27.

Edwards, W. and M. Guttentag. 1975. "Experiments and Evaluations: A Reexamination." Pp. 409-63 in *Evaluation and Experiment*, edited by C. A. Bennett and A. A. Lumsdaine. New York: Academic Press.

Edwards, W., M. Guttentag, and K. Snapper. 1975. "A Decision-Theoretic Approach to Evaluation Research." In *Handbook of Evaluation Research*. Vol. 1, edited by E. L. Streuning and M. Guttentag. Beverly Hills, CA: Sage.

Einhorn, H. J. and R. M. Hogarth. 1986. "Judging Probable Cause." *Psychological Bulletin* 99(1):3-19.

Eisenberg, M., L. Bergner, and A. Hallstrom. 1979. "Paramedic Programs and Out-of-Hospital Cardiac Arrest: II. Impact on Community Mortality." *American Journal of Public Health* 69(1):39-42.

Etzioni, A. 1960. "Two Approaches to Organizational Analysis: A Critique and a Suggestion." *Administrative Science Quarterly* 5:257-58.

Ferber, R. and W. Z. Hirsch. 1982. *Social Experimentation and Economic Policy.* New York: Cambridge University Press.

Fetterman, D. M. 1981. "Blaming the Victim: The Problem of Evaluation Design and Federal Involvement and Reinforcing World Views in Education." *Human Organization* 40(1):67-77.

Fiene, R. J. and H. G. Nixon. 1981. "An Instrument-Based Program Monitoring System." Washington, DC: Children's Services Monitoring Transfer Consortium.

Fink, A., J. Kosecoff et al. 1984. "Consensus Methods: Characteristics and Guidelines for Use." *American Journal of Public Health* 74(September):979-83.

Finney, J. W. and R. H. Moos. Forthcoming. "Theory and Methods in Treatment Evaluation." In special issue for the Theory Driven Evaluation. *Evaluation and Program Planning.*

Fisher, R. A. 1935. *The Design of Experiments.* 1st ed. London: Oliver and Boyd.

Foster, G. H. 1973. *Traditional Societies and Technological Change.* New York: Harper & Row.

Foxx, R. M. and N. H. Azrin. 1973. "Dry Pants: A Rapid Method of Toilet Training Children." *Behavior Research and Therapy* 11:435-42.

Garfield, S. and A. Bergin, eds. 1978. *Handbook of Psychotherapy and Behavior Change.* New York: John Wiley.

Gavin, J. F. and D. L. O'Toole. 1973. "Validity of Aptitude Tests for the 'Hardcore Unemployed.' " *Personal Psychology* 27(1):139-46.

Georgopoulous, B. S. 1973. *An Open System Theory Model for Organizational Theory.* Kent, OH: Kent State University Press.

Giles, M. W. 1978. "White Enrollment Stability and School Desegregation: A Two-Level Analysis." *American Sociological Review* 43:848-64.

Glass, G. V., B. McGaw, and M. L. Smith. 1981. *Meta-Analysis in Social Research.* Beverly Hills, CA: Sage.

Goode, W. J. 1971. "Force and Violence in the Family." *Journal of Marriage and the Family* 33:624-36.

Gramlich, E. M. and P. P. Koshel. 1975. *Educational Performance Contracting: An Evaluation of an Experiment.* Washington, DC: Brookings Institution.

Grant, D. I. 1978. *Monitoring Ongoing Programs.* San Francisco: Jossey-Bass.

Groeneveld, L. P., N. B. Tuma, and M. T. Hannan. 1980. "The Effects of Negative Income Tax Programs on Marital Dissolution." *Journal of Human Resources* 15(4):654-74.

Guba, E. G. and Y. S. Lincoln. 1981. *Effective Evaluation: Improving the Usefulness of Evaluation Results Through Responsive and Naturalistic Approaches.* San Francisco: Jossey-Bass.

Guttentag, M. 1973. "Subjectivity and Its Use in Evaluation Research." *Evaluation* 1(2):60-65.

Guttentag, M. and E. L. Struening, eds. 1975. *Handbook of Evaluation Research.* Beverly Hills, CA: Sage.

Hall, G. E. and S. F. Loucks. 1977. "A Developmental Model for Determining Whether the Treatment Is Actually Implemented." *American Educational Research Journal* 14(3):263-76.

Hall, R. H. 1982. *Organizations: Structure and Process.* Englewood Cliffs, NJ: Prentice-Hall.

Harlow, H. F. and M. K. Harlow. 1962. "Social Deprivation in Monkeys." *Scientific American* 207:137-47.

Hausman, J. A. and D. A. Wise. 1985. *Social Experimentation.* Chicago: University of Chicago Press.

Hawley, A. 1950. *Human Ecology.* New York: Ronald.

Heckman, J. J. 1979. "Sample Bias as a Specification Error." *Econometrica* 47:153-62.

Heckman, J. J., V. J. Hotz, and M. Dabos. 1987. "Do We Need Experimental Data to Evaluate the Impact of Manpower Training on Earnings?" *Evaluation Review* 11(4):395-427.

Heise, D. R. 1975. *Causal Analysis.* New York: Wiley-Interscience.

Hemple, C. 1965. *Aspects of Scientific Explanation.* New York: Free Press.

Herzberg, F. 1966. *Work and the Nature of Man.* New York: World.

Holzner, B. and E. Fisher. 1979. "Knowledge in Use: Considerations in the Sociology of Knowledge Application." *Knowledge* 1:219-44.

House, E. R. 1976. "Evaluation as Justice." *Evaluation Studies Review Annual* 1:75-100 (edited by G. V. Glass).

———. 1980. *Evaluating with Validity.* Newbury Park, CA: Sage.

House, J. 1981. *Work Stress and Social Support.* Reading, MA: Addison-Wesley.

Hultsch, D. F. and T. Hickey. 1978. "External Validity in the Study of Human Development: Theoretical and Methodological Issues." *Human Development* 21:76-91.

Jacob, J. 1961. *The Death and Life of Great American Cities.* New York: Random House.

Janzen, C. 1977. "Families in the Treatment of Alcoholism." *Journal of Studies on Alcohol* 38:114-30.

Jellson, I. A. 1975. "The National Drug Abuse Policy Delphi: Progress Report and Findings to Data." In *The Delphi Method—Techniques and Applications*, edited by H. A. Lindstone and M. Turuff. Reading, MA: Addison-Wesley.

Jöreskog, K. G. and D. Sörbom. 1979. *Advances in Factor Analysis and Structured Equation Models.* Cambridge, MA: Abt Books.

Kassebaum, G., D. Ward, and D. Wilner. 1971. *Prison Treatment and Parole Survival.* New York: John Wiley.

Keeney, R. L. and H. Raiffa. 1977. *Decisions with Multiple Objectives: Preferences and Value Tradeoffs.* New York: John Wiley.

Kempthorne, O. 1961. "The Design and Analysis of Experiments with Some Reference to Educational Research." In *Research Design and Analysis*, edited by R. O. Collier, Jr., and S. M. Elm. Bloomington, IN: Phi Delta Kappa.

Kerlinger, F. N. 1986. *Foundations of Behavioral Research.* 3rd ed. New York: Holt, Rinehart & Winston.

Kerr, D. M., L. Kent, and T. C. M. Lam. 1985. "Measuring Program Implementation with a Classroom Observation Instrument: The Interactive Teaching Map." *Evaluation Review* 9(4):461-82.

Kershaw, D. N. 1972. "Issues in Income Maintenance Experimentation." In *Evaluating Social Programs: Theory, Practice, Politics*, edited by P. H. Rossi and W. Williams. New York: Seminar.

Kershaw, D. and S. Fair. 1976. *The New Jersey Income-Maintenance Experiment.* Vol. I. New York: Academic Press.

Klatzky, S. R. 1970. "Organizational Inequality: The Case of the Public Employment Agencies." In *Human Service Organizations*, edited by Y. Hasenfeld and R. A. English. Ann Arbor: University of Michigan Press.

Klein, R. E. 1979. "Malnutrition and Human Behavior: A Backward Glance at an Ongoing Longitudinal Study." In *Malnutrition, Environment, and Behavior*, edited by D. A. Levitsky. Ithaca, NY: Cornell University Press.

Kmenta, J. 1986. *Elements of Econometrics.* 2nd ed. New York: Macmillan.

Kress, G., G. Kohler, and J. F. Springer. 1981. "Policy Drift: An Evaluation of the California Business Enterprise Program." In *Implementing Public Policy*, edited by D. J. Palumbo and M. A. Harden. Lexington, MA: D. C. Heath.

Kruglanski, A. W. and M. Kroy. 1976. "Outcome Validity in Experimental Research: A Reconceptualization." *Representative Research in Social Psychology* 7:166-76.

Kuhn, T. 1970. *The Structure of Scientific Revolutions.* Chicago: University of Chicago Press.

Kutchinsky, B. 1973. "The Effects of Easy Availability of Pornography on the Incidence of Sex Crimes: The Danish Experience." *Journal of Social Issues* 29:163-81.

Lalonde, R. J. and R. Maynard. 1987. "How Precise Are Evaluations of Employment and Training Programs: Evidence from a Field Experiment." *Evaluation Review* 11(4):428-51.

Larson, R. C. 1975. "What Happened to Patrol Operations in Kansas City: A Review of the Kansas City Preventive Patrol Experiment." *Journal of Criminal Justice* 3:267-97.

Lave, C. A. and James G. March. 1975. *An Introduction to Models in the Social Sciences.* New York: Harper & Row.

Lawler, E. E., III. 1973. *Motivation in Work Organizations.* Monterey, CA: Brooks/Cole.

Lawrence, P. R. and J. W. Lorsch. 1967. *Organization and Environment: Managing Differentiation and Integration.* Boston: Harvard University Press.

Leigh, J. P. 1983. "Direct and Indirect Effects of Education on Health." *Social Science and Medicine* 17(4):227-34.

Leithwood, K. A. and D. A. Montgomery. 1980. "Evaluating Program Implementation." *Evaluation Review* 4:193-214.

Lenihan, K. J. 1977. *Unlocking the Second Gate.* Washington, DC: Government Printing Office.

Lewin, K. 1947. "Frontiers in Group Dynamics: Concept, Method and Reality in Social Science; Social Equilibria and Social Change." *Human Relations Journal* 1:5-41.

Lincoln, Y. S. and E. G. Guba. 1985. *Naturalistic Inquiry.* Beverly Hills, CA: Sage.

———. 1986. "But Is It Rigorous? Trustworthiness and Authenticity in Naturalistic Evaluation." Pp. 73-84 in *Naturalistic Evaluation. New Directions for Program Evaluation* (No. 30), edited by D. D. Williams. San Francisco: Jossey-Bass.

Lindblom, C. E. and D. K. Cohen. 1979. *Useable Knowledge.* New Haven, CT: Yale University Press.

Lipsey, M. 1987. "Theory as Method: Small Theories of Treatments." Paper presented at the National Center for Health Services Research Conference, "Strengthening Causal Interpretations of Non-Experimental Data," Tucson, AZ.

Lipsey, M. W., D. S. Cordray, and D. E. Berger. 1981. "Evaluation of a Juvenile Diversion Program: Using Multiple Lines of Evidence." *Evaluation Review* 5:283-306.

Lipsey, M. W., S. Crosse, J. Dunkle, J. Pollard, and G. Stobart. 1985. "Evaluation: The State of the Art and the Sorry State of the Science." Pp. 7-28 in *Utilizing Prior Research in Evaluation Planning. New Directions for Program Evaluation* (No. 27), edited by D. S. Cordray. San Francisco: Jossey-Bass.

Lipsey, M. W. and J. A. Pollard. Forthcoming. "Driving Toward Theory in Program Evaluation: More Models to Choose From." In special issue for the Theory Driven Evaluation. *Evaluation and Program Planning.*

Lipsky, M. 1974. "Toward a Theory of Street-Level Bureacracy." In *Theoretical Perspectives on Urban Politics*, edited by Willis Hawley and Michael Lipsky. Englewood Cliffs, NJ: Prentice-Hall.

———. 1980. *Street-Level Bureaucracy.* New York: Russell Sage.

Litwin, H. 1987. "Applying Theories of Aging to Evaluation of Social Programs for the Elderly." *Evaluation Review* 11(3):267-80.

Maddala, G. S. 1983. *Limited-Dependent and Qualitative Variables in Econometrics.* Cambridge: Cambridge University Press.

Malcolm, M. T. and J. S. Madden. 1973. "The Use of Disulfiram Implantation in Alcoholism." *British Journal of Psychiatry* 123:41-45.

Malcolm, M. T., J. S. Madden, and A. E. Williams. 1974. "Disulfiram Implantation Critically Evaluated." *British Journal of Psychiatry* 125:485-89.

Mark, M. M. 1983. "Treatment Implementation, Statistical Power and Internal Validity." *Evaluation Review* 7(4):543-49.

Mark, M. M. and R. L. Shotland, eds. 1987. *Multiple Methods in Program Evaluation. New Directions for Program Evaluation* (No. 35). San Francisco: Jossey-Bass.

Marvel, Mary K. 1982. "Implementation and Safety Regulation: Variations in Federal and State Administration Under OSHA." *Administration and Society* 14(1):15-33.

Maslow, A. H. 1943. "A Theory of Human Motivation." *Psychological Review* 50:370-96.

McClintock, C. 1987. "Conceptual and Action Heuristics: Tools for the Evaluator." In *Using Program Theory in Evaluation. New Directions for Program Evaluation* (No. 33), edited by L. Bickman. San Francisco: Jossey-Bass.

McCord, J. 1978. "A Thirty-Year Follow-Up of Treatment Effects." *American Psychologist* 33:284-91.

McCrone, D. J. and R. J. Hardy. 1978. "Civil Rights Policies and the Achievement of Racial Economic Equality, 1948-1975." *American Journal of Political Science* 22(1):1-17.

McLaughlin, M. W. 1975. *Evaluation and Reform: The Elementary and Secondary Education Act of 1965, Title I.* Cambridge, MA: Ballinger.

Meyer, H. J., E. F. Borgatta, and W. C. Jones. 1965. "Girls at Vocational School: An Experiment in Social Work Intervention." In *Examining Deviance Experimentally*, edited by D. J. Steffensmeier and R. M. Terry. Port Washington, NY: Alfred.

Mielke, K. W. and J. W. Swinehart. 1976. *Evaluation of the Feeling Good Television Series.* New York: Children's Television Workshop.

Miles, M. B. and A. M. Huberman. 1984. *Qualitative Data Analysis: A Sourcebook of New Methods.* Beverly Hills, CA: Sage.

Minuchin, S. 1974. *Families and Family Therapy.* Boston: Harvard University Press.

Mitroff, I. and T. V. Bonoma. 1978. "Psychological Assumptions, Experimentations, and Real World Problems." *Evaluation Quarterly* 2(2):235-59.

Mook, D. G. 1983. "In Defense of External Invalidity." *American Psychologist* 38(4):379-87.

Moos, R. H. 1974. *Evaluating Treatment Environments: A Social Ecological Approach.* New York: John Wiley.

———. 1988. "Assessing the Program Environment: Implications for Program Evaluation and Design." In *Evaluating Program Evaluation* (No. 40), edited by K. J. Conrad and C. Roberts-Gray. San Francisco: Jossey-Bass.

Moos, R. H. and E. J. Trickett. 1987. *Classroom Environment Scale Manual.* 2nd ed. Palo Alto, CA: Consulting Psychologists Press.

Murnane, R. J. 1985. "Comparing Public and Private Schools: The Puzzling Role of Selectivity Bias." *Journal of Business and Economic Statistics* 3(1):23-35.

Mushkin, S. J. 1973. "Evaluations: Use with Caution." *Evaluation* 1(2):30-35.

Naegele, K. D. 1955. "A Mental Health Project in a Boston Suburb." In *Health, Culture, and Community*, edited by B. D. Paul. New York: Russell Sage.

Nagel, E. 1979. *The Structure of Science.* Indianapolis: Hackett.

Nakamura, R. T. and F. Smallwood. 1980. *The Politics of Policy Implementation.* New York: St. Martins.

Neyman, J. 1952. "Some Controversial Matters Relating to Agricultural Trials." Pp. 67-84 in *Lectures and Conferences on Mathematical Statistics and Probability.* Washington, DC: U.S. Department of Agriculture, Graduate School.

Nicholson, W. and S. R. Wright. 1977. "Participants' Understanding of the Treatment in Policy Experimentation." *Evaluation Quarterly* 10:245-68.

Olsen, L. 1981. "Optimizing Child-Welfare Policy Through Research and Demonstration Projects." Pp. 129-38 in *Implementing Public Policy*, edited by D. J. Palumbo and M. A. Harden. Lexington, MA: D. C. Heath.

Orne, M. T. 1962. "On the Social Psychology of the Psychological Experiment with Particular Reference to the Demand Characteristics and Their Implications." *American Psychologist* 17:776-83.

Palumbo, D., S. Maynard-Moody, and P. Wright. 1984. "Measuring Degrees of Successful Implementation: Achieving Policy Versus Statutory Goals." *Evaluation Review* 8(1):45-74.

Palumbo, D. J. and A. Oliver. Forthcoming. "Implementation Theory and the Theory-Driven Approach to Validity." *Evaluation and Program Planning.*

Parlett, M. and D. Hamilton. 1978. "Evaluation and Illumination: A New Approach to the Study of Innovatory Programmes." In *Beyond the Numbers Game*, edited by D. Hamilton et al. Berkeley, CA: McCutchan.

Patton, M. Q. 1980. *Qualitative Evaluation Methods.* Beverly Hills, CA: Sage.

———. 1986. *Utilization-Focused Evaluation.* 2nd ed. Beverly Hills, CA: Sage.

———. Forthcoming. "A Context and Boundaries for Theory-Driven Approach to Validity." *Evaluation and Program Planning.*

Paul, G. L. 1966. *Insight Versus Densensitization in Psychotherapy.* Stanford, CA: Stanford University Press.

Pearson, E. S. 1970. "William Sealy Gosset, 1876-1937." Pp. 360-95 in *Studies in the History of Statistics and Probability*, edited by E. S. Person and M. C. Kendall. London: Charles Griffin.

Pearson, K. 1937. "Some Aspects of the Problem of Randomization." *Biometrika* 29:53-64.

Perrow, C. 1961. "The Analysis of Goals in Complex Organizations." *American Sociological Review* 26:855.

————. 1967. "A Framework for the Comparative Analysis of Organizations." *American Sociological Review* 32:194-208.

Popper, K. 1968. *The Logic of Scientific Discovery.* New York: Harper & Row.

Posavac, E. J. and R. G. Carey. 1989. *Program Evaluation: Methods and Case Studies.* 3rd ed. Englewood Cliffs, NJ: Prentice-Hall.

Power, E. and H. Witmer. 1951. *An Experiment in the Prevention of Delinquency.* New York: Columbia University Press.

Pressman, J. and A. Wildavsky. 1973. *Implementation.* Berkeley: University of California Press.

Quinn, B., A. Van Mondfrans, and B. R. Worthen. 1984. "Cost-Effectiveness of Two Math Programs as Moderated by Pupil SES." *Educational Evaluation and Policy Analysis* 6(1):39-52.

Quinn, J. B. 1978. "Strategic Choice: 'Logical Incrementation.'" *Sloan Management Review* 20:7-21.

Raizen, S. and P. H. Rossi. 1981. *Program Evaluation in Evaluation: Why? How? To What End?* Washington, DC: National Academy Press.

Reichardt, C. S. and T. D. Cook. 1979. "Beyond Qualitative Versus Quantitative Methods." In *Qualitative and Quantitative Methods in Evaluation Research,* edited by T. D. Cook and L. S. Reichardt. Beverly Hills, CA: Sage.

Reicken, H. W. 1972. "Memorandum on Program Evaluation." In *Evaluating Action Programs,* edited by C. H. Weiss. Boston: Allyn & Bacon.

Reicken, H. W. and R. F. Boruch, eds. 1974. *Social Experimentation: A Method for Planning and Evaluating Social Intervention.* New York: Academic Press.

Reynolds, K. D. and S. G. West. 1988. "A Multiplist Strategy for Strengthening Nonequivalent Control Group Designs." *Evaluation Review* 11(6):691-714.

Rodgers, C. S. 1981. "Work Tests for Welfare Recipients: The Gap Between the Goal and the Reality." *Journal of Policy Analysis and Management* 1(1):5-17.

Roethlisberger, F. J. and W. Dickson. 1939. *Management and the Worker.* Cambridge, MA: Harvard University Press.

Rosenberg, M. J. 1969. "The Conditions and Consequences of Evaluation Apprehension." In *Artifacts in Behavioral Research,* edited by R. Rosenthal and R. L. Rosnow. New York: Academic Press.

Ross, H. S., D. T. Campbell, and G. V. Glass. 1970. "Determining the Social Effects of Legal Reform: The British Breathalyzer Crackdown of 1967." *American Behavioral Scientist* 3:494-509.

Rossi, P. H., R. A. Berk, and K. J. Lenihan. 1980. *Money, Work, and Crime.* New York: Academic Press.

Rossi, P. H. and H. E. Freeman. 1985. *Evaluation: A Systematic Approach.* Beverly Hills, CA: Sage.

Rossi, P. H. and K. C. Lyall. 1976. *Reforming Public Welfare: A Critique of the Negative Income Tax Experiment.* New York: Russell Sage.

Rudner, R. 1966. *Philosophy of Social Science.* Englewood Cliffs, NJ: Prentice-Hall.

Rutman, L. 1980. *Planning Useful Evaluation: Evaluability Assessment.* Beverly Hills, CA: Sage.

Sabatier, P. A. and D. A. Mazmanian, eds. 1982. *Effective Policy Implementation.* Lexington, MA: Lexington Books.

Sadler, D. R. 1981. "Intuitive Data Processing as a Potential Source of Bias in Naturalistic Evaluations." *Educational Evaluation and Policy Analysis* 3(4):25-31.

St. Clair, Harakal C., M. J. Silver, and G. Spivack. 1975. "An Instrument to Assess Staff Time Utilization in a Community Mental Health Center." *Community Mental Health Journal* 11(4):371-80.

Scheirer, M. A. 1987. "Program Theory and Implementation Theory: Implications for Evaluators." In *Using Program Theory in Evaluation. New Directions for Program Theory* (No. 33), edited by L. Bickman. San Francisco: Jossey-Bass.

Scott, A. G. and L. Sechrest. Forthcoming. "Strength of Theory and Theory of Strength." *Evaluation and Program Planning.*

Scriven, M. 1967. "The Methodology of Evaluation." In *Perspectives on Curriculum Evaluation. AERA Monograph Series on Curriculum Evaluation* (No. 1), edited by R. E. Stake et al. Chicago: Rand McNally.

———. 1971. "Objectivity and Subjectivity in Educational Research." In *Philosophical Redirection of Educational Research (71st Yearbook of the National Society for the Study of Education,* Part I), edited by L. G. Thomas. Chicago: University of Chicago Press.

———. 1972. "Pros and Cons About Goal-Free Evaluation." *Evaluation Comment* 3:1-4.

———. 1981. *Evaluation Thesaurus.* 3rd ed. Pt. Reyes, CA: Edgepress.

———. 1983. "Evaluation Ideologies." Pp. 229-60 in *Evaluation Models: Viewpoints on Educational and Human Services Evaluation,* edited by G. F. Madaus, M. Scriven, and D. L. Stufflebeam. Boston: Kluwer-Nijhoff.

Seaver, W. B. and A. H. Patterson. 1976. "Decreasing Fuel-Oil Consumption Through Feedback and Social Commendation." *Journal of Applied Behavior Analysis* 9:147-52.

Sechrest, L. and R. Redner. 1979. "Strength and Integrity of Treatments in Evaluation Studies." In *How Well Does It Work? Review of Criminal Justice Evaluation, 1978.* Washington, DC: Department of Justice, U.S. National Criminal Justice Reference Service.

Shadish, W. R., Jr. 1986. "Planned Critical Multiplism: Some Elaborations." *Behavioral Assessment* 8:75-103.

———. 1987. "Program Micro- and Macrotheories: A Guide for Social Change." In *Using Program Theory in Evaluation. New Directions for Program Evaluation* (No. 33), edited by L. Bickman. San Francisco: Jossey-Bass.

Shadish, W. R. and T. D. Cook. 1986. "Program Evaluation: The Worldly Science." *Annual Review of Psychology* 37:193-232.

Shadish, W. R., Jr., T. D. Cook, and A. C. Houts. 1986. "Quasi-Experimentation in a Critical Multiplist Mode." In *Advances in Quasi-Experimental Design and Analysis. New Directions for Program Evaluation* (No. 31), edited by W. M. K. Trochim. San Francisco: Jossey-Bass.

Shadish, W. R. and C. S. Reichardt. 1987a. "The Intellectual Foundations of Social Program Evaluation: The Development of Evaluation Theory." Pp. 13-30 in *Evaluation Studies Review Annual.* Vol. 12, edited by W. R. Shadish and C. S. Reichardt. Newbury Park, CA: Sage.

———, eds. 1987b. *Evaluation Studies Review Annual.* Newbury Park, CA: Sage.

Shapiro, J. P., C. Secor, and A. Butchart. 1983. "Illuminative Evaluation." *Educational Evaluation and Policy Analysis* 5(4):465-71.

Shapiro, J. Z. 1982. "Evaluation as Theory Testing: An Example from Head Start." *Evaluation and Policy Analysis* 4(3):341-53.

————. 1984. "The Social Costs of Methodological Rigor: A Note on the Problem of Massive Attrition." *Evaluation Review* 8(5):705-12.

————. Forthcoming. "Contextual Limits on Validity Attainment: An Artificial Science Perspective on Program Evaluation." *Evaluation and Program Planning.*

Shotland, R. L. and M. M. Mark. 1987. "Improving Inferences from Multiple Methods." In *Multiple Methods in Program Evaluation. New Directions for Program Evaluation* (No. 35), edited by M. M. Mark and R. L. Shotland. San Francisco: Jossey-Bass.

Simon, H. A. 1955. "A Behavioral Model of Rational Choice." *Quarterly Journal of Economics.* 69:99-118.

————. 1956. "Rational Choice and the Structure of the Environment." *Psychological Review* 63:129-38.

Singh, R. D. 1952. "The Village Level: An Introduction of Green Manuring in Rural India." In *Human Problems in Technological Change*, edited by E. H. Spicer. New York: Russell Sage.

Sloane, R. B., F. R. Staples, A. H. Cristol, N. J. Yorkston, and K. Whipple. 1975. *Psychotherapy Versus Behavior Therapy.* Cambridge, MA: Harvard University Press.

Smith, M. L. 1986. "The Whole Is Greater: Combining Qualitative and Quantitative Approaches in Evaluation Studies." Pp. 37-54 in *Naturalistic Evaluation. New Directions for Program Evaluation* (No. 31), edited by D. D. Williams. San Francisco: Jossey-Bass.

Smith, M. and J. Bissell. 1970. "Report Analysis: The Impact of Head Start." *Harvard Educational Review* 40:51-104.

Somers, G. and E. Stromsdorfer. 1972. "Cost-Effectiveness Analysis of In-School and Summer Neighborhood Youth Corps." *Journal of Human Resources* 7:446-59.

Stake, R. E., ed. 1975. *Evaluating the Arts in Education: A Responsible Approach.* Columbus, OH: Merrill.

————. 1978. "Responsive Evaluation." In *Beyond the Numbers Game*, edited by D. Hamilton et al. Berkeley, CA: McCutchan.

————. 1986. *Quieting Reform.* Urbana: University of Illinois Press.

"Student." 1936a. "Co-Operation in Large-Scale Experiments." *Journal of the Royal Statistical Society* (Series B) 3:115-36.

————. 1936b. "The Half-Drill System Agricultural Experiments." *Nature* 138:971-72.

Stufflebeam, D. L. 1974. "Comment by Daniel L. Stufflebeam: Should or Can Evaluation Be Goal-Free." In *Evaluation in Education*, edited by W. J. Popham. Berkeley, CA: McCutchan.

Suchman, E. 1967. *Evaluation Research.* New York: Russell Sage.

————. 1969. "Evaluating Educational Programs." *Urban Review* 3(4):15-17.

————. 1970. "Action for What? A Critique of Evaluative Research." In *The Organization, Management, and Tactics of Social Research*, edited by R. O'Toole. Cambridge, MA: Schenkman.

Talmage, H. 1982. "Evaluation of Programs." In *Encyclopedia of Educational Research.* 5th ed., edited by H. E. Mitzel. New York: Free Press.

Tatsuoka, M. M. 1988. *Multivariate Analysis.* New York: Macmillan.

Taylor, F. W. 1947. *Scientific Management.* New York: Harper & Row.

Thompson, B. and M. Swisher, 1983. "An Assessment, Using the Multiphasic Environmental Procedure (MEAP), of a Rural Life-Care Residential Center for the Elderly." *Journal of Housing for the Elderly* 1:41-56.

Thompson, J. D. 1967. *Organizations in Action.* New York: McGraw-Hill.

Tornatzky, L. G. and E. E. Johnson. 1982. "Research on Implementation: Implications for Evaluation Practice and Evaluation Policy." *Evaluation and Program Planning* 5:193-98.

Trist, E. L., G. W. Higgin, H. Murray, and A. B. Pollack. 1963. *Organizational Choice.* London: Tavistock.

Trites, D. K., F. D. Galbraith Jr., J. F. Leckwart, and M. Sturdavant. 1969. "Radial Nursing Units Prove Best in Controlled Study." *Modern Hospital* 112(April):94-99.

Trochim, W. M. K. 1985. "Pattern Matching, Construct Validity, and Conceptualization in Program Evaluation." *Evaluation Review* 9(5):575-604.

——. ed. 1986a. *Advances in Quasi-Experimental Design and Analysis. New Directions for Program Evaluation* (No. 31). San Francisco: Jossey-Bass.

——. 1986b. "Editors Notes." In *Advances in Quasi-Experimental Design and Analysis. New Directions for Program Evaluation* (No. 31), edited by W. M. K. Trochim. San Francisco: Jossey-Bass.

——. Forthcoming. "Outcome Pattern Matching and Program Theory." *Evaluation and Program Planning.*

Valle, S. K. 1981. "Impersonal Functioning of Alcoholism Counselors and Treatment Outcome." *Journal of Studies on Alcohol* 42(9):783-90.

Van de Ven, A. H. and A. L. Delbecq. 1972. "The Nominal Group as a Research Instrument for Exploratory Health Studies." *Exploratory Health Studies* (March):337-42.

Waldo, G. P. and T. G. Chirico. 1977. "Work Release and Recidivism." *Evaluation Quarterly* 2(1):87-108.

Wang, M. C. and H. J. Walberg. 1983. "Evaluating Educational Programs: An Integrative, Causal-Modeling Approach." *Educational Evaluation and Policy Analysis* 5(3):347-66.

Ward, D. A. 1961. "The Influence of Family Relationships on Social and Psychological Functioning: A Follow-Up Study." *Journal of Marriage and the Family* 23(November):807-15.

Warriner, C. K. 1965. "The Problem of Organizational Purpose." *Sociological Quarterly.* 6:139-46.

Weatherly, R. and M. Lipsky. 1977. "Street-Level Bureaucrats and Institutional Innovation: Implementing Special Education Reform." *Harvard Educational Review* 42(2):171-97.

Weber, M. 1947. *The Theory of Social and Economic Organization,* edited by A. M. Henderson and T. Parsons. Glencoe, IL: Free Press.

Weiss, C. H. 1972. "Evaluating Educational and Social Action Programs: A 'Treeful of Owls.' " In *Evaluating Action Programs: Readings in Social Action and Education,* edited by C. H. Weiss. Boston: Allyn & Bacon.

——. 1975. "Evaluation Research in the Political Context." In *Handbook of Evaluation Research.* Vol. 1, edited by E. L. Struening and M. Guttentag. Beverly Hills, CA: Sage.

——. ed. 1977. *Using Social Research in Public Policy Making.* Lexington, MA: Lexington.

Weiss, C. H. and M. J. Bucuvalas. 1980a. *Social Science Research and Decision-Making.* New York: Columbia University Press.

——. 1980b. "Truth Tests and Utility Tests: Decision-Makers' Frames of Reference for Social Science Research." *American Sociological Review* 45(April):302-13.

Weiss, R. S. and M. Rein. 1969. "The Evaluation of Broad-Aim Programs: A Cautionary Case and a Moral." *Annals of the American Academy of Political and Social Science* 385:133-42.

White, W. D. 1978. "The Impact of Occupational Licensure of Clinical Laboratory Personnel." *Journal of Human Resources* 13(1):91-102.

Wholey, J. S. 1979. *Evaluation: Promise and Performance.* Washington, DC: Urban Institute.

―――. 1987. "Evaluability Assessment: Developing Program Theory." In *Using Program Theory in Evaluation. New Directions for Program Evaluation* (No. 33), edited by L. Bickman. San Francisco: Jossey-Bass.

Wholey, J. S., J. W. Scanlon, H. Duffy, J. S. Fukumoto, and L. M. Vogt. 1970. *Federal Evaluation Policy.* Washington, DC: Urban Institute.

Williams, D. D. 1986a. "When Is Naturalistic Evaluation Appropriate?" In *Naturalistic Evaluation. New Directions for Program Evaluation* (No. 30), edited by D. D. Williams. San Francisco: Jossey-Bass.

―――. 1986b. "Naturalistic Evaluation: Potential Conflicts Between Evaluation Standards and Criteria for Conducting Naturalistic Inquiry." *Educational Evaluation and Policy Analysis* 8(1):87-99.

Williams, W. 1975. "Implementation Analysis and Assessment." *Policy Analysis* 1:531-66.

Williams, W. 1980. *The Implementation Perspective.* Berkeley: University of California Press.

Williams, W. and R. F. Elmore. 1976. *Social Program Implementation.* New York: Academic Press.

Williams, W. et al. 1982. *Studying Implementation.* Chatham, NJ: Chatham House.

Wilner, D. M. et al. 1962. *The Housing Environment and Family Life.* Baltimore: Johns Hopkins University Press.

Windle, C. and S. S. Sharfstein. 1978. "Three Approaches to Monitoring Mental Health Services." In *Monitoring Ongoing Programs. New Directions for Program Evaluation,* edited by D. I. Grant. San Francisco: Jossey-Bass.

Woodward, J. 1965. *Industrial Organization: Theory and Practice.* New York: Oxford University Press.

Wortman, P. M. 1983. "Evaluation Research: A Methodological Perspective." *Annual Review of Psychology* 34:223-60.

Wortman, P. M., C. S. Reichardt, and R. G. St. Pierre. 1978. "The First Year of the Education Voucher Demonstration: A Secondary Analysis of Student Achievement Test Scores." *Evaluation Quarterly* 2:193-214.

Wright, J. D., P. H. Rossi, K. Daly, and E. Weber-Burdin. 1981. *Weapons, Crime, and Violence in America.* Amherst, MA: Social and Demographic Research Institute.

Yates, F. 1939. "The Comparative Advantages of Systematic and Randomization Arrangements in the Design of Agricultural and Biological Experiments." *Biometrika* 30:440-66.

Yin, R. K. 1984. *Designing and Doing Case Studies.* Beverly Hills, CA: Sage.

Yuchtman, E. and S. E. Seashore. 1967. "A System-Resource Approach to Organizational Effectiveness." *American Sociological Review* 32:891-903.

Zald, H. 1963. "Comparative Analysis and Measurement of Goals: The Case of Correctional Institutions for Delinquents." *Sociological Quarterly* 4:206-30.

Name Index

Subject Index

About the Author

HUEY-TSYH CHEN is Associate Professor in the Department of Sociology at the University of Akron. He was born and raised in Taiwan. He received his Ph.D. in sociology from the University of Massachusetts at Amherst. He has taught at the National University of Singapore and has been an Associate Research Scientist at Johns Hopkins University. Among other topics, he is interested in constructing models and strategies for integrating theory into evaluation processes to expand the scope and usefulness of program evaluation. In the past several years, he has been working with Peter H. Rossi in developing the theory-driven perspective. He was a guest editor for a special issue of *Evaluation and Program Planning*, which focused on the theory-driven approach. He is currently engaged in a number of research projects including an evaluation of a treatment program for abusive men and a study of the impact of unemployment.

Printed in the United States
18300LVS00002B/108